D1255797

Images of Children in American Film

A Sociocultural Analysis

by
Kathy Merlock Jackson

The Scarecrow Press, Inc.
Metuchen, N.J., & London
1986

The author gratefully acknowledges permission to reprint the following:

Extracts from C. John Sommerville's The Rise and Fall of Childhood, Sage Library of Social Research, vol. 140, 1982, pp. 12-13, 14, 175, 204, and 219. Used by permission of the author.

Extracts from Norman Zierold's The Child Stars (New York: Coward-McCann, 1965), pp. 12, 16, 20, 23, 44, 57, 75, 98-99, 100, and 188. Used by permission of the author.

Jackson, Kathy Merlock, 1955-
  Images of children in American film.

  Originally presented as the author's thesis (doctoral-- Bowling Green State University)
  Bibliography: p.
  Filmography: p.
  Includes index.
  1. Children in motion pictures. 2. Moving-pictures-- United States. I. Title.
  PN1995.9.C45J27 1986 791.43'09'09352054 86-6751
  ISBN 0-8108-1901-5

TABLE OF CONTENTS

1. INTRODUCTION   1
   Notes   10

2. CHILDREN, INNOCENCE, AND THE
   AMERICAN TRADITION   14
   Notes   28

3. IMAGES OF CHILDREN IN PRE-WORLD
   WAR II FILMS: UNQUALIFIED INNOCENCE   31
   America Before World War I   31
   World War I and the Age of Prosperity   37
   The Child-Star Era and Depression America   56
   World War II America   72
   Notes   81

4. IMAGES OF CHILDREN IN POST-WORLD
   WAR II FILMS: NEW VARIATIONS   86
   Postwar America, the Baby Boom, and
      the Grasp for Stability   86
   The Disney Films   118
   The 1960s and the End of the Baby Boom   126
   The Child-As-Monster Film   137
   The Precocious Imp and Other Images   154
   The Age of Spielberg   165
   Notes   174

5. CONCLUSION   183
   Notes   189

Bibliography   190

Filmography   200

Index   213

ACKNOWLEDGMENTS

This book began as a Ph.D. dissertation in American culture at Bowling Green State University, and, as all dissertations do, it reflects the suggestions and support of many people. I am especially indebted to Dr. Jack Nachbar, a conscientious and perceptive reader whose continuous enthusiasm for my topic provided me with lasting encouragement. My appreciation is further extended to Professors Ray Browne, Gary Edgerton, Barbara McMillen, and Art Neal; their guidance and constructive criticisms led to the betterment of this project. While these individuals can share in the credit for this work's merits, I assume all responsibility for its shortcomings. In addition, I would like to thank the Graduate College at Bowling Green State University for awarding me a nonservice fellowship for the 1983-84 academic year as well as a dissertation research support grant that enabled me to do research at the Motion Picture, Broadcasting, and Recorded Sound Division of the Library of Congress in Washington, D.C. There I encountered friendly and helpful librarians who were kind enough to assemble dozens of films for my personal viewing during one of their busiest seasons. Virginia Wesleyan College, which financed the preparation of the final manuscript, and Dorothy Hilliard, who did the actual typing, deserve my warmest thanks. So, too, do Virginia Wesleyan College librarian Theresa Dunleavy, who generously offered me her time, expertise, and friendship during the most stressful of times, and my colleague Michael Hall, whose extensive knowledge of the college's word processing system--and seemingly endless hours implementing it--proved invaluable to me. Sincere appreciation is also expressed to my wonderful parents and to my brother, Ray Merlock, whose endless supply of understanding and confidence proved to be a great inspiration. It was Ray who, when I was a child, sparked my interest in movies and nurtured it over the years. Finally, this work is dedicated to Joe Jackson, who in addition to discussing with me the ideas and concepts that eventually made their way into the following pages, offered me the emotional support that was necessary to maintain my sanity. Without him, this work would never have reached completion.

Chapter 1

INTRODUCTION

Prior to World War II, the image of children in American films
was one of unqualified innocence. The early successes of
D. W. Griffith, represented by The Adventures of Dolly
(1908), The Lonely Villa (1909), and The Battle at Elderbush
Gulch (1913), featured young, helpless children in danger.
In 1921, Charlie Chaplin released The Kid, co-starring five-
year old Jackie Coogan whose ragamuffin role helped make
for a box-office success. In subsequent years, young Coogan
was cast in several films in which, according to Norman Zierold, he invariably "played the poor, but lovable orphan waif,
whose innocence was elemental, whose love was boundless."1
Coogan paved the way for the child-star era, a time when
children's cherubic faces, often involved in saccharine plots,
graced the screen, and names like Jackie Cooper, Jane Withers, Freddie Bartholomew, Judy Garland--and most notably,
Shirley Temple--became familiar household words. In essence,
children in pre-World War II movies were happy, basically
good, and endowed with a sense of childlike tenderness and
wonder.

This image of childhood innocence has continued to dom-
inate the screen. Blockbuster films such as The Yearling
(1947), Shane (1953), Old Yeller (1958), Toby Tyler (1960),
To Kill a Mockingbird (1963), Oliver! (1969), Close Encounters
of the Third Kind (1977), and E.T. (1982) attest to the fact
that audiences remain intrigued by the idea of childhood innocence and find in it a special charm. However, after World
War II, some significant variations began to occur in the phenomenon of children in the movies.

First, the child-star era, which began around 1925,
sharply declined following the war's end in 1945. Although
children have continued to appear in popular films of the

postwar period, they have not held the box-office appeal of
their predecessors. Between 1934 and 1946, Shirley Temple,
Jane Withers, Mickey Rooney, Judy Garland, and Margaret
O'Brien made the list of the top ten box-office stars at least
twice, in Temple's case for six consecutive years.[2] In 1946,
Margaret O'Brien was the only child star to place, and since
then, the only child to be a major box-office success has been
Tatum O'Neal, the ten-year-old star of Paper Moon (1973); she
made the list for a single year, 1976.[3] In place of children,
adolescents like Brooke Shields and Jodie Foster have captured
a larger portion of the movie audience and brought with them
more mature themes. Instead of espousing the simple beauty
of childhood innocence, their films focus on the traumas of
growing up and the pangs of sexual awareness.[4]

    Secondly, following World War II, new images of children
slowly began to appear on the screen, ones that would have
been unthinkable in the years prior. Most striking was The
Bad Seed (1956), which featured a seemingly demure eight-
year-old girl who turned out to be a malicious murderess. In
1962, The Miracle Worker--a chronicle of the relationship between the blind, deaf, and mute Helen Keller and her dedicated teacher, Anne Sullivan--became a success. It brought
to bear the fact that all children are not happy and healthy
and living rosy lives; instead, some have problems and disabilities so severe that the children become incorrigible. In
years to come, this darker view of childhood hinted at in The
Miracle Worker hit full force with a barrage of child-as-demon
films, among them Rosemary's Baby (1968), The Exorcist
(1973), and The Omen (1976). Concurrent with the child-as-
monster image, more savvy and precocious--and less innocent--
children appeared on the screen, perhaps best represented by
smoking, swindling, sexually aware Addie Loggins in Paper
Moon (1973). Other movies reflective of this trend include
The Sailor Who Fell from Grace with the Sea (1976), Gloria
(1980), Shoot the Moon (1982), and Author! Author! (1982).
The youngsters in these films have an insight into the adult
world; they are not fully innocent. As Edward Edelson observes, "By 1970, both on and off screen, innocence was out
of style."[5] Although this is not totally true, as evidenced
by the success of Steven Spielberg's work and of several
other recent films pronouncing the innocence theme, one cannot deny the variations that have occurred in the way that
children are portrayed on the screen. These images reflect
the changing attitudes toward childhood and innocence that
have been taking place in America.

It is important to note, of course, that children in films are not representative of real-life children; instead, they tend to be stereotypes, caricatures, or symbols. Movies, like other narrative art forms, create their own world, and, although it is not a realistic one, it is nevertheless useful to observe, especially for the issues and attitudes that these screen images suggest. As Joseph Featherstone notes,

> Images of childhood fashioned by artists and writers are important sources because they sometimes influence and reflect popular thought and because they often constitute profound imaginative explorations of unacknowledged cultural dilemmas and tensions.[6]

Films, because they are the product of several creators' efforts and ideas and because they are designed to appeal to a mass audience, are perhaps more reflective of a collective unconscious than other more individualistic art forms. Thus, images of children in film provide a cultural shorthand for determining attitudes toward childhood; they transmit some of the important social values, fears, and concerns that Americans have regarding children. In his introduction to Corruption in Paradise: The Child in Western Literature (1982), Reinhard Kuhn writes, "It is my intention to take a modest step toward a better comprehension of the real child by proposing a phenomenological description of his fictional counterpart."[7] The same goal applies to a study of filmic children. By looking at the recurring narrative images of children in the movies and tying these images to the changing times, one can gain insight into the history of mass attitudes toward childhood in twentieth-century America.

The idea of analyzing particular images in films as a reflection of cultural trends is not new. Movies, especially those that do well at the box office, at least since Lewis Jacobs' The Rise of the American Film (1939),[8] have been studied as cultural artifacts, as mirrors of their culture--the social milieu of their filmmakers as well as the hopes, dreams, fears, values, and expectations of their audience. Approaching films in this way, called sociocultural criticism, has produced several valuable works. Siegfried Kracauer in From Caligari to Hitler (1947),[9] examined Weimar Germany via its films. In We're in the Money (1971) Andrew Bergman looks at Depression America in the same way:

> As films are not viewed in a void, neither are they

created in a void. Every movie is a cultural artifact ... associated with pottery shards, stone
utensils, and so on--and as such reflects the values, fears, myths and assumptions of the culture
that produces it.[10]

For the sociocultural film scholar, films, and the images
generated in them, are representative of the underlying
beliefs of the people who make and view them.

Since Kracauer and Bergman, several other important
sociocultural studies have emerged; these have taken various
approaches. Andrew Dowdy's The Films of the Fifties: The
American State of Mind (1973)[11] focuses on a particular decade. Robert Sklar takes a broader approach in Movie-Made
America (1975),[12] a cultural history of the development of
film in this country. Molly Haskell's From Reverence to Rape
(1974),[13] Thomas Cripps' Slow Fade to Black (1977),[14] and
Vito Russo's The Celluloid Closet (1981)[15] discuss how society's attitudes toward women, blacks, and homosexuals, respectively, are reflected in their stereotypical portrayals in
the movies. More recently, Michael T. Marsden, John G.
Nachbar, and Sam L. Grogg, Jr. have produced Movies as
Artifacts: Cultural Criticism of Popular Film (1982),[16] a collection of twenty articles which appeared in the pages of
The Journal of Popular Film and Television from 1972 to 1982,
all utilizing the sociocultural perspective. As the editors
write in their introduction, "To view an American film is to
witness the dreams, values, and fears of the American people, to feel the pulse of American culture."[17]

Undoubtedly, there is ample reason for the proliferation
of sociocultural criticism: it takes film out of a vacuum and
places it in the realm of history, politics, economics, literature, art, music, and other far-reaching cultural factors. In
essence, it looks squarely at the relationship between films
and the social milieu of the people who produce and consume
them. It is important to acknowledge, however, the possible
pitfalls of this approach. One must be extremely cautious in
interpreting filmic images; often they are not what they seem.
For example, as Molly Haskell points out in From Reverence
to Rape, mothers in 1940s' women's films seemed obsessively
devoted to their children. During a time when more women
were entering the workplace and spending less time with their
children, this portrayal may have been more representative of

women's guilt and ensuing cultural tensions than of the reality of the time.[18] Filmic images, as has been stated, are not
realistic; instead, they come in response to culturally held
beliefs. These responses may be directly reflective, conflicting, or symbolic. Because movie images do not wear
identity tags, it is often difficult to determine what social
messages are being transmitted.

A second precaution when attempting sociocultural
criticism is to avoid overgeneralization. It would be rash to
assume that blockbuster films such as Shane (1953), Mary
Poppins (1965), Paper Moon (1973), and E.T. (1982) were
popular simply because their portrayals of childhood hit a
chord among American movie audiences. People may have
gone to see Shane because of its Western hero; Mary Poppins because of its music and star, Julie Andrews; Paper
Moon because of its Depression setting and Ryan O'Neal;
and E.T. because of its special effects and extensive advertising campaign. However, if a particular image of childhood appears in several top-grossing films as well as influ-
ences an entire trend of subsequent films, it would be equally rash to dismiss it as pure coincidence. This argument
recalls that of Andrew Bergman's in We're in the Money.
Faced with the claim that Depression moviegoers attended
films simply for escape, Bergman counters that people do not
escape into something they cannot relate to: "The movies
were meaningful because they depicted things lost or desired."[19] Such is the case with children in films. Their
recurring portrayals are indicative of the inner workings of
American culture.

Despite the fact that there is justification for looking
at the images of children in films in order to determine the
latent cultural attitudes being expressed, few works have
addressed this issue. In 1954, Martha Wolfenstein published
an essay entitled "The Image of the Child in Contemporary
Films,"[20] in which she compares the portrayals of children
in selected Italian, French, British, and American films of
the 1950s. Children in the American films, she concludes,
embody "the American legend of the self-sufficient child
...."[21] "... [T]he child is the bearer of the heroic image.
In a prosaic world, he dreams of a man surpassing his
father, who would combine masculine strength and tenderness."[22] In essence, the focus in American films is on the
child's independence and ability to achieve more than his or

her parents, both commonly held American beliefs. In another essay, "Images of Childhood" (1976),[23] Robin Wood
takes a similar intercultural approach to children in film.
His analysis of the child in the American cinema emphasizes
the child's role within the family. As Wood writes,

> The concept of Family--a motif that cuts across all
> genres in the Hollywood cinema, informing and
> structuring westerns, musicals, comedies, gangster
> films, melodramas alike--is obviously basic to Amer-
> ican ideology, and in the American film the Child
> has his full meaning only in relation to it.[24]

Wood then proceeds to compare the child's familial role in
four films, Meet Me in St. Louis (1944), Night of the Living
Dead (1968), My Darling Clementine (1946), and High Plains
Drifter (1973). In 1980, Ruth M. Goldstein and Edith Zornow produced The Screen Image of Youth: Movies About
Children and Adolescents,[25] a reference work "concerned not
with films for children but with films that have something to
tell us about children."[26] The book outlines recommended
films but is not concerned with an in-depth social interpre-
tation. Most recently, a few writers have contemplated the
meaning of children in the intensely popular works of Steven
Spielberg and the later films featuring children that were
inspired by them.[27]

    While little has been done in the area of sociocultural
criticism on children in film, it is important to note that the
relationship between children and film has not gone unac-
knowledged. Past research, however, has taken only a few
established directions. Earliest studies on movies and children focused on the effects, almost always negative, of the
medium on its child audience. This approach has a great
deal to do with another emerging phenomenon of the twentieth century--social science research. Because movies were
new on the American social scene and clearly making an impact, they became the subject of several early studies. The
most prominent of these, made available through a grant
from the Payne Study and Experimental Fund, was conducted
between 1929 and 1932 and the bulk of its findings made
available in 1933. The Payne Fund Studies, which utilized
laboratory tests, questionnaires, and interviews, determined
that motion pictures had decidedly detrimental effects on
children; these included loss of sleep, heightened sexual
awareness, and tendency toward violence.[28]

As social science techniques became more sophisticated, researchers began to find problems with the Payne Fund studies. The studies blamed children's social and moral problems squarely on movies without considering any other factors. In Our Movie Made Children (1933), Henry James Forman rectified this situation by placing the movies in a social context before examining their effects on children.[29] By the 1950s, researchers agreed that the effects of movies on children were not as detrimental as they previously had thought. Thus, fewer and fewer studies tracing movie effects were published, the interest having shifted to other newer media, among them comic books[30] and television.[31]

Once movies' negative effects on their child audience ceased to be an issue of concern, research on the relationship between movies and children took another direction. Done primarily by teachers and librarians, it focused on the positive effects--the educational and entertainment values-- of movies for children. Notable studies of this kind include Films Kids Like (1963) by Susan Rice,[32] More Films Kids Like (1977) by Maureen Gaffrey,[33] and Movies for Kids (1973) by Ruth M. Goldstein and Edith Zornow,[34] all of which catalogue recommended movies for children. A related area of research discusses filmic adaptations of children's literature,[35] again with their acceptability to the child audience a paramount concern.

A final area of research on the relationship between children and movies, which proliferated in the 1970s, focuses on child stars and is primarily biographical in nature. Marc Best's Those Endearing Young Charms (1971)[36] and its sequel, Their Hearts Were Young and Gay (1975),[37] provide short biographical sketches on well-known child stars. The Child Stars (1965) by Norman Zierold[38] and Great Kids of the Movies (1979) by Edward Edelson[39] take a similar approach although their descriptions offer greater detail. Hollywood's Children (1979) by Diana Serra Cary[40] (formerly Baby Peggy of movie fame) lends insight into the lives of child stars and the impact that their early careers had on their adult lives; impeccably researched and well written, it is one of the best books available on children in the movies. The remaining sources focus on particular child stars. Representative of these are a host of books on Shirley Temple, including Shirley Temple (1974) by Jeanine Basinger,[41] The Shirley Temple Scrapbook (1975) by Loraine Burdick,[42] The Shirley Temple Story by Lester and Irene David (1983),[43] and <u>The Films of Shirley Temple</u> by Robert Windeler (1981).[44]

While past studies have focused on the positive and negative effects of films on their child audiences as well as on biographical accounts of child stars, it is necessary to delve further into the relationship between children and the movies in order to determine how children--defined as pre-adolescents twelve years of age and under--have been portrayed in the movies, and how these portrayals reflect changing attitudes toward childhood and historical trends in general. The justification for this research is clear. First, at the turn of the century when movies appeared on the American social scene, childhood was exalted,[45] and the idea of childhood innocence prevailed. In a country which had always looked to the future with optimism, the innocent child, whose whole life lay before him or her and who provided the key to future generations, became an important symbol of the American ideal. With the spread of industrialization, men left their homes for the workplace, motherhood became a full-time career, and families became child-centered;[46] thus, the innocent child provided the emotional core of the family. In the decades that followed, movies grew into a major mass medium; simultaneously, American attitudes toward childhood, never static, underwent various developments. By looking at the images of children on the screen, one can gain insight into the changing beliefs about the child and the family in twentieth-century America.

Further, the American family is a microcosm for society as a whole. What happens within the family becomes a marker for what is happening culturally. Children and their parents do not live in a vacuum; they are affected by general historical trends, and the twentieth century--fraught with rising industrialization, a major depression, two world wars, the Vietnam war, and rapidly changing life-styles-- has been a turbulent time. The American family has not escaped the impact of a century's worth of historical and social events, and the issues and attitudes influenced by them have made their way to the movie screen.

Prior to World War II, filmic portrayals of children were characterized by unerring innocence. These fictional representations reflected the charm, goodness, and limitless hope for the future that Americans saw in their children.

The movie images embodied American optimism and confidence
in what was to come. As Charlton Heston once remarked,
"Movies didn't always get history straight. But they told
the dream."[47] Slowly, beginning after World War II, movie
portrayals of children underwent some changes; the bright
side of childhood in some cases gave way to the darker side.
The glories of childhood innocence were downplayed as demon children and tough, precocious imps inhabited the screen.
These images no longer told of the dream. Instead, they
revealed societal fears; they foretold the nightmare.

There is no single reason for the emergence of this
new, darker dimension of filmic portrayals of children, ones
seemingly void of the innocence that was so endemic to the
earlier American vision. One reason, suggested by Neil
Postman, points to the fact that children have changed.
Postman argues that the rise of television, and its ability to
provide children with a source of information previously off
limits to them, has led to children's becoming more adultlike
and, consequently, to society's altered view toward them.[48]
In light of this observation, it is not surprising that as the
first generation raised on television reached adulthood, more
people began to scrutinize the institution of childhood--and
demand that children be granted the same basic rights as
adults.[49] At the same time, many parents expected their
children to be more precocious and take on greater responsibilities at an earlier age. Children, it seems, were maturing
sooner than they ever had before.

Other explanations for the new portrayals of filmic
children hinge not so much on changes in real children as
in the society around them. Postwar America saw the beginning of several cultural changes that intensified in the
decades that followed. After World War II, Americans
plunged into a great baby boom that lasted for the next
twenty years, and children became factors in overpopulation
and diminishing resources. By the 1970s, as Americans
faced soaring inflation and a rising cost of living, they saw
children as a greater financial burden. At the same time,
the traditional American family was undergoing transition.
First, women's roles took on a new aura. As motherhood as
a full-time career was questioned, new thoughts on the value
of children and their role in the family began to take hold.
Second, divorce became more prevalent, thus causing strain
within the traditional American family and making way for

new household structures. As the family changed, so, too,
did cultural attitudes toward children.

    While these social phenomena suggest reasons for vari-
ation in the child's image on the movie screen, they do not
explain changes in Americans' attitudes toward innocence, a
characteristic that has been traditionally associated with children. For this reason, it is essential to point to other factors, especially the atomic bomb--a device which threatens
not only to destroy human life but also to eradicate future
generations. A hope for the future has always been at the
core of childhood innocence, as embodied by children both
on screen and off. In a very real and powerful way, the
atomic age has threatened the future with the possibility of
no future. This realization, coupled with a growing loss of
confidence as a consequence of the Cold War, the Kennedy
slayings, defeat in Vietnam, and the Watergate scandal, has
contributed to a sense of pessimism and a mistrust in innocence; it has altered the American perception of children
and what they represent.

Notes

1. Norman Zierold, The Child Stars (New York: Coward-
    McCann, 1965), p. 44.
2. Cobbett Steinberg, Reel Facts, updated ed. (New York:
    Vintage Books, 1982), pp. 57-58.
3. Steinberg, p. 61. Feminist Molly Haskell has expressed
    extreme dismay over the fact that child star O'Neal was
    the only female to make the 1976 list, having unseated
    Barbra Streisand, the only woman named to the list the
    year before. See Molly Haskell, "Jodie Foster and Tatum
    O'Neal," in The National Society of Film Critics on the
    Movie Star, ed. Elisabeth Weis (New York: Viking,
    1981), pp. 227-231.
4. National Velvet (1945) and its sequel, International Vel-
    vet (1978), reflect this changing trend. The original,
    which focuses on the theme of childhood obsession,
    features a twelve-year-old protagonist. In the sequel,
    the emphasis shifts to teenage adjustment and finding
    oneself, and the protagonist is a sixteen-year-old orphan.
5. Edward Edelson, Great Kids of the Movies (Garden City,
    N.Y.:   Doubleday, 1979), p. 113.

6. Joseph Featherstone, "Children and Youth in America," in The Rights of Children. Reprint Series No. 9, ed. Harvard Educational Review (Cambridge: Harvard Educational Review, 1974), p. 357.

7. Reinhard Kuhn, Corruption in Paradise: The Child in Western Literature (Hanover, N.H.: Univ. Press of New England, 1982), p. 3.

8. Lewis Jacbos, The Rise of the American Film: A Critical History (New York: Teacher's College Press, 1982).

9. Siegfried Kracauer, From Caligari to Hitler (Princeton, N.J.: Princeton Univ. Press, 1947).

10. Andrew Bergman, We're in the Money: Depression America and Its Films (New York: Harper and Row, 1971), p. xii.

11. Andrew Dowdy, The Films of the Fifties: The American State of Mind (New York: William Morrow, 1973).

12. Robert Sklar, Movie-Made America: A Cultural History of American Movies (New York: Random House, 1975).

13. Molly Haskell, From Reverence to Rape (New York: Holt, Rinehart, and Winston, 1974).

14. Thomas Cripps, Slow Fade to Black (New York: Oxford Univ. Press, 1977).

15. Vito Russo, The Celluloid Closet: Homosexuality in the Movies (New York: Harper and Row, 1981).

16. Michael T. Marsden, John G. Nachbar, and Sam L. Grogg, Jr., eds., Movies as Artifacts (Chicago: Nelson-Hall, 1982).

17. John G. Nachbar and Sam L. Grogg, Jr., "Introduction," in Movies as Artifacts, ed. Michael T. Marsden, John G. Nachbar, and Sam L. Grogg, Jr. (Chicago: Nelson-Hall, 1982), p. 5.

18. Haskell, Reverence, pp. 153-188.

19. Bergman, p. xii.

20. Martha Wolfenstein, "The Image of the Child in Contemporary Films," in Childhood in Contemporary Cultures, ed. Margaret Mead and Martha Wolfenstein (Chicago: Univ. of Chicago Press, 1955), pp. 277-293.

21. Wolfenstein, p. 290.

22. Wolfenstein, p. 292.

23. Robin Wood, "Images of Childhood," in Personal Views: Explorations in Film by Robin Wood (London: Gordon Fraser, 1976), pp. 153-172.

    See also Woods' chapters in Andrew Britton, Richard Lippe, Tony Williams, and Robin Wood, American Nightmare: Essays on the Horror Film (Toronto: Festival of Festivals, 1979).

24. Wood, "Images." p. 163.
25. Ruth M. Goldstein and Edith Zornow, The Screen Image of Youth: Movies About Children and Adolescents (Metuchen, N.J.: Scarecrow, 1980).
26. Goldstein and Zornow, p. viii.
27. See Marina Heung, "Why E.T. Must Go Home: The New Family in American Cinema," The Journal of Popular Film and Television, 11, no. 2 (Summer, 1983), pp. 79-85. Also of interest is Vincent Canby, "Finding the Way to the Heart of Childhood," New York Times, 27 June 1982, Sec. 17, p. 1, col. 1.
28. The following sources, some of them outgrowths of the Payne Fund studies, outline the negative effects of movies on children:

    Blumler, Herbert. Movies and Conduct. New York: Macmillan, 1962.

    Blumler, Herbert and Philip M. Hauser. Movies, Delinquency, and Crime. New York: Macmillan, 1933.

    Charters, W. W. Motion Pictures and Youth: A Summary. New York: Macmillan, 1933.

    Dysinger, Wendell S. and Christian A. Ruckmick. The Emotional Responses of Children to the Motion Picture Situation. New York: Macmillan, 1933.

    Ford, Richard. Children in the Cinema. London: George Allen and Unwin, Ltd., 1939.

    Mitchell, Alice. Children and Movies. Chicago: Univ. of Chicago Press, 1929.

    Peterson, Ruth C. and L. L. Thurstone. Motion Pictures and the Social Attitudes of Children. New York: Macmillan, 1933.
29. Henry James Forman, Our Movie Made Children (New York: Macmillan, 1933).
30. See, for example, Frederic Wertham, Seduction of the Innocent (New York: Holt, Rinehart, and Winston, 1954).
31. Much has been written on the effects of television on children. For a good overview, see Robert M. Liebert, John M. Neale, and Emily S. Davidson, The Early Window: Effects of Television on Children and Youth (New York: Pergamon, 1978).
32. Susan Rice, comp. and ed., Films Kids Like (Chicago: ALA. The Center for Understanding Media, Inc., 1963).
33. Maureen Gaffrey, comp. and ed., More Films Kids Like (Chicago: ALA, 1977).

34. Ruth M. Goldstein and Edith Zornow, Movies for Kids (New York: Ungar, 1973).
35. See, for example, Douglas Street, ed., Children's Novels and the Movies (New York: Ungar, 1983).
36. Marc Best, Those Endearing Young Charms (New York: A.S. Barnes, 1971).
37. Marc Best, Their Hearts Were Young and Gay (New York: A.S. Barnes, 1975).
38. Norman Zierold, The Child Stars (New York: Coward-McCann, 1965).
39. Edward Edelson, Great Kids of the Movies (Garden City, N.Y.: Doubleday, 1979).
40. Diana Serra Cary, Hollywood's Children (Boston: Houghton Mifflin, 1979).
41. Jeanine Basinger, Shirley Temple (New York: Pyramid, 1974).
42. Loraine Burdick, The Shirley Temple Scrapbook (Middle Village, N.Y.: Jonathan David, 1975).
43. Lester and Irene David, The Shirley Temple Story (New York: Putnam, 1983).
44. Robert Windeler, The Films of Shirley Temple (Secaucus, N.J.: Citadel, 1981).
45. John Sommerville, The Rise and Fall of Childhood, Sage Library of Social Research, No. 140 (Beverly Hills: Sage, 1982).
46. Tamara K. Hareven, "American Families in Transition: Historical Perspectives on Change," in The Development of an American Culture, ed. Stanley Coben and Lorman Ratner (New York: St. Martin's, 1983), p. 350.
47. Charlton Heston, narrating America on Film, 1976, as quoted in Vito Russo, The Celluloid Closet: Homosexuality in the Movies (New York: Harper and Row, 1981), p. 4.
48. Neil Postman, The Disappearance of Childhood (New York: Delacorte, 1982).
49. See John Holt, Escape from Childhood (New York: Dutton, 1974).

Chapter 2

CHILDREN, INNOCENCE, AND THE AMERICAN TRADITION

The image of the child as innocent that has become so apparent in American movies over the years is not a mere coincidence. In America, children and innocence are highly valued; indeed, their significance is just as firmly woven into the fabric of American thought as it is into American movies. This, however, has not always been the case. In order to understand the twentieth-century belief in childhood innocence, it is necessary to look at its development in prefilmic days.

Traditionally, two opposing viewpoints have been associated with childhood. On one hand, the child is wild and needing to be tamed; on the other, the child is tender and innocent.[1] As David Grylls writes, "There are two perennial pictures of children: one tends to stress their incapacity for evil, the other their incapacity for good. The second of these was incorporated in the Christian doctrine of original sin. The first surfaced in resistance to this as a version of primal innocence."[2] In America, both of these images have persisted.

In colonial times the idea of the bad child prevailed. The Puritans, mindful of the doctrine of original sin, regarded children as innately depraved and requiring strict control.[3] Thus, they treated their children with little tenderness or affection; instead, they disciplined them, sometimes harshly, in order to teach them to be obedient, respectful, hardworking, and God-fearing. Warned against laxity, parents strove to make their children fit into the world of pious, responsible adults.[4] The Puritans believed this to be in the best interests of the child, especially if the child were to die, and this was not a matter to be taken lightly. Prior to the Industrial Revolution, families could

expect infection and other pestilence to take the lives of
more than half of their children, for little was known about
sanitation and nothing about immunization.[5] Because children were believed to be born sinful, they were not assured
a place in heaven. One popular writer, James Janeway,
warned that children "are not too little to die, they are not
too little to go to Hell."[6] Thus, Puritans felt a moral obligation to guard their children from a similar fate by ensuring their virtue.

By the time movies appeared on the American social
scene, the image of the bad child had receded into the background of American thought, where it has remained ever
since. Traces of it, however, always linger. In the early
twentieth century, as movies were gaining popularity, the
Progressive movement gained momentum. Concerned with at-
tacking social ills in order to bring about reform, the Progressives devoted some of their efforts to establishing playgrounds for children. On the surface, the "child savers,"[7]
as they were called, seemed to be goodheartedly trying to
provide recreational spots for city children. The real reason
for their efforts, however, centered around their belief in
the Puritan idea of the bad child. As one New York City
mother stated, "Why should I have children?... They say
the children here is all ruined--I know it.... They makes
'em thieves."[8] In essence, the child savers fought for institutions that would keep children in check; this particularly applied to poor immigrant children, whom some middle-
class mothers would chase away before they could contami-
nate their own children with "bad blood."[9] As Barbara Kaye
Greenleaf states, "It was hoped that supervised playgrounds,
by filling both the disciplinary and recreational voids in city
life, would make children 'good.'"[10] In more recent times,
vestiges of a belief in the bad child remain. In American
society, where childhood goodness and innocence are openly
professed, the myth of the bad child--the juvenile delinquent
--remains in the background. This becomes especially apparent with the introduction of new media--movies, radio,
comic books, television; each one, some fear, will bring out
the latent evil that lurks inside America's children. The co-
existence of the bad child with the good has characterized
America; it is the good child, however, who has been the
more dominant image in America for the past two centuries.

An affirmation of childhood innocence took hold in the

nineteenth century. The belief that the child is inherently
evil was supplanted by its opposite, a clear affirmation of
the child's basic goodness. According to Robert E. Stone,
the Romantic imagination reversed the traditional Puritan
family order of things:

> ... children, far from being little limbs of Satan,
> were in fact innately superior to adults, closer to
> Nature and hence to God, more alive to sensuous
> emotional and moral experience.[11]

This idea made its way into the American home. Adhering
to a belief in the good child, parents were able to treat
their children with more tenderness than was previously accorded them. Further, this realization seems to have had an
effect on the parental role: instead of concerning themselves
primarily with being disciplinarians, parents took a greater
interest in being protectors of the innocent. However, childhood innocence functioned on a symbolic level as well. In a
new land, innocence had become a national trait, and the
child--an embodiment of innocence--became an appropriate
symbol of the American frontier spirit, one which focused on
the future.

The concept of American innocence that took hold in
the nineteenth century is rooted in two central thoughts.
The first of these focuses on America's youthfulness as a
nation and its optimism in the future. After the War of 1812,
an air of hopefulness became apparent in American life and
letters, one which expressed the sense of enormous possibility that Americans were beginning to share about the future
of their new country.[12] Unlike its European counterparts,
America did not have a past to revert to for confidence and
comfort; more importantly, though, America did not have a
past looming over it to remind it of its mistakes and failures.
Thus, the future became all important. As R. W. B. Lewis
writes,

> As an index to the "hopeful" stand on national
> morality, I cite the editorial (of 1939) which hailed
> the birth of America of "a clear conscience unsullied
> by the past." The national and hence the individual
> conscience was clear just because it was unsullied
> by the past, but only a present and a future. The
> key term in the moral vocabulary of Emerson, Thoreau,

> Whitman, and their followers and imitators conse-
> quently was "innocence."[13]

Like the child, then, America lacked history and experience.
Marked by innocence and optimism, it set its sights on the
future.

This idea became further solidifed by America's image
as a virgin land.[14] Not only did America not have a history, but it was still primarily uncharted wilderness; thus,
like a child, it was still in the state of physical and moral
growth. Frederick Jackson Turner affirmed in 1893 that
America's character can be explained by the westward movement:

> Up to our own day American history has been in a
> large degree the history of the colonization of the
> Great West. The existence of an area of free land,
> its continuous recession, and the advance of Amer-
> ican settlement westward, explain American develop-
> ment.[15]

To Americans, the frontier stood for unlimited possibilities.
This was apparent not only in its vast physical dimensions
but also in its natural abundance. Thus, like the child, the
American West represented future potential, an optimistic belief in what lay ahead.

Innocence and an eye on the future also characterized
America's mythic heroes. The perfect American hero lacked
education and experience. Rugged and stalwart, he greeted
his lush environment with an unbiased vision and a child's
sense of wonder. As R. W. B. Lewis observes, the image
of this national hero takes its form from the prelapsarian
Adam:

> It was not surprising, in a Bible-reading genera-
> tion, that the new hero (in praise or disapproval)
> was most easily identified with Adam before the Fall.
> Adam was the first, the archetypal, man. His moral
> position was prior to experience, and in his very
> newness he was fundamentally innocent. The world
> and history lay all before him. And he was the
> type of creator, the poet par excellence, creating
> language itself by naming the elements of the scene

about him. All this and more were contained in the image of the American as Adam.[16]

Childlike in his innocence, Adam became a new hero for a new land. He existed, it seemed, outside of history; the world of total possibility lay before him.[17] Daniel Boone, as he has come down in legend, exemplified the American Adamic spirit.

> Boone enters the wilderness in a state of innocence and naivete, unsure of his own motivations and of the ultimate outcome of his adventures, but trusting in the strength of his own character and the goodness of nature to create ultimate good out of present confusion. This trusting immersion in the wilderness ultimately results in the attainment of self-knowledge and an understanding of the design of God--a state of awareness which Boone attains when he is able to stand above his experience, view it from the outside, and exercise his reason upon it in order to reduce it to its essential order.[18]

This modern critical assessment of Boone sounds more like that of the traditional "good" child: Boone and the child are characterized by an innate innocence that allows them to behold nature with no preconceptions, thus resulting in a state of goodness, trust, and wonder. This vision, unmuddled by past experience, brings the innocent observer closer to nature and ultimately to God.

Several themes emerged concurrently in nineteenth-century American thought and mythology. These included primal innocence, a hope in the future, the importance of a clear vision, and a sense of trust and wonder in nature. The child represented all of these values. Thus, the image of the child earned a special place in American Romantic literature, one richly reflective of the concerns of its time.

The American literary tradition of the innocent child found a voice among American transcendentalists. Ralph Waldo Emerson, whose writing revealed a disdain for conformity, realized his age's fascination with childhood. In "Self-Reliance" (1841) he wrote, "Infancy conforms to nobody; all conform to it; so that one babe commonly makes four or five out of the adults who prattle and play with

it."[19]   Interested in seeing the birth of a truly national literature, Emerson believed that America had to escape the
clutches and confining ideas of the past by looking forward.
The child, a symbol of the future, thus became an apt symbol for expressing the attitudes of the time.   Emerson also
found special appeal in the child's unbiased point of view
and keen perception.   Called "the innocent eye," this idea
found its roots among European Romantic writers--among
them, William Wordsworth, John Stuart Mill, and Thomas
Carlyle.[20]   Tony Tanner describes the child's special interest for the Romantic writer thusly:

> Not only because of his putatively innocent heart,
> not only because he seems free of all besetting
> doubts and distress of adult life, but also because
> of his point of view, his visual relationship with
> reality.   The distrust of judgement and analysis,
> the conviction of the need for a renewed sense of
> wonder and admiration, a new stress on "the pas-
> sive susceptibilities," a longing to feel the whole-
> ness of the universe rather than merely understand
> it--almost inevitably writers who embraced this
> cluster of ideas fastened on the child's relationship
> with nature as a symbol of their own aspirations.
> The child's wondering eye offered the romantic
> writer an avenue back to a reality from which he
> felt fast becoming alienated.   By recapturing a
> naive vision he might once again enjoy an untram-
> melled intimacy with nature.   There would be a
> new reverence, a new quietude, a new sense of
> glory.[21]

The oneness with nature made possible by looking through
"the innocent eye" held special significance for Emerson and
other American Romantics.   Just as an unlimited wilderness
characterized their new land, so too did a clear appreciation
of nature enhance their thoughts.   Thus, the child's
perspective--an ability to perceive nature more acutely and
fully--became an important literary motif.

Like Emerson, Henry David Thoreau felt a special
kinship with nature.   The West, which he saw as supremely
good, held a great attraction for him.   As he wrote in the
nature essay "Walking,"

> The future lies that way to me, and the earth seems
> more unexhausted and richer on that side.... East-
> ward I go only by force; but westward I go free.
> Thither no business leads me. It is hard for me to
> believe that I shall find fair landscapes or sufficient
> wildness and freedom behind the eastern horizon.
> I am not excited by the prospect of a walk thither;
> but I believe that the forest which I see in the
> western horizon stretches uninterruptedly toward
> the setting sun, and there are no towns or cities
> in it of enough consequence to disturb me. Let me
> live where I will, on this side is the city, on that
> the wilderness, and ever I am leaving the city more
> and more, and withdrawing into the wilderness.[22]

Thoreau, who believed "that every child begins the world
again,"[23] wrote in Walden, "I have always been regretting
that I was not as wise as the day I was born."[24] In essence, he affirmed the child's naive vision, one marked by
keen perception and an intimacy with nature, as clearly
superior to the adult's experienced one. Thoreau also noted
in Walden, "Children, who play life, discern its true law and
relations more clearly than men, who fail to live it worth-
ily."[25] Thus, from the Romantic viewpoint, the child, characterized by innocence, confronts life and nature more hon-
estly; it is in the child that one need look for the answers
to life's hidden mysteries.

In the tradition of Emerson and Thoreau, other
nineteenth-century writers turned to the child for inspiration. Walt Whitman's Leaves of Grass, characterized by
themes of individualism, progress, and optimism, paints the
image of the perfect national hero, the innocent, solitary,
forward-thrusting American Adam.[26] Whitman, who saw innocence as a replacement for sinfulness as the first attribute
of the American character,[27] regarded the innocence of childhood as parallel to Adam's own prelapsarian state. In "There
Was a Child Went Forth" (1855, 1871), one of Whitman's best-
known poems, he paid a special tribute to the child, who
"... went forth every day, / And the first object he look'd
upon that object he became, / And that object became part
of him for the day or a certain part of the day, / Or for
many years or stretching cycles of years."[28] In essence,
Whitman regarded the child as a blank slate who experienced
stimuli in the environment and was shaped by them; in turn,

the child became a part of his or her surroundings and affected them. Whitman, then, made the child's intimacy with nature, that which Emerson and Thoreau alluded to, complete: the child is nature, and nature is the child.

Nineteenth-century American fiction writers were also attracted to the ideal of childhood. Less optimistic than their counterparts in poetry and essay writing, however, they were more likely to balance the bright vision of childhood innocence with its darker side. In 1832, Nathaniel Hawthorne wrote "The Gentle Boy" containing a portrait of the innocent child; in The Scarlet Letter (1850), he created the opposite, the wild child Pearl, who functioned as a symbol of the sin inherent in her parents' adulterous love affair. Apparent in the fiction of Mark Twain is the nostalgia of childhood. Living in a world that was becoming increasingly technological and complex, Twain attached great beauty to the simple domain of children. However, like Hawthorne, he did not accept wholeheartedly the optimism of the Romantic imagination. Unlike his transcendental predecessors, Twain took the child out of nature and used the child's innocent perspective and keen perception to bring to the surface social ills; thus, the child functioned as a moral commentator on adult society. In Huckleberry Finn (1885), for example, Twain addressed the issue of slavery by showing it through the eyes of a child. Twain's youthful characters were not idealized; his best-known creations--among them Tom Sawyer, Huckleberry Finn, and Puddin'head Wilson--were frequently mischievous, even morally deficient. Another fiction writer to confront his age's intrigue with childhood innocence was Henry James, and for him, the idea took on a darker significance. While previous writers recognized a profound vision in the child's "innocent eye," James perceived a blindness; thus, the innocent was frequently portrayed as a victim, a theme expressed in The Turn of the Screw (1898), in which real children cannot live up to their governess' exalted conception of childhood innocence. James put innocence into a more realistic perspective. He tempered the unlimited possibility inherent in childhood innocence with the vulnerability that it necessarily entailed.

At the same time children were making their way into the thoughts and works of the nation's serious writers in nineteenth-century America, the virtue of innocence became a national trait. However, just as fictional children were

gaining more critical attention in America, so were real ones.
Beginning in the 1830s and 1840s, the importance of the
child's formative years began to be felt in other areas of
American life: Catharine Beecher, Elizabeth Peabody, and
Horace Mann in education; Horace Bushnell in theology;
Samuel Goodrich and Jacob Abbott in magazine writing; and
Erastus Field and Henry Walton in portrait painting.[29] In
the field of human development, scientists engaged in a vig-
orous debate over which was more important--heredity or
environment--in shaping a child's personality; leading the
nature side was Francis Galton, opposed by behaviorist
John B. Watson, who spoke out in favor of the nurture concept. Owing to all of the interest accorded to children, by
the end of the century they had come into their own as special and unique human beings. In America, as Neil Postman
comments, "successful attempts were made ... to get all
children into schools and out of factories, into their own
clothing, their own furniture, their own literature, their
own games, their own social world."[30] Child welfare, pedi-
atric medicine, the campaign for clean milk, and the movement to build more playgrounds became topics of concern.[31]
Further, through the work of G. Stanley Hall and Sigmund
Freud, children were accorded their own psychology. The
former, considered to be the founder of child psychology in
the United States, oversaw the design, distribution, and
analysis of sophisticated questionnaires about children and
started a journal to provide a forum for speculation and con-
crete findings on child behavior.[32] He was also responsible
for bringing noted Viennese psychiatrist Sigmund Freud to
America to speak.[33] Freud, who was met with mass opposition when he tried to dispel the popular myth that children
were sexless and innocent, was especially influential in establishing childhood as the most critical period of life in
terms of psychological development.[34]

It could not be denied that children were making an
impact in the humanities and social sciences in nineteenth-
century America. Not surprisingly, then, images of children, characterized by the prevailing notion of primal innocence, also appeared in the mass-produced, popular arts
of the time; these works, especially popular books and
plays, provided material from which the early silent movies
frequently drew their plots.[35] In 1832, Jacob Abbott published The Young Christian, which concluded as follows:

> Childhood is a most fertile part of the vineyard of
> the Lord. The seed which is planted there vege-
> tates very soon, and the weeds which spring up are
> easily eradicated. It is in every respect an easy
> and pleasant spot to till; and the flowers and fruits
> which, with proper effort, will bloom and ripen there
> surpass all others in richness and beauty. [36]

In its profession of the innocence of childhood, this guide-
book to Christian life, which sold at least a quarter of a
million copies, [37] started the mass attitudes toward childhood
which characterized popular images for the remainder of the
nineteenth century.

In the 1840s, sentimental books became popular in
America, and innocent child characters--often dying children
or impoverished orphans--flourished. This trend is evidenced
in the work of Charles Dickens, who frequently addressed
the theme of injustice against children. Sixteen of Dickens'
books qualified as American best-sellers, [38] thus making him
one of the most widely read authors in America. In The Old
Curiosity Shop, which first appeared as a magazine serial,
Dickens introduced Little Nell, the epitome of childhood innocence and vulnerability. The popularity of her character is
legendary: Americans lined New York's docks for the final
number of the series, shouting at the approaching steamer,
"Is Little Nell dead?" [39] Published as a book in 1841, The
Old Curiosity Shop sold over a million copies. In 1844,
Dickens' A Christmas Carol, which had also been serialized,
appeared in book form. It featured another innocent child--
crippled Tiny Tim, who was also in danger of dying. This
story sold over two million copies and became Dickens' top-
selling work in America. [40] His best-selling longer novel,
David Copperfield (1850), [41] also addressed the issue of
childhood, as did several of his other novels, including
Oliver Twist (1838), which sold over a million and a half
copies. [42] Given Dickens' popularity among readers, it is
not surprising that every one of his novels and six of his
stories were adapted for the American stage, [43] thereby
bringing his child characters to an even larger popular
audience.

By the 1850s, as the trend toward sentimentality continued, domestic novels predominated. These books, written

primarily by women, explored the women's world, especially
the American home; children, of course, occupied an important part in this world. Frank Luther Mott notes,

> The middle-class American home was one of the chief
> focal points of the best seller literature of this
> great book boom. The home, with a saintly mother,
> a father saintly or otherwise, and a family of grow-
> ing children one of whom is the heroine formed the
> basis for many a popular novel. Or to emphasize
> the home still more, an author sometimes showed an
> orphan growing up in an alien family. This Home-
> and-Jesus formula, emphasizing the strains of fam-
> ily life, and the education of youth, with religious
> solution for all problems, filled books which found
> hundreds of thousands of purchasers. [44]

The popularity of these books was unmistakable. Susan
Warner's The Wide, Wide World (1850) told the story of innocent little Ellen who, despite tragedy after tragedy, finds
strength in God and doing good for others. In America
alone, the novel sold over a half million copies[45] and earned
for Warner $4,500 in six months. [46] Her next novel, Queechy
(1852), also sold briskly. Like The Wide, Wide World, Maria
Susanna Cummins' book, The Lamplighter (1854), was a moralistic romance chronicling the virtuous but problem-riddled
life of an orphan girl; it sold forty thousand copies within
the first eight weeks after its publication and a hundred
thousand within the first decade. [47] In each of these books,
the underprivileged heroine triumphs in the end, as was the
case in Augusta Jane Evans' Beulah (1859) and St. Elmo
(1867) and E. D. E. N. Southworth's The Hidden Hand
(1859), all of which qualified as best-sellers in their time.

    Although the domestic novel featuring innocent, saintly
children reached a peak in the 1850s, its sales continued
throughout the century, as evidenced by such popular novels
as A. D. T. Whitney's Faith Gartney's Girlhood (1863), John
Habberton's Helen's Babies (1876) and Louisa May Alcott's
Little Women (1868) and Little Men (1871). Many domestic
novels were designed with a juvenile as well as an adult audience in mind; best-sellers in this category included The
Five Little Peppers and How They Grew (1880) by Margaret
Sidney, Heidi (1884) by Johanna Spyri, and Little Lord
Fauntleroy (1886) by Frances Hodgson Burnett, the last of

which also became immensely popular as a Broadway play. [48]
In the first two decades of the twentieth century, at precisely the time when movies were beginning, sentimental,
domestic novels reached another height of popularity. Like
the family novels of the 1850s, many of these included child
protagonists who, through their goodness, overcame all odds
and assured themselves of a happy, secure future. The
popularity of Alice Hegan Rice's Mrs. Wiggs of the Cabbage
Patch (1901), Kate Douglas Wiggin's Rebecca of Sunnybrook
Farm (1903), Gene Stratton Porter's Freckles (1904), Lucy M.
Montgomery's Anne of Green Gables (1908), Jean Webster's
Daddy Long-Legs (1912), and Eleanor H. Porter's Pollyanna
(1913) attest to this trend.

Images of innocent children also figured prominently
in crusade-books of the nineteenth century. Similar to domestic novels in their presentation of the American family,
these books were most notable for their devotion to causes.
Published in 1852, Harriet Beecher Stowe's Uncle Tom's Cabin
proved to be one of the most popular crusade-books of all
time. A simple, moralistic, antislavery tale, it featured a
paragon of childhood virtue, saintly Little Eva, a vulnerable,
helpless innocent who was willing to do anything, even sacrifice herself, if necessary, in order to bring her father closer
to God and thereby eliminate the evil of slavery. Uncle Tom's
Cabin immediately became a best-seller; more than 300,000
copies were bought in less than a year after it appeared, and
it quickly became the most popular work of fiction in America. [49] A dramatic version of the novel, produced by George
Aiken in 1852, began a nationwide tour and met with audience
acclaim everywhere; the stage version further helped to sell
more copies of the book. [50] By the second half of the nineteenth century, except for the Bible and selected evangelical
hymns, Uncle Tom's Cabin, as a book or play, was often the
only form of literary art familiar to hundreds of thousands of
Americans. [51] As her popularity attested, Little Eva had an
unmistakable audience.

So too did Little Mary Morgan in T. S. Arthur's Ten
Nights in a Bar-Room and What I Saw There (1854), another
popular crusade-book. Published at the height of the temperance movement, it told the story of three men who were
affected by drink, one of whom had a daughter, Little Mary
Morgan. Embossed in gold on the cover of the black bound
book was a scene from the bar-room showing Little Mary

tugging at her father's arm. The caption beneath the picture read, "Father, come home!" Ten Nights in a Bar-Room
became a best-seller of the era, second only to Uncle Tom's
Cabin; it sold a steady 100,000 a year for twenty years, and
after it was turned into a play in 1858 remained on the stage
circuit for another fifty.[52] Although it was the most popular temperance novel to use innocent children to show the
dismal effects of drink on family life, it was not the only
one. In Walt Whitman's novel, Franklin Evans, Little Jane's
last act before dying was to deposit in her alcoholic brother's
hand a tiny temperance tract.[53] In another popular novel,
a drunken mother who was rocking her infant near the
hearth accidentally dropped it into the fire, thus sending
the baby to a fiery demise.[54] In temperance novels, then,
children frequently suffered or died as a result of their
family members' drunkenness and neglect; in essence, their
deaths served as punishment for cruel adults.

Sentimental, domestic, and crusade novels were not
the only best-sellers to feature children in the nineteenth
century. Other books, diverse in their subject matter and
style, also featured children. Among the more literary
writers, Mark Twain achieved popular success with Tom
Sawyer (1876) and Huckleberry Finn (1885), Robert Louis
Stevenson with Treasure Island (1884), and Rudyard Kipling
with The Jungle Books (1894-95) and Captains Courageous
(1897). In 1867, Horatio Alger published Ragged Dick, the
story of a poor bootblack who, through practicing the American virtues of hard work, thrift, honesty, and self-reliance,
achieved success. The book led to a profitable series of
Horatio Alger rags-to-riches novels, thus making the author
when he died in 1899 as much of a success as his boyhood
characters. Lewis Carroll's Alice in Wonderland (1866) and
L. Frank Baum's The Wonderful Wizard of Oz (1900), each
chronicling the fantasy-filled journey of a young, curious
child, appealed to audiences in a child-oriented era.

Children figured prominently in nineteenth-century
books and plays, and they also made their mark in another
popular art, the comics. On February 16, 1896, Richard
Outcault unveiled "The Yellow Kid," thus giving birth to
the image of the tough, mischievous, street kid, one that
would characterize comics for years to come. Prompted by
the success of "The Yellow Kid," the New York World signed
Outcault on to do another comic strip based on the same

theme. The result was "Buster Brown" (1902), the story of
a mischievous boy and his equally conniving dog who together
outwit all of the adults around them in order to get their way.
In 1897, another mischievous-kid comic strip, "The Katzenjammer Kids," appeared in William Randolph Hearst's New
York Journal. Drawn by Rudolph Dirks, this strip, which
enjoyed a long and successful run, featured two devilish
boys who wreaked havoc everywhere they went, much to the
dismay of Mamma, Der Captain, and the other household members. Windsor McKay's "Little Nemo" (1905), which portrayed
a young boy in the strange but wonderful dream world of
slumberland, was an especially eloquent example of the continuing trend of the mischievous child in American comics.
The fact that audiences took delight in the frolicsome antics
of these devilish little mischief-makers seems, at first glance,
to contradict the prevalent belief in the good, innocent child
as reflected in the other popular arts. This, however, is
not the case. John Sommerville explains the nineteenth-
century attraction for the mischievous child thusly:

> Apparently, it was precisely as these children were
> being "naughty" that they seemed most precious to
> adults. Of course, it was exactly at that point in
> their own childhood activities that they had always
> been stopped. Authors were almost too eager to
> assure their readers that this mischief does not
> show a really bad heart. Quite the contrary, it
> demonstrates the child's innocence by showing him
> to be unconscious of the effects of his actions.[55]

In essence, readers enjoyed "The Yellow Kid," "Buster Brown,"
"The Katzenjammer Kids," and "Little Nemo" because the children in them were mischievous; however, the children were
not as much bad as they were rambunctious, curious, fun-
loving, and spirited. The little rascals simply added a new
dimension to the pervading belief in the carefree, innocent
days of childhood.

At the turn of the century, childhood reached the
highest point it has ever occupied in Western culture.[56]   In
both serious and popular literature, children were exalted as
embodiments of innocence. At the same time, lavish attention was being paid to the special needs and psychology of
real children. This was the cultural climate when movies
took hold in America. For this reason, movies, following the

lead set by other cultural indicators, adopted the popular
image of the child as innocent.

Notes

1. Frederick Elkin and Gerald Handel, The Child and
    Society: The Process of Socialization (New York:
    Random House, 1980), p. 4.
2. David Grylls, Guardians and Angels: Parents and
    Children in Nineteenth Century Literature (Boston:
    Faber & Faber, 1978), p. 24.
3. Grylls, p. 24.
4. Grylls, p. 42.
5. Ann L. Clark, "Childrearing in Matrix America," in
    Culture and Childrearing, ed. Ann L. Clark (Philadel-
    phia: F. A. Davis, 1981), p. 43.
6. James Janeway, A Token for Children: Being an Exact
    Account of the Conversion, Holy and Exemplary Lives,
    and Joyful Deaths of Several Young Children, as
    quoted in Grylls, p. 26.
7. See Anthony Platt, The Child Savers: The Invention
    of Delinquency (Chicago: Univ. of Chicago Press,
    1969).
8. Greenleaf, Barbara Kaye, Children Through the Ages:
    A History of Childhood (New York: McGraw-Hill,
    1978), p. 107.
9. Greenleaf, p. 108.
10. Greenleaf, p. 107.
11. Albert E. Stone, The Innocent Eye: Childhood in Mark
    Twain's Imagination (New Haven: Yale Univ. Press,
    1961), p. viii.
12. R. W. B. Lewis, The American Adam: Innocence,
    Tragedy and Tradition in the Nineteenth Century
    (Chicago: Univ. of Chicago Press, 1955), p. 13.
13. Lewis, p. 7.
14. See Henry Nash Smith, Virgin Land: The American
    West as Symbol and Myth (New York: Vintage Books,
    1957).
15. Frederick Jackson Turner, "The Significance of the
    Frontier in American History," reprinted in The Fron-
    tier in American History (New York: 1920; republished,
    New York: Holt, Rinehart, and Winston, 1962), p. 1.

16. Lewis, p. 5.

17. David W. Noble, The Eternal Adam and the New World Garden (New York: George Braziller, 1968), p. 6.

18. Richard Slotkin, Regeneration Through Violence: The Mythology of the American Frontier (Middletown, Conn.: Wesleyan Univ. Press, 1973), p. 280.

19. Ralph Waldo Emerson, "Self-Reliance," in The Complete Writings of Ralph Waldo Emerson, Vol. I (New York: William H. Wise & Co., 1929), p. 139.

20. Tony Tanner, The Reign of Wonder: Naivety and Reality in American Literature (Cambridge: Cambridge Univ. Press, 1965), p. 13.

21. Tanner, p. 7.

22. Henry Davis Thoreau, "Walking," in The Works of Thoreau, ed. Henry Seidel Canby (Boston: Houghton Mifflin, 1937), pp. 667-668.

23. Henry David Thoreau, Walden, in Canby, p. 262.

24. Henry David Thoreau, Walden, in Canby, p. 310.

25. Henry David Thoreau, Walden, in Canby, p. 308.

26. Lewis, p. 28.

27. Lewis, p. 28.

28. Walt Whitman, "There Was a Child Went Forth," in Walt Whitman: Complete Poetry and Collected Prose, ed. Justin Kaplan (New York: Library of America, 1982), p. 138.

29. Stone, p. viii.

30. Neil Postman, The Disappearance of Childhood (New York: Delacorte, 1982), p. 67.

31. Greenleaf, p. 122. In the area of child welfare, it is also interesting to note that the Society for the Prevention of Cruelty to Children was founded in 1875--nine years after the establishment of the American Society for the Prevention of Cruelty to Animals.

32. Greenleaf, p. 126.

33. Greenleaf, p. 126.

34. Greenleaf, p. 127.

35. Russel B. Nye, The Unembarrassed Muse; The Popular Arts in America (New York: Dial, 1970), p. 365.

36. Jacob Abbott, The Young Christian, as quoted in Frank Luther Mott, Golden Multitudes: The Story of Best Sellers in the United States (New York: Macmillan, 1947), p. 97.

37. James D. Hart, The Popular Book: A History of America's Literary Taste (Berkeley: Univ. of California Press, 1963), p. 87.

38. Mott, p. 87.
39. Hart, p. 102.
40. Mott, p. 83.
41. Mott, p. 83.
42. Mott, p. 87.
43. Hart, p. 103.
44. Mott, p. 122.
45. Mott, p. 124.
46. Hart, p. 93. In contrast, Hart notes that Nathaniel Hawthorne received only $144.09 in royalties on Mosses from an Old Manse in twice the time period (p. 93).
47. Mott, p. 125.
48. Hart, p. 187.
49. Arthur Pollard, gen. ed., Webster's New World Companion to English and American Literature (New York: Popular Library, 1976), p. 650.
50. Hart, p. 112.
51. Pollard, p. 650.
52. Nye, pp. 29-30.
53. Hart, p. 108.
54. Hart, p. 108.
55. John Sommerville, The Rise and Fall of Childhood, Sage Library of Social Research, No. 140 (Beverly Hills: Sage, 1982), p. 175.
56. Sommerville, p. 177.

Chapter 3

IMAGES OF CHILDREN IN PRE-WORLD WAR II FILMS:

UNQUALIFIED INNOCENCE

America Before World War I

Since the earliest days of commercial motion pictures, filmmakers have been portraying children. In France during
the 1890s, brothers Louis and Auguste Lumiere took a special delight in capturing the spontaneity of children on film,
not unlike, today, an overzealous parent with a happy baby
and a home-movie camera. In Feeding the Baby (1898), one
of the first film documentaries, the Lumiere Brothers recorded
an everyday occurrence, an infant being fed by two persis-
tent parents. Although this was a deliberately staged performance,[1] what made it memorable was the baby's natural
reactions--and total nonchalance for the parents' efforts.
Children did not even have to act; they were entertaining
by just being themselves. In one of the first film comedies,
Watering the Gardener (1895), the Lumiere Brothers devised
a story that focuses on a child's penchant for mischief. A
young boy places his foot on a garden hose, thus blocking
the flow of water. When the gardener examines the clogged
hose to determine the problem, he gets soaked by a quick
torrent of water. The young boy, of course, is amused.
This short incident underscores the child's early known ca-
pacity for humorous, trickster roles.

   As the showing of motion pictures gained momentum in
America, so did children's filmic roles. Almost from the
start, though, American filmmakers were interested in telling
stories, and this required character development. Filmmakers
had to learn how to translate into visual, cinematic images
that intangible quality of innocence that had become so clearly associated with children. One of the most obvious ways

to dramatize innocence--and one which was being used with
much success already in popular books and stage melodrama
--was to concentrate on the child's vulnerability by placing
him or her in a dangerous situation. In the first decade of
the twentieth century, several images of children emerged
concurrently in American novels. Of these, the helpless,
threatened child, frequently one who spends little time on
the screen but around whose rescue the entire plot revolves,
became one of the most popular.

    This image appeared in the early films of Edwin S.
Porter, one of America's first influential filmmakers, and set
a general trend for what was to come. In The Life of an
American Fireman (1902), usually considered to be the first
film of a dramatic nature made in the United States,[2] Porter
carefully created the scene of a child in jeopardy. Sitting
at his desk in the police station, the police chief dozes off
and dreams of a woman putting a child to bed. Suddenly,
he awakens from the peaceful domestic scene, only to wonder nervously who might be in danger from fire at that moment. Abruptly, the fire alarm goes off, and the next several scenes depict the Newark, New Jersey, Fire Department,
complete with a wide array of fire-fighting apparatus, de-
parting for the blaze. Upon their arrival, the firemen find
a burning building with a mother and her child trapped inside. A fireman first rescues the woman, who, once safely
on the ground, begs him to return for her imperiled child.
The fireman reenters the smoke-filled building and several
tense moments later emerges with the child and delivers it
safely to its mother. The film ends, as Lewis Jacobs notes,
as "the child, being released and upon seeing its mother,
rushes to her and is clasped in her arms, thus making a
most realistic and touching ending of the series."[3]

    This simple, melodramatic plot emphasizes several char-
acteristics of the child's early image in American films. First,
the relationship between mother and young child is clearly
established. In the beginning, both are depicted as helpless
and in danger while men work to rescue them; in essence,
the woman and child are of one domain, the men of another.
Upon the mother's rescue, her only thought is of her child;
she is obsessive and hysterical while the men are calm and
deliberate. Within this film, the point of view lies with the
fire fighters. As Lewis Jacobs notes of the film's release,

The Life of an American Fireman aroused excitement
wherever it was shown. Audiences, as if viewing a
real crisis, could not remain passive. They identified themselves with the fireman and the rescue on
the screen. The fire engines simply had to get to
the fire on time! The mother and child must not
perish! Such intense personal reactions to a movie
were unprecedented.[4]

Like the fire fighters, then, the audience members assumed
the role of protector while they watched the helpless child
languish on screen. This reaction suggests a necessary
counterpart to the child-as-innocent image. If children are
helpless innocents, they must be protected; it is up to adults
to guide, aid, and ultimately protect the child. A final observation on The Life of an American Fireman lies with its
depiction of an urban setting, complete with modern fire-
fighting technology. At the turn of the century, when the
film was made, rapid urbanization and industrialization characterized America, and many people questioned the acceptability of the city as a place to raise children. This film
points to one of the dangers of the city--the possibility of
fire in a multistory dwelling. However, tragedy never occurs. With their apparatus--engines, ladders, and hoses--
the fire fighters reach the fire in a matter of seconds and
are able to rescue the mother and child. Thus, the child
born into a world of technology is saved by technology.
The future remains secure.

The Great Train Robbery (1903), Porter's best-known
adventure film, featured another child, again in a minor
role. Her portrayal, however, is significant. Immediately
upon her appearance on the screen, she is placed in a difficult situation: as she enters the station to bring her
father, the telegraph operator, his dinner pail, she discovers him bound, gagged, and unconscious after a robbery. In a moment of panic, she scurries about trying to
revive him. She then frees him from the ropes, throws a
glass of water in his face, and restores him to consciousness so that he can report the robbery to the townspeople.
In essence, the little girl in The Great Train Robbery is
one of the film's first child fix-it characters. Although
initially put into a situation of helplessness, she relies on
herself to correct it. The film ends happily: a posse of

townsmen defeats the bandits. This outcome could not have been accomplished had the little girl not revived her father so that he could summon help. She, in a sense, saves the day. Thus, concurrent with the helpless child in film, another image emerged on screen: the self-reliant fix-it character.

Following Edwin S. Porter's lead, D. W. Griffith featured a child in his first directorial effort for American Biograph, The Adventures of Dolly (1908). Griffith, no doubt recalling plot conventions of stage melodramas, believed that a child in jeopardy could hold his audience's attention. Adhering to the turn-of-the-century idea of the child as vulnerable and in need of protection, he told the story of Baby Dolly, who is kidnapped by a band of gypsies as she plays happily along a riverbank. The gypsies deposit the child in a water cask, place it in the back of their wagon, and go speeding off. Moments later, the cask falls into the river and travels briskly downstream through rapids and over a waterfall. Meanwhile, Dolly's parents, realizing she is missing, embark on a frantic search. Finally, some boys fishing on the riverbank find the cask that has washed downstream, hear sounds in it, and open it--to find the child cheerful and well. In the film's final scene, Dolly is reunited with her overjoyed parents.

Griffith's intuition proved correct: Dolly was a success, and Biograph immediately had Griffith sign a contract at $45 a week plus royalties.[5] Of course, the presence of a child character was not the only reason for Dolly's recognition. Movies, because they were so new, were exciting to their audiences, almost regardless of their content. Still, Dolly struck on some major trends. As with The Life of an American Fireman, the audience watching Dolly identified with the rescuers, not the little baby or the gypsy villains; thus, the viewers, like Dolly's parents, assumed the role of protector. It is important to note that unlike the imperiled child in The Life of an American Fireman, Dolly is the victim of adult treachery, not a natural occurrence. Her parents, however, are not the aggressors. This underscores a common theme in films featuring victimized children: although parents may be weak or ineffectual, they are rarely the cause of their children's mistreatment; instead, parents try to protect and save the child from evil forces. In later years, even as reports of parent-child abuse were more

frequently reported, this undaunting image of the good,
watchful parent remained with few exceptions.

Following The Adventures of Dolly, Griffith's cinematic
methods, especially his use of cross-cutting, close-ups, and
lighting, became more sophisticated. Still, he maintained an
interest in simple plots featuring victimized children, sometimes with their equally victimized mothers in tow. In The
Lonely Villa (1909), a woman and her young daughters are
alone in their home when burglars attack. In an excellent
use of cross-cutting, Griffith captured the terror and intensity of the situation by alternating shots of the mother
and children moving from room to room to escape the burglars and the father hurrying home to rescue his endan-
gered family. This film presents some common images.
First, the mother, by nature of her helplessness in a traumatic situation, is likened to her daughters; both need the
protection of a strong male figure. Second, two entities
are formed: the child/female world versus the male world.
This division is further established in a later Griffith film,
The Battle at Elderbush Gulch (1913). Here a family in a
cabin fears an attack by Indians. The main concern, however, lies with a mother and her infant, both embodiments
of innocence. In one particularly striking scene, a man in
the cabin points a gun at the young mother's head. If he
cannot protect her from the Indians, she is better off dead
than to risk her and her child's goodness and innocence at
the hands of savages. The world of the mother and infant
in this film is juxtaposed with that of the men who hold the
responsibility for protecting them. The child/female world
is further established by its visual relationship to two cute
puppies; in essence, both groups are characterized by innocence, helplessness, and a lack of obligation.

In the early days of silent film, then, the innocent
child in jeopardy, as popularized by premier film directors
Edwin S. Porter and D. W. Griffith, was a popular celluloid
image. There was ample reason for this phenomenon. As
America became more urbanized and industrialized, many
people enjoyed a lessened work week which allowed for more
leisure hours. At the same time, they had little money to
spend on traditional entertainments such as the theatre and
vaudeville. The first American motion picture audiences
were composed primarily of members of this large urban
working class, many of them immigrants whose command of

the English language and knowledge of the manners and cus-
toms of their new environment were limited.[6] Thus, they
needed simple melodramatic plots, with clearly defined moral
conflict, typed characters, and a one-dimensional story. Motion picture narratives revolving around children in danger
fit the bill. They were easily translatable into filmic images
(e.g., the happy beginning, the child in jeopardy, the frantic rescue, and the happy ending) that the immigrant audience could comprehend without difficulty. Further, movies
of this type emphasized two underlying American beliefs:
first, the importance of family and second, the innocence
and vulnerability of childhood.

By 1910, the popular image of imperiled children became further entrenched in film due to two simultaneous occurrences. Almost from the beginning of the film industry,
nickelodeon owners were interested in expanding their audience by attracting the middle class, including women and
entire families.[7] In 1907 and 1908, a censorship attack flared
up;[8] this resulted in the passage of censorship laws in 1910.[9]
Thus, in order to attract the middle class as well as meet the
growing demand for acceptable, often moralistic stories, moviemakers realized they had to upgrade content while adhering
to the melodramatic format. Frequently, they turned to popular literature and the classics where images of the innocent,
vulnerable child already flourished.[10] This image, then, became standard fare for early movie audiences.

Other reasons for the presence of innocent children in
early films lie with the important cultural developments that
were occurring in America. By bringing to the silent screen
images of children in danger, Porter, Griffith, and their motion picture contemporaries were not only telling melodramatic
stories to an immigrant audience but were also drawing attention to a growing social phenomenon--concern over the treatment of children. During the first fifteen years of the century, Progressivism, with its emphasis on social reform to
build a better society, took hold in America. Among the
Progressives' concerns were the effects of motion pictures
on youth, preservation of morality for children, and the
mistreatment of children, especially those who worked in
factories and coal mines. In 1909, a series of White House
Conferences for consideration of the child, one to be held
each decade, was begun; the first focused on Americans'
responsibilities toward dependent children. Indeed,

Americans began to see child care and welfare as ongoing
concerns. During the second decade of the century, when
movies began to take hold firmly and Griffith reached his
peak of popularity, children gained unprecedented social
attention. The first state bureau of child hygiene was established.[11] The Children's Bureau of the United States
Government was formed, conducted its first infant mortality
study, and published the best-selling child-care manual Infant Care.[12] Several child welfare boards were begun.[13]
Child labor was regulated,[14] and the second White House
Conference for Children, devoted to improving the standards
of child welfare, was held. Thus, the innocent child in
jeopardy was not only a screen image but also a social reality that was gaining attention and being investigated.

One of the reasons that Americans in the early years
of the twentieth century fought so vigorously for improved
welfare standards for children was that they saw the child
as a hope for the future. As industrialization and urbanization threatened to alter the face of American life, people
saw in their children the last vestiges of simplicity and pur-
ity in a rapidly changing society. Theodore Roosevelt, for
example, regarded the American youth as a maintainer of
the democratic life. In an attempt to preserve the national
character, he urged native-born Americans to have more
children so as to counteract the influx of recent immigrants.[15]
Also characteristic of the early 1900s was a drive to develop
the child's aptitude, achievement, and physical growth. Seeing children as a hope for the future, Americans wanted
them fit and ready should twentieth-century warfare strike.[16]

World War I and the Age of Prosperity

As American participation in World War I seemed more and
more inevitable, the vision of children as future soldiers
took on ominous connotations, as exemplified by Herbert
Brenon's 1916 pacifistic film, War Brides. This film, as
Lewis Jacobs notes, "purported to show the unwillingness
of the German people at large to participate in war, although
the reference to Germany was veiled."[17] Its plot revolves
around a spirited young woman named Joan (Alla Nazimova),
who incites a strike among mistreated factory workers, and,
in the course of her gallant efforts, falls in love and marries
a farmer. Soon after, war is declared, and her husband,

along with his three brothers, is killed in battle. The king
then decrees that all women will marry available men in order
to produce offspring to fight future wars. Joan, who is
pregnant, balks at the projected future of her unborn child
and organizes the townswomen in an attempt to stop the war.
She is arrested for her actions but, because she is expectant
with a potential soldier, cannot be executed. After escaping
from prison, Joan leads the women in an antiwar demonstra-
tion before the king, who tells her firmly that there will always be war. Convinced of the fate of her unborn child,
Joan shouts "No more children for war!" and shoots herself.
Then, as Jacobs describes the dramatic scene, "The women
take up her body, hold it aloft as a symbol, and with renewed courage determine to carry on their campaign."[18]

    Although the on-screen presence of children in War
Brides is minimal, what the film says about parental expectations of children is significant. When this film was released, it met with both wide popularity and critical acclaim,
no doubt in part because of its accurate portrayal of parental hopes and, most poignantly, fears. Upon America's en-
try into World War I, the film was banned from movie theatres on the grounds that "the philosophy of this picture is
so easily misunderstood by unthinking people that it has
been found necessary to withdraw it from circulation for the
duration of the war."[19] Had American parents not been so
obsessed with the culturally embedded idea of children being
the key to a hopeful future, this film would not have been
as influential as it evidently was.

    Following World War I, great changes continued to oc-
cur in the fabric of American culture. War veterans returned with a worldliness from having been other places and
seen other things and with a confidence in America's triumph.
Indeed, America and its people, relieved to see the war ended
and content with its outcome, were anxious to begin anew.
There was much reason for their optimism. After a brief
postwar recession, 1920s America--called the Age of Prosperity
--was characterized by a booming economy and unlimited opportunity, and the stock prices proved it. On August 2,
1923, United States Steel (paying a five-dollar dividend)
stood at 87, Atchison (paying six dollars) at 95, New York
Central (paying seven) at 97, and American Telephone and
Telegraph (paying nine) at 122.[20] This was the age of the
self-made businessman. Banks lent money on easy terms,

thereby giving such capable entrepreneurs as Henry Ford
and F. W. Woolworth a chance to become millionaires.[21]
Along with the emphasis on making money, Americans were
hit with a potent surge of consumerism and easy access to
credit, and they wanted to spend. After the war, many
Americans were not content to return to a humdrum, routine
life-style and old-fashioned Victorian morality.[22] Instead,
they craved speed, excitement, and passion, and a growing
technology helped to fulfill these needs.[23] The popularity
of the automobile, sales of which more than tripled between
1919 and 1929, made people more mobile.[24] The development
of motion pictures (by 1929, an average of fifty million Americans attended weekly[25]) provided a unique window on the
world. In America, the decade following World War I was
charged with energy and an emphasis on youth. Childhood
found a special place in this world and in its movies.

The on-screen time of children increased significantly
after World War I. In earlier films, plots frequently re-
volved around children in danger, but the motion picture
camera remained primarily on the adult rescuers. By the
dawn of the 1920s, more substantive children's roles proliferated in films; however, they were frequently played by
adult performers. In 1919, D. W. Griffith made Broken
Blossoms, adapted from Thomas Burke's story, "The Chink
and the Child," in Limehouse Nights.[26] This film is a tale
of parent-child abuse, which makes it a rarity among films.
Griffith tempered the impact of this message by combining
it with a simple love story. In Broken Blossoms, the child
Lucy, played by adult actress Lillian Gish,[27] is the victim
of frequent beatings by her cruel, temperamental father,
Battling Burrows. Cheng Huan, the "Chink" (Richard
Barthelmess), a kind, Oriental shopkeeper, sees the poor,
unjoyful child, and, one day after she has been brutally
beaten by her father, takes her to a room above his store
to take care of her. It is difficult to determine Lucy's age.
Although gentle Cheng Huan makes no physical advances
toward Lucy, he has an undeniable longing for her. However, Lucy, characterized by childlike optimism and wonder,
remains girlish. Even when her life is too despairing for
her to smile naturally, she pushes up the corners of her
mouth with her fingers to create one. Edward Wagenknecht
observes,

Take the scene in which Lucy and Cheng Huan first

look at each other--he in his shop, she in the street
outside. The audience looks through the eyes of
each, seeing the girl as the man looks at her and
the objects in the shop window as Lucy's delighted
gaze travels over them. Later he remembers the
flower she had wanted and been unable to buy and
brings it to her in her sanctuary. There is a delightful, subdued humor in these scenes, along with
all their lyricism and danger, for the girl is still a
child, and the doll Cheng Huan brings her is the
climax of all her joys.[28]

What is significant about this film is the continuous on-screen
presence of a child character; Lucy dominates the screen until the tragic ending when Battling Burrows, upon discovering her whereabouts, takes her home and beats her to death,
and Cheng Huan carries her poor, battered body to his room,
where he stabs himself in the heart. Thus, the camera, in
frequently assuming Lucy's point of view, chronicles a child's
own feelings and observations. Also of note in this film is
an important child-welfare issue circa 1920: Should outsiders
intervene on the behalf of children who are mistreated by
their parents?

One of the most popular films of 1921, Tol'able David,
directed by Henry King, also featured an adult actor playing
a child character. Tol'able David tells of the quest of a boy
(Richard Barthelmess) to grow up and gain maturity. In the
beginning of the film, young David frolics with his dog,
Rocket, and comically tries to impress the neighbor's grand-
daughter. After ruffians threaten the security of David's
rural homestead, he acquires the responsibility of avenging
their villainy and supporting his family. In a tense, adventurous climax, David, who has taken over his injured brother's position as mail carrier, is confronted by the villains as
he attempts to deliver the mail to its specified destination.
In order to fulfill his duties, he must kill the man who crippled his brother and escape with his own life. By the film's
conclusion, David has, despite all odds, fulfilled his obligation of delivering the mail. In essence, he has learned responsibility; he has made the transition from boyhood to man-
hood. As in Broken Blossoms, the point of view of Tol'able
David lies frequently with the child. Seen through David's
eyes, the film is a story of the rites of passage that come
with growing up.

In an age characterized by an emphasis on youth, several actors and actresses who began stage and movie careers as children continued to play children's roles well into adulthood. Marguerite Clark, who placed second in a 1918 Motion Picture Magazine star-popularity contest, was five feet tall and weighed less than a hundred pounds; she had no difficulty looking like a child even when in her thirties.[29] Her screen credits between 1915 and 1919 included Uncle Tom's Cabin (in which she played both Topsy and Little Eva), The Prince and the Pauper (in which she again played a dual role as both of Mark Twain's boys), Snow White, The Seven Swans, A Poor Little Rich Girl, and The Blue Bird. Another actress to attract children's roles was Mary Miles Minter:

> ... a golden, peaches-and-cream kind of girl, in whom all the sweet, innocent charms of youth were embodied as irresistibly as in any human being this generation has seen, and those who did not like her might quite reasonably, have gone on to declare that they did not like sunshine either ... besides being a girl, she was girlhood itself.[30]

Minter, who began her screen work as a child, continued to play children in the movies until her career was abruptly cut short in 1922 when she was implicated in the murder of director William Desmond Taylor. The movie public was taken with Minter's childlike charms, but after her association with a sex-related shooting (for which she was never convicted), it could no longer accept her innocent on-screen persona.[31] In addition to Clark and Minter, other actresses to cash in on the adult-child trend in silent films included June Caprice, Jewel Carmen, Vivian Martin and Gladys Lester.[32]

The 1920s intrigue with youth is best exemplified by the on- and off-screen persona of Mary Pickford, the most popular actress of the silent era. Like so many other performers on the silent screen, Pickford began her acting career during childhood, first on the stage, where she eventually worked under the distinguished direction of Broadway's David Belasco. In 1909, a slow season on Broadway, Pickford, who stood at a mere sixty inches, delivered herself to Biograph Pictures and confidently asked D. W. Griffith for a job. Surmising that the petite, pretty-featured young woman would make a smash on the movie screen, Griffith offered her

a job at the standard five dollars a day. Pickford demanded
twice as much, and Griffith, impressed with her energy and
spunk, agreed to meet her terms.[33] Griffith's intuition
proved correct. After casting Pickford (who, like other
performers, was not given any billing) in several short pro-
ductions, audiences began to take notice. Who, they asked,
was the lovely, doll-like actress with the blond, cascading
curls? Mary Pickford became a star. Dubbed "America's
Sweetheart" in 1914, she began appearing without fail in the
many fan magazines that were springing up in America, magazines that were just as interested in reporting the details of
her personal life as her movie roles. By 1914, Pickford had
married Owen Moore, one of Hollywood's most handsome leading men, and was making an unprecedented movie star's
salary of $104,000 annually.[34] Her drive and pluck had
achieved for the petite, seemingly demure, little actress exactly what she wanted.

The movie magazines' accounts of Pickford's personal
characteristics did not differ significantly from her screen
roles. Diana Serra Cary writes of the early Pickford screen
persona:

> She was a spunky girl, someone that the immigrant,
> the country folk, and the self-made man could all
> believe in: everything was possible for little Mary
> and the land in which she pursued her happy end-
> ings. Obviously, both America and the girl who
> became America's sweetheart were born to win.[35]

Pickford radiated a sense of innocence and independence; in
her, and people like her, Americans felt an optimism in the
good that could be accomplished. Adhering to her established screen image, Griffith, and later Carl Laemmle and
Adolph Zukor, cast Pickford most frequently in ingenue
roles--ones that commonly involved a young woman with special problems who, after overcoming her handicaps, is well
on her way to maturity and, most likely, marriage.[36] It
soon became apparent, though, that Pickford's screen persona could be best used to enhance children's roles; thus,
in response to her own diminutive stature and her time's
obsession with childhood, Pickford took on primarily children's parts. While in her twenties and thirties, she developed her little-girl persona in films such as Cinderella
(1914), Rags (1915), Rebecca of Sunnybrook Farm (1917),

Stella Maris (1917), Pollyanna (1920), Through the Back
Door (1921), Little Lord Fauntleroy (1921), and Little Annie
Rooney (1925). As Raymond Lee notes, Pickford played "a
child most of her reel life."[37]

It was within her children's roles that Mary Pickford's
plucky persona found its most successful vehicle. In order
to examine Pickford's tremendous success as a child on the
screen, it is useful to look at two of her representative roles.
In 1920, Pickford starred in Pollyanna, her first production
at United Artists, the studio that she, Douglas Fairbanks,
Charlie Chaplin, and D. W. Griffith had formed the year
before. In Pollyanna, directed by Paul Powell, Pickford took
the child-as-fix-it role introduced in The Great Train Robbery and expanded and personalized it. The film begins on
an optimistic note with the image of a rainbow. Immediately,
the scene turns to sorrow as Pollyanna Whittier (Mary Pickford) sings to her poor, aged father, an Ozark Mountain
missionary, who is dying. This initial scene underscores
the father/daughter relationship; throughout the film, Pollyanna's admiration for her father and his impact on her life
are established. Upon his death, orphaned Pollyanna is left
to fend for herself. In the American tradition, she must be
independent and self-reliant. She has outlived her father
and vows that she will always follow his wisdom: She will
be glad, no matter what happens. Her childlike affirmation
of optimism is reminiscent of Lucy in Broken Blossoms who,
despite her despair, pushes up the corners of her mouth to
form a smile.

Shortly after her father's death, Pollyanna is sent to
live with her rich, snobbish Aunt Polly in New England.
There she makes a series of blunders. She falls into a rain
puddle, tracks water and mud into Aunt Polly's elegant home,
and, unknowingly, catches and unravels Aunt Polly's knitting
--all much to the dismay of her very proper, decorous aunt.
Further, Pollyanna greets her aunt with unbounded affection,
an emotion which Aunt Polly, who sticks the child away in a
small, dark attic room, cannot reciprocate. Among themselves, the servants criticize Aunt Polly's treatment of her
niece. This scene sets up some interesting opposites: the
poor Ozark community versus the rich New England town;
the child's enthusiasm, outward displays of affection, and
inattention to what is proper versus the adult's coldness,
restraint, and obsession with decorum; and the moral

superiority of the less fortunate--the poor, the servants--
over the wealthy and privileged.

Although initially distraught over Aunt Polly and her
new home, Pollyanna soon returns to her spirited, optimistic
self by remembering the glad game, a game her father had
taught her, in which one takes something bad and turns it
into something good. Reiterating her father's central belief
that "The Lord told us eight hundred times to be glad; he
must have wanted us to do it some," Pollyanna begins to
transcend through kindness and natural innocence the barriers set up by age and social class. Subsequent scenes in
the film show Pollyanna cheering up a crotchety old woman,
befriending Jimmy Bean, a poor orphan boy, and converting
stern, reclusive Mr. Pendleton into a truly sympathetic and
caring old man.

These incidents are only a few of Pollyanna's fix-it
activities. In one of the film's crucial scenes, Pollyanna is
badly injured when she darts out in front of a speeding car
to rescue an imperiled baby. In the scenes that follow, Pollyanna's injury becomes a sacrifice (not unlike Little Eva's in
Uncle Tom's Cabin) to right the wrongs of the community.
Seeing her injured niece, Aunt Polly realizes how much the
child means to her. Pollyanna, it turns out, is glad she was
hurt: It made Aunt Polly love her. Although paralyzed,
Pollyanna finds reason to be glad and eventually learns to
walk again. Her courage and undaunted spirit help to con-
vert the townspeople to her optimistic way of thinking, and
they, too, learn to be happy, thankful, and caring. Thus,
through her pluck and determination, Pollyanna proves to be
a perfect fix-it. In the film's final scene, a grown-up Pollyanna and her husband, Jimmy Bean, happily take their several children for a streetcar ride, thereby assuring the movie
audience that, thanks to the power of youth, the future remains secure.

Pollyanna is a typical rags-to-riches story, one reflective of the Horatio Alger myth of the self-made man that was
popular in America in the 1920s. A poor child, through her
own basic goodness, determination, and pluck, makes it in
the world. Although the plot is simplistic and sentimental,
Mary Pickford brings to the role of Pollyanna unmistakable
energy and mischief, again characteristics clearly valued in
the youth-dominated era of the 1920s. Pollyanna, while well

meaning and loving, is not always well behaved. She fist
fights with Jimmy Bean, disobeys her aunt, and trespasses
onto Mr. Pendleton's property to steal apples from his tree.
It seems, though, that Pollyanna's misbehavior inevitably
results in good. The happy-go-lucky street gamin ultimately achieves more than a socially conscious Aunt Polly, who is
motivated by community obligation rather than a genuine concern. Of further importance is Pollyanna's physical sacrifice.
Although she espouses gladness and goodness throughout the
film, no one responds fully until after her life is threatened.
Thus, words are insigificant; actions lead to realization. In
essence, through her inherent innocence, Pollyanna is able
to traverse many worlds: rich and poor, young and old,
rural and urban. Her ability to bring together the people
of these diverse worlds underlies her fix-it role. Once she
has fixed things, the future remains secure.

A similar fix-it role prevails in a later, equally successful Pickford film, Little Annie Rooney (1925), directed
by William Beaudine. In this film, Annie (Mary Pickford),
whose mother is dead, lives with her father, a jolly policeman, and brother, who is trying to decide whether to follow
in his father's occupational footsteps or to join the local gang.
Just like her brother, Annie has two sides to her. In one
sense, she is a little homemaker devoted to providing a comfortable life for her father and brother. On the other hand,
she is a crusty neighborhood kid who likes to join in the
ruckus by fighting and throwing bricks.

One day, as Annie is at home preparing a surprise
for her father's birthday, another policeman arrives to tell
her that her beloved father has been shot and killed. Joe,
a good friend of Annie's brother and someone whom Annie
has long admired, is the prime suspect, although he claims
his innocence. Annie, in her faith and goodness, believes
him, but her brother does not. So, to avenge his father's
death, he goes off to shoot Joe. In the meantime, Annie
works behind the scenes trying to prove Joe's innocence.
She finally does, but it is too late; her brother has already
shot Joe, who is now badly in need of a blood transfusion.
Annie and her friends arrive at the hospital, and Annie offers to donate her blood to save Joe's life. Ignorant of the
transfusion process, however, she assumes she will die;
thus, she fully believes that she is sacrificing her life for
Joe. Bidding a tearful farewell to her neighborhood friends,
brave little Annie is wheeled away for the transfusion.

As the film ends, Annie, like Pollyanna, has fixed
everything. Of course, Annie has survived the blood dona-
tion, and, even though she did not have to sacrifice her
own life, she did save Joe's, and she realizes how much she
cares for him. Her brother has followed in his father's footsteps and become a proud policeman. With Joe and her
friends, Annie is happy; the future looks secure for all.

In Little Annie Rooney, Mary Pickford sustains the
same screen persona that made her so popular in Pollyanna.
She fights with the neighborhood kids, throws bricks, even
breaks a few windows. Ultimately, though, she is just,
caring, and good-hearted, even to the point of consenting
to sacrifice her life for someone she believes in and admires.
Hers is a child's undaunted faith; if she believes the best
of someone, nothing will mar her opinion. Like Pollyanna,
Annie Rooney becomes an orphan, and, through her own independence and self-reliance, carries on her father's work;
she maintains peace and justice. Interestingly, though,
while Annie's personal initiative is responsible for the positive outcome of this story, so is technology. Blood trans-
fusions, relatively new in the early 1920s when Little Annie
Rooney was released, attest to the life-saving powers of
medical technology. Hence, like Pollyanna, Little Annie
Rooney ends on an optimistic note for the future: in a
world with plucky Annie Rooneys and the best of technology, the possibilities for a good tomorrow remain unlimited.

In the 1920s, Americans were feeling the flux of urbanization and industrialization--and holding on to vestiges
of youth and simplicity. Mary Pickford's screen roles represent these virtues. The tremendous appeal of the Mary
Pickford child-character has always been its duality. With
her lovely long curls and petite, pretty features, she is
perfection--the ultimate good child. In her films, this characteristic is enhanced by soft back lighting that makes her
appear almost angelic. However, Pickford is the mischievous
child as well, one whose fists are always poised for a good
fight. In essence, the Pickford persona combines the two
popular images of childhood: the virtuous little girl and the
rambunctious street urchin. Ultimately, though, the Pickford character is seeped in innocence, which she puts to use
to solve everyone else's problems. Her box-office success
attests not only to her remarkable talent but also to her
time's obsession with innocence and youth. As Wagenknecht

affirms, "More than any great star, Mary Pickford really did belong to the Age of Innocence."[38]

Even when Pickford was not playing children's roles herself, she frequently remained associated with childhood. In Daddy Long Legs (1919), she is constantly surrounded by children. In Sparrows (1926), she escapes with several little children through a swamp, as alligators snap at their heels. These films provided a practical advantage to real child performers. When Pickford played a little-girl role, anywhere from ten to a hundred atmosphere children, in the schoolroom, orphanage and other scenes, were needed.[39] Thus, thanks to Pickford, and the many other adult performers who played children's roles, audiences became accustomed to seeing children on the screen. The time was right for a real child to play a starring role in a major film.

In 1921, Charlie Chaplin made The Kid, introducing five-year-old Jackie Coogan. This proved to be a landmark film for child performers: It was the first full-length movie to feature a child in a starring role. Immediately, young Jackie Coogan was catapulted to fame. A 1923 poll rated him the number-one box-office star in America, leading both Rudolph Valentino and Douglas Fairbanks.[40]

Chaplin first discovered Coogan when the child was working as an added attraction to his father's vaudeville act at the Orpheum Theatre in Los Angeles. After his father completed his final dance number, he called to his son, who appeared on stage doing the shimmy, a popular dance of the time; the child brought the house down. Chaplin was immediately taken by little Jackie, whose performance hit a certain chord in the comedian's memory of his own boyhood as the son of poor vaudevillians in London.[41] As Chaplin later remarked,

> What first attracted me to the boy was a whimsical, wistful quality, a genuineness of feeling.... He is a loveable child, carried to the nth power, yet endowed with not a letter of the self consciousness of an artist, and with a hundred resources as an actor. What a marvelous understanding, what delicacy of feeling. Jackie is inspiring and inspired. Just to be in his presence is to feel inspiration.[42]

A few weeks after Chaplin saw Jackie Coogan's dance number, he sent for the boy's father and asked if he could borrow the child to star in his next picture. The elder Coogan
agreed; thus, his son, who had no formal acting background,
went to work with the most famous comedian in the world.

Chaplin's selecting a child to act as a sidekick to his
well-established Tramp character was a stroke of pure genius. Inherent in the Tramp are the same simplicity, innocence, and subsequent vulnerability that traditionally characterize screen children. Although the Tramp is obsessed
with genteel manners, he remains naive in social situations,
and, as a result, he blunders. As a waiter, for example,
he acts with supreme politeness and dignity, only to spill
soup on his customer's lap. In romantic encounters, he
practices all the right moves, but in the end he is sadly rejected. In essence, the Tramp is familiar with the facade of
the adult social world, but he lacks experience with it;
hence, he is vulnerable to its disappointments. In addition
to his childlike naivete, the Tramp has a child's lack of responsibility. Sauntering on his merry way, he takes things
as they come: He is not bounded by obligation or routine.
He is not particularly selfish but rather egocentric in the
same way that a young child, unaware of the larger world,
invariably is. Further, the Tramp radiates a spectrum of
natural emotions; like a child, he is not afraid to feel, and
his eyes are open to experience and wonder. All of these
are traits associated with childhood. Thus, by co-starring
with a real child, Chaplin intensified his own screen persona.
He also created a superb vehicle for comedy. In The Kid,
an innocent tries to rear an innocent; as a result, their
roles are frequently muted, reversed, displaced. Together,
the Tramp and the Kid must face the more sophisticated world-
at-large. This creates uncomfortable situations for them and,
often, hilarious scenes for their movie audience. In The Kid,
Chaplin took to its logical end the child's possibility for humor that the Lumiere Brothers, in Watering the Gardener,
hinted at a quarter of a century before.

The opening scene of The Kid recalls an underlying
cultural belief in wanting the best for one's children, no
matter what the sacrifice. Edna, a young, attractive woman,
is being released from a maternity hopsital with her precious
infant cradled in her arms--and no husband to take her home.
Chaplin's title defines her predicament: "Her only crime--that

she is a mother." For the sake of her child's future, she
makes a painful sacrifice: She gives up her infant. Seeing
a stylish limousine, she carefully places the child in it, believing that a wealthy family will provide him with the life-
style and opportunities that she cannot give him. Unfortunately, and without her knowledge, her plan misfires.
Thieves steal the limousine and, upon discovering the child,
immediately unload him. Thus, the child, which the mother
cherished, suddenly becomes refuse, a worthless object to
be disposed of. Cars are of value, not children. The child
ends up in a back-alley garbage heap where Charlie Chaplin,
the Tramp, comes upon him.

After discovering the baby, the Tramp looks up, won-
dering who might have thrown this bit of garbage out. Then,
not being one motivated by social obligation, he must decide
what to do with his newest find. Walter Kerr notes the impact of this situation on Chaplin's Tramp who

> has been placed in a situation utterly serious, one
> with which he is presumably unequipped to deal
> but with which he must deal. He is confronted with
> a living, breathing infant for whom he must assume
> some responsibility. The narrative moment calls for
> a deeply human response--he cannot simply run
> away and leave the baby to die of starvation, ex-
> posure, or rat-bite--and he is, in this narrative,
> going to make an appropriate response, accept a
> serious burden seriously.[43]

This, however, is not within his basic character; thus, to
lighten and undercut the gravity of the obligation, he tries
to rid himself of this burden. His attempt to place the baby
in the carriage of a woman passing by proves unfruitful; un-
impressed with the infant's cuteness, she cares only about
her own child, not someone else's. The Tramp even considers dropping the infant down a sewer, but he cannot.
Inherently innocent, he has a basic sense of right and wrong:
He can try to extricate himself from the child, but he cannot
harm it. Thus, when he finds no takers, he does what he
knows is morally right: He takes the child to his own modest
home. In doing so, he feels none of the child's mother's
feelings of inability to give her son a proper life. Telling
the bums who are sitting on the steps to his hovel, "It's
mine. I found it," the Tramp enters his small room. Using

his natural ingenuity, he fashions the child's necessities out
of what is available: Old clothes become diapers, a strung-
up coffee pot, a baby bottle, and a chair with a circular
hole cut in it, a potty chair.   The child is happy enough,
and the Tramp believes he is doing an adequate job of parenting.

In the next scene, five years have passed, and a little
boy who is almost a miniature Tramp, with baggy pants, an
old sweater, and a tattered, oversized cap, appears on the
screen.   He has adopted the Tramp's life-style as well as his
appearance.   By occupation, the Tramp fixes broken window
panes; the Kid is his apprentice.   His job is to throw stones
at windows and break them and then run off quickly before
his vandalism is discovered.   The Tramp then comes ambling
by, replacement window panes in tow, and graciously offers
to repair the damage, thereby making his day's wages.   This
scene serves to establish the fact that the Tramp and the
Kid have clearly assumed the traditional relationship of father
and son: The child is learning his father's trade, following
in his father's footsteps, albeit bizarre ones.   When <u>The Kid</u>
was released in 1921, a son's assuming his father's occupation was often expected, especially in immigrant families where
it was believed that family contacts were essential in secur-
ing a steady job. [44]   This humorous scene speaks to this
widespread belief.   It also points, in a comic way, to the
specifics of teaching a child to succeed in a capitalistic society.   The Tramp's advice to the Kid is to create a need,
no matter how, so their services will be sought.

As the Tramp and the Kid go about their day's work,
a policeman senses something is amiss and watches the child.
After the Kid tosses a stone through a window and breaks a
pane, he runs to the man equipped with replacements; thus,
the policeman is on to their scheme, as the Tramp realizes.
The Kid, however, shows his innocence.   He knows that he
should run after breaking a window but is not aware that
his walking alongside the window repairman will incriminate
both of them.   In essence, he does not understand certain
tenets of the adult world, of what is proper and not proper,
suspected and not suspected.   The Tramp, however, fully
grasps the situation and kicks the anxious boy away as he
scampers at his feet.   As Kerr notes of the scene,

To kick a trusting child away is--if taken seriously,

> and this relationship is a serious one--a bewildering
> and painful thing for a child. Jackie's "father" is
> denying him, at least thrice. But we look at the
> betrayal and laugh uproariously. Our focus is en-
> tirely on Charlie's predicament, on the increasing
> pace of their leavetaking and the obvious rhythmic
> promise of coming chase. There is even a saving
> sense in which Charlie is trying to protect Jackie
> from the danger of being identified with him. But
> all threads are one, and the thread is--in its ab-
> solute need to disassociate rock-throwing from
> window-mending--uncorruptedly funny.45

This scene is essential in establishing the Kid's image as an
innocent child. He is totally trusting of his admired "father"
and naive to the adult world's specifications as to what is
acceptable and what is not. Further, the Tramp, by "deny-
ing his son," actually assumes the parental role of protector.

      In subsequent scenes, this distinction wavers. The
Tramp is insistent on teaching the child good manners. When
the Kid eats his pancakes with a knife, the Tramp corrects
him--for bringing the sharp, rather than the dull, edge of
the knife to his mouth. He also makes sure that the boy
washes behind his ears and coaches him on how to fight the
town bully. Yet the boy takes care of the Tramp as well.
He prepares his breakfast and rouses him out of bed to eat
it. Theirs is a reciprocal relationship, and the longer they
remain together, the stronger the father-son bond becomes.

      In one of the film's key scenes, the Kid becomes ill,
and the Tramp, very concerned, sends for a doctor to examine him. The image of the sick child is a common one in
film, often played up for its sentimental and melodramatic
effects; such is not the case in The Kid. Instead, the
scene humorously emphasizes the natural similarities--almost
to a oneness--that have emerged between the Tramp and the
Kid. As the incompetent doctor begins to examine the child,
mix-ups occur: It is the Tramp who gets the thermometer in
his mouth and whose heartbeat the doctor's stethoscope records. Because of what has come before, this interplay is
acceptable to Chaplin's audience. Because the Tramp and
the Kid have so much in common--because they are both
innocents--one can easily assume the functions of the other.

As the physician attempts to learn the nature of the
Kid's illness, he asks the Tramp how he came to get the
child, and the Tramp describes his discovery in the garbage
heap. Upon leaving, the doctor reports the case to the police, and the rest of the film revolves around the Tramp's
fighting to keep the child while the authorities try to wrest
him away to an orphanage. A truck arrives to take the Kid
away, and Jackie and the Tramp do what they can to fight
off the police. Of note here is the Kid's total innocence as
to what is happening. Knowing no parent other than the
Tramp nor life-style other than poverty, he has no idea that
either could be insufficient. He understands only what he
has experienced and, in his love for the Tramp, wants nothing different. Unsuccessful at fighting off the police, the
Kid is dragged to an orphanage truck while the Tramp is
left alone--not, however, to be outdone. Through a tremendous feat of acrobatics, he reaches the truck and spirits the
boy away, thus kidnapping his own child. Knowing the authorities are after them, the Tramp sneaks the Kid into a
flophouse, but, during the night, the proprietor, anxious
for the generous reward offered by police for the child's
return, discovers him and takes him from the Tramp. Upon
awakening the next morning, the Tramp finds the child gone
and dejectedly goes home to his flat where, outside in the
courtyard, he has a dream in which he sees himself in a
beautiful garden filled with flowers and angels. This idealized world, marked by innocence, goodness, and honesty,
has the virtues lacking in the Tramp's real world. It is into
this world that the Tramp fits. Upon losing the boy, he
does not respond with anger and hostility; instead, through
his dream, he points longingly to a happy, carefree place.
This scene, considered by many critics to be pompous and
unnecessary to the action of the film, takes on greater importance when one focuses on the clear development of the
Tramp character, one charged with the same childlike innocence as the infant he rescued from the garbage heap.

A policeman wakes the Tramp from his wondrous dream
and leads him to the elegant home of the Kid's natural mother, Edna, who has become a successful singer. There the
Tramp and the Kid are reunited, but it is uncertain for how
long. As Edna, the Tramp, and the Kid move inside, the
door closes. Thus, the three gather to discuss the child's
custody. The outcome is to be their secret, one not to be
shared with Chaplin's audience.

When Chaplin's The Kid was released, it was a tremendous success, perhaps because it had special meaning for its
1921 audiences. While making the film, Chaplin frequently
recalled his own poor childhood in London and his dreadful
experiences in a workhouse. In fact, in order to prepare
Jackie Coogan for the crucial scene in which the officials try
to drag the Kid away to the orphanage, Chaplin took the
child aside and graphically described for him the horrors of
life in a London workhouse, explaining all the pain that lay
ahead for the Kid once he was torn from even those few comforts supplied by the Tramp.[46] The issue regarding institu-
tionalism versus parental custody for impoverished children
was a pertinent one in Chaplin's own childhood, and it remained so in America in the first few decades of the twentieth century. As educator Elwood Patterson Cobberly lamented
at the time: "Each year the child is coming to belong more
and more to the state and less and less to the parent."[47]
In 1909, the first White House Conference on the Care of
Dependent Children declared that poverty alone should not
be grounds for removing children from their families.[48] Two
years later, two states enacted "mothers' pensions" laws per-
mitting assistance from public funds for parents to maintain
children in their own homes.[49] Between 1914 and 1916, the
New York charities controversy revealed the poor conditions
in subsidized institutions for children,[50] and in the years
that followed several child-welfare boards were established
to look into institutional care for children. In essence,
Chaplin's The Kid reflected many concerns of the time regarding children. First, who has the right to custody of a
poor child, the parents or the state? Second, how miserable
are the conditions in public institutions for children? Should
children be placed in them if any other alternatives exist?
In a humorous way, Chaplin's The Kid brings to the surface
these raging issues.

Following The Kid, Jackie Coogan's career soared. In
the next few years, Coogan made several films, among them
Peck's Bad Boy (1921), Oliver Twist (1922), My Boy (1922),
Trouble (1922), Daddy (1923), and Circus Days (1923). In
all of them, he maintained the same screen persona that made
such a hit with audiences who saw The Kid--the tough little
street gamin marked with a childlike innocence and a touch
of mischief. Approving of the characterization, Coogan's
father, Jack Coogan, Sr., proclaimed:

> I don't want my son to be a Little Lord Fauntleroy.
> I want him to be the sort of a child that he por-
> trays on the screen--robust and appealing and
> muddy--and if necessary, a little bad.... If he
> grows up to be a real person and a hundred per-
> cent American citizen, I won't ask for anything
> else. I'm strong for American things.[51]

In his son, then, the elder Coogan saw a hope for the future and a belief in the preservation of American ideals.
Tough, energetic children, even ones marked with a certain
naughtiness, will make respectable adults, ones with whom
the future can be entrusted. Unlike Coogan's father, though,
others preferred not to visualize the rambunctious child as
ever becoming an adult. As one magazine writer invoked,
"Dear child, we have only one prayer to offer.... Don't
grow up."[52] Coogan's innocent but mischievous portrayal
and his natural on-screen spontaneity were perfectly in
sync with the time. In an age that valued youth and energy,
Jackie Coogan was an apt hero, and many of his fans hoped
that he, like themselves and their ideals, would never grow
old.

Inspired by the success of The Kid, comedy producer
Hal Roach recognized the comic potential for a long-term
series featuring children. Roach began interviewing youngsters for the roles, only to be disappointed with their made-
up appearances and stilted performances. After listening to
one little girl's overrehearsed, uninteresting audition, Roach
walked over to his window and happened to see a group of
children arguing over sticks in the lumber yard across the
street. As he later reminisced,

> Now this amused me. The littlest kid claimed the
> biggest stick, and the oldest kid wanted it. Now
> they were going to throw the sticks away as soon
> as they walked another block but the most impor-
> tant thing in the world right then was who could
> have which stick. All of a sudden I realized I'd
> been watching this silly argument for fifteen min-
> utes. I'd spent fifteen minutes because these are
> real kids. I mean they're on the square. They're
> just kids being kids. So I thought if I could find
> some clever street kids to just play themselves in
> films and show life from a kid's angle, maybe I

could make a dozen of these things before I wear
out the idea.[53]

Out of this casual observation emerged the concept for Our
Gang--hiring real kids to act as real kids. Roach assembled
his original cast rather haphazardly. Although some of his
young performers had previous acting experience, many did
not; they were friends or relatives of people Roach knew
and were hired simply for their spontaneity and all-American
looks.[54] Roach's collection of randomly selected children,
touted as "a cast of just kids, tattered and full of spirits,"[55]
was a tremendous success. Effectively resembling a typical
neighborhood gang, the children were able to capture on
screen the same scruffiness and naturalness that had made
Jackie Coogan a big hit.

Roach believed that both child and adult audiences
would be amused by the antics of typical street children,
especially ones who use boundless imagination in absurd
circumstances. In the Our Gang short comedies, the focus
is on a children's peer group; thus, the series addresses
common childhood problems, fears, wishes, nightmares, and
dreams--always in a humorous context. In its portrayal,
Our Gang points to several trends that were popular in the
1920s. First, its detailed characterizations of child personalities reflect the pronounced interest in child psychology
that was taking shape, as evidenced by the work of notables
John B. Watson and Jean Piaget. As child study became an
accepted field of research, people took a greater interest in
the child's thoughts, identity, problems, and development.
Our Gang, by focusing on the child's point of view and placing the child among his or her peers, responds to this growing fascination. Our Gang also represents the American ideal
of the happy childhood, one fraught with mischief and good
times. During an age obsessed with youth and fun, Americans looked at childhood as the best years of one's life, the
time prior to adult problems and obligations. Indeed, it was
a time to be enjoyed, and to be extended for as long as possible. Lastly, Our Gang underlies the democratic belief in
the desirability of a classless society. In Our Gang, the
poor are happy and able to have fun, while the rich, with
their stuffiness and material concerns, cannot.

This simple idea was the perfect vehicle for catapulting
the popularity of the Our Gang series from the 1920s into the

Depression and beyond. In all, the series ran from 1922 to
1944, an unprecedented 221 comedies, and continued to hold
its appeal for decades later, perhaps attesting to the age-
lessness of childhood fantasy. At any rate, Hal Roach's
thesis proved correct: Children were entertained by Our
Gang; so, too, however, were adults, who recognized vestiges of their own childhoods, as well as those of their
children, in the amusing antics of the delightful street kids
who inhabited the screen.

The Child-Star Era and Depression America

Sparked by Jackie Coogan's success in The Kid, as well as
in his post-Kid features, and the initial appeal of Our Gang,
images of children in the movies became more common than
ever before. By 1925, the child-star era, which would en-
compass the next two decades, had hit Hollywood, and such
stars as Baby Peggy Montgomery, Baby June Hovick, the
Parrish Children, and Mickey Rooney became an important
part of America's early film legacy. In 1927, spurred by the
growing popularity of radio, sound reached the movies, and
two years later, the stock market crashed, plunging America
into the worst depression it has ever known. Both of these
seemingly unrelated incidents increased the demand for child
stars, especially those who could optimize the new medium
with their singing and dancing skills. While the 1920s had
been characterized by carefree, often opulent living, the
1930s took on the graver tones of hardship and, in many
cases, poverty. Children, however, found a place in the
entertainment of this world too. As Americans endured their
economic struggle, they looked two ways: to the past for
the security of tradition and to the future for hope in a better world. Children, who are the continuation of past generations and the key to future ones, represented both of
these comforting perspectives. Further, in the midst of a
depression, America realized that there were more important
things in life than money and material goods and looked with
renewed interest at the institution of the family.[56] Children,
who provided the nucleus of the family, occupied a great
place in their lives. At the same time, they continued their
popularity in their movies.

When the Depression hit, sound films were still a
novelty to many moviegoers; thus, for a few years, the

movie industry was able to hold its own in the midst of a
broken economy. It did, however, adhere to its tried-and-
true successes in an attempt to keep audiences coming, and,
because children had fared well on the screen in the 1920s,
movie producers supplied a steady stream of them in the
1930s. Many parents, dazzled by the screen performances
of children, and by the money the movie magazines reported
that the young tots were making, looked at their own children and saw, perhaps, an easy way to beat the Depression.
Throughout America, dancing schools flourished, and soon
came the natural consequences--the convergence of child-
star hopefuls on Hollywood. Hedda Hopper marveled at their
arrival

> ... like a flock of hungry beasts driven by the
> gale winds of their pushing, prompting, ruthless
> mothers. One look into the eyes of those women
> told you what was on their minds: "If I can get
> this kid of mine on the screen, we just might make
> it big." I used to wonder if there wasn't a special
> superhuman species of womankind that bred children
> for the sole purpose of dragging them to Hollywood.
> Most of the women showed no mercy. They took
> little creatures scarcely old enough to stand or
> speak, and like buck sergeants drilled them to
> shuffle through a dance step or mumble a song.
> They robbed them of every phase of childhood to
> keep the waves in the hair, the pleats in the dress,
> the pink polish on the nails.[57]

During the child-star era, it is estimated that every fifteen
minutes one hundred children poured into Hollywood with
their driven parents, many of whom hoped to fulfill their
own frustrated desires for fame and fortune through their
child prodigies.[58] In essence, many parents had subscribed
wholeheartedly to the child in the fix-it characterization that
the Mary Pickford films professed; they believed that children could solve all problems, even the dismal financial ones
brought on by the Great Depression. Unfortunately, this
was rarely the case. Even at the height of the child-star
craze, it is estimated that only one juvenile performer in
15,000 earned enough in a year from movie work to cover a
single week's expenses.[59] Of the 140,000 children to interview for parts in the Our Gang series over a period of
seventeen years, only 176 appeared on the screen, and a

scant forty-one were put under contract; that put the
chances for any remuneration at all at 3,400 to one.[60]

Despite the odds, some children did make it in the
movies--and make it big. Shirley Temple--who became not
only a highly paid actress and top box-office attraction but,
more importantly, a unique symbol of the Depression era--is
a case in point. Even prior to the baby's birth, her mother,
desperately hoping for a daughter, tried to prepare her unborn child for a theatrical career, which she herself had always wanted but never achieved. As Gertrude Temple would
later make public, "Long before she was born I tried to influence her life by association with music, art, and natural
beauty."[61] The practice of prenatal stimulation--based on a
belief that the fetus will absorb the elements in its environ-
ment--was in vogue at the time, and in Gertrude Temple's
case, it may just have worked. Shirley Temple was born
in 1928, the year that sound films really took over,[62] and
by the time she was six, after having appeared in several
one- and two-reelers for Educational Pictures, she stole the
show with her song-and-dance number in Stand Up and Cheer
(1934), a Fox feature film. Immediately, Shirley's salary was
upped to $150 a week, and Fox signed her to a seven-year
contract. The lengthy association proved beneficial for both
parties. Fox, which was undergoing a box-office crisis after
the death of Will Rogers in an airplane crash,[63] found a gold
mine in the gifted young actress. And Shirley benefited
from the studio system then in operation. Banking on her
eventual success, Fox took the gamble of signing the child
to a long-term contract, thereby incurring the expense of
training and promoting her. As it turned out, though, Fox
did not make much of a gamble; instead, the studio made a
wise financial investment.

Following Stand Up and Cheer, Shirley Temple became
a hot property in Hollywood. Fox, however, was unsure
how to deal with its new find. In Hollywood it is said that
stars of repute are reluctant to play with children (or animals) because of their tendency to steal scenes.[64] Further,
children on the set could be temperamental, unprofessional,
and overall difficult to work with.[65] While assessing Shirley's potential, Fox lent her out to Paramount for two feature films, Little Miss Marker (1934) and Now and Forever
(1934). In the first of these, in which she co-starred with
Adolphe Menjou, she plays an orphan whose father leaves

her with a bookie as a marker for a gambling debt before he
commits suicide. Shirley's memorable performance, in which
she reforms the crusty bookie, solidified her "little miss fix-
it" screen image as well as her star status. As New York
Times critic Mordaunt Hall wrote of Shirley in Little Miss
Marker, "No more engaging child has ever been seen on the
screen."[66] In 1934, Shirley made eight films, an astounding
number for any film star, let alone a young child. She also
appeared in the number eight spot of the annual top box-
office stars; the following year, she took over first place, a
position she occupied for four consecutive years before slip-
ping to fifth place in 1939.[67] Along with her mounting popularity came an increase in earnings. In 1936, she earned
$121,422; in 1937, $161,500; and in 1938, $307,014, the
seventh-highest salary in the country.[68] It is further estimated that she made as much as fifteen times more from such
Shirley Temple by-products as dolls, records, and assorted
playthings.[69]

Shirley Temple's was a classic success story, an affirmation that America's capitalistic system could really work.
Depression America thrived on success stories to uplift it
during the hard times, and Shirley Temple's personal achievement, as frequently reported in the popular publications of
the 1930s, was no exception.[70] She was, for example, Time's
"cinemoppet," and the youngest person ever to appear on the
magazine's cover.[71] She was also a celebrity, more photographed than President Franklin Delano Roosevelt.[72] In her
film roles, Shirley Temple told similar success stories. She
usually played an orphan or the child of a widowed parent
(Hollywood in the 1930s did not openly acknowledge divorce[73]), who makes it in the world by her own self-reliance,
determination, and wits and, in the process, brings happiness to others. Her formula for success was to adhere to
basic American values of independence, hard work, honesty,
fairness, wholesomeness and patriotism--ones that Americans
clung to during the hard times of the Great Depression.

This was the image created for Shirley Temple in
Bright Eyes (1934), the first film written expressly for her
and in which she received top billing; it established some of
the characteristics that became common in later vehicles designed for her. This film underscored Shirley's fix-it persona and the regenerative nature of a child's love. As the
film begins, Shirley lives with her mother, a maid, in the

home of the wealthy Smythes, their bratty daughter, Joy,
and crotchety, wheelchair-ridden Uncle Ned. Joy, played
by Jane Withers, is the antithesis of angelic little Shirley.
She noisily imitates a machine gun, rejects box after box of
expensive Christmas toys, and wants to play burglars long
after bedtime (while devout Shirley dutifully says her
prayers). Early in the film Shirley's mother is hit by a
car and killed, thus making Shirley's custody the main crux
of the plot. Mr. and Mrs. Smythe want no part of the orphan; however, Uncle Ned, whose money they want, has
taken a liking to the child and plans to adopt her. At the
same time, Loop--Shirley's godfather, a pilot and former
best friend of her deceased father--wants to give Shirley
the best home he can provide in a barracks filled with bache-
lor pilots. In an intricately contrived plot, Adele, Loop's
former lover who jilted him many years ago, has come to
visit the Smythes, and the couple is reunited through their
mutual love for the child. The film's final scene involves
Shirley's court custody case. Sitting on the judge's knee,
Shirley says she prefers to live with Loop, Adele, and Uncle
Ned. In a private meeting in the judge's chambers, the
group reaches a solution: Loop and Adele will marry, and
both Shirley and Uncle Ned will come to live with them.
Thus, Shirley has solved her own custody problem, and, in
the process, played matchmaker and brought love into the
life of a lonely old man.

        In this film, Shirley shows her self-reliance. In the
film's initial scene she is seen hitchhiking alone to the air-
port to visit Loop. This underscores the Shirley Temple
persona. Frequently in her films, either one or both of her
parents have died, thus suggesting that the child must be
independent and able to take care of herself. The absent
father also sheds light on a prevalent fear in Depression
America: In an economic system gone sour, fathers were
often unable to support the families to whom they owed a
responsibility; thus, in a sense, they were absent. The
Shirley Temple persona is further enhanced by her association with men. Loop and his fellow pilots dote on the child,
constantly hugging her, kissing her, fondling her. Simply
to please her, they spend an entire afternoon with her in an
airplane on the ground. Totally enraptured by the child,
they hang on her every word as she sings to them "On the
Good Ship Lollipop." In essence, it is the child, not a
woman more suitable to their age, who brings brightness

into their lives, thus suggestive of the male fantasy of the woman as child.

Also of note in Bright Eyes is the basic duality of Shirley Temple. She is independent and able to take care of herself; however, she remains very much a child. She needs love and someone to look up to; thus, she makes adults feel worthwhile and needed. Further, Shirley remains an innocent. When Loop must tell Shirley that her mother is dead, he cannot do so realistically. Instead, he must treat her like a child by softening the truth: He tells her that her mother became lonesome for her father and went to heaven to see him. In her films, then, Shirley Temple represents the ideal; she is the self-reliant child with whom the future can be entrusted as well as the innocent child who needs an adult's love and guiding hand.

In one of Shirley's later films, Rebecca of Sunnybrook Farm (1938), the same image prevails. In this film, which bears little resemblance to the book of the same name from which it was adapted, Shirley plays the role of Rebecca Winstead, a talented little singer whose stepfather (her mother is dead) wants only to cash in on her success. When he cannot land any parts for her, he takes her to live with her Aunt Miranda and cousin Gwenn at Sunnybrook Farm. There she meets a neighbor, Tony Kent, who runs a radio show. Impressed with her singing ability, he wants her to appear on his show, but strict, staid Aunt Miranda says no. The rest of the film revolves around Gwenn's and Tony's plotting to get Rebecca on the show despite Aunt Miranda's objections, and later, after Rebecca becomes a big hit, trying to save her from being taken away once again by her conniving, money-hungry stepfather. As it turns out, however, Rebecca is quite capable of taking care of herself.

In Rebecca of Sunnybrook Farm, the Shirley Temple character is hardworking but espouses that work is fun, not unlike the real Shirley Temple who adhered to the Depression work ethic by putting in endless numbers of hours and asserting that work to her was so enjoyable that it seemed like play. She is wholesome; she drinks her milk right down, savoring every drop. She is polite and appreciative of a life of rural simplicity. Further, as she outrightly proclaims, "I am very self-reliant." Thus, she not only makes sure that she gets herself a suitable guardian but along the way she

saves a radio show, plays matchmaker for both Tony and
Gwenn and Aunt Miranda and her estranged sweetheart from
decades before, and ultimately, teaches her crusty aunt the
importance of tenderness and love.

All told, Shirley Temple starred in twenty-one feature
films before she reached adolescence and the demand for her
services lessened. Each of her pictures dealt with the same
story--of a little girl who righted the world around her--thus
prompting Times critic Frank S. Nugent to conclude, "The
sensible thing to do would be to announce Shirley Temple in
Shirley Temple and let it go at that."74 In Now and Forever
(1934), she helps to keep her father from a life of crime.
The same year, in Baby, Take a Bow, she clears her father,
an ex-convict who has been framed for robbery, by catching
the real thief. The Littlest Rebel (1935), a film reflective
of the 1930s emphasis on national history and spirit, has her
playing the daughter of a captured Confederate soldier who
marches to Washington to plead with President Lincoln for
her father's release. Her fix-it roles continue in Wee Willie
Winkie (1937) and Susannah of the Mounties (1939), in which
she prevents wars, and in Heidi (1937), in which she teaches
a lame girl to walk. She is, however, most skillful at getting
lovers together, which she accomplishes in Curly Top (1935),
Poor Little Rich Girl (1936), and Stowaway (1936), the last
of which also has her demonstrating keen business sense and
ability to speak Chinese. Like Mary Pickford, Shirley Temple was a consummate fix-it. Thus, she became a matchmaker, peacemaker, even a money-maker. As Norman Zierold
notes, Shirley Temple "did more good deeds in one picture
than the Boy Scouts of America brought off in an entire
year."75

There has been much speculation over the reasons for
Shirley Temple's phenomenal popularity during the Depression
years. On the surface, much of her appeal had to do with
her cuteness and, of course, her remarkable talent. Dubbed
"One-Take Temple" by John Ford, Shirley proved herself to
be a fast learner and a true professional. Perhaps her greatest tribute came from fellow actor Lionel Barrymore, who
raved,

> Talent drips from her fingertips. She has an ex-
> traordinary instinct for acting, a real naturalness....
> Her talent is God-given.76

Shirley Temple obviously had talent. While her ability on
screen was unquestionable, it seems too easy to say that it
was the only reason for her popularity. The success of her
on-screen persona suggests something more complex: Her
films reflect the cultural milieu of the 1930s, now concerns
as well as continuing preoccupations from the 1920s.

Coming as it did after the prosperous 1920s, Depression America seemed to be a world gone wrong. By the
spring of 1933, estimates of unemployment ranged from thir-
teen million to well over sixteen million, and one fourth of
the nation was made up of families with no regular income.[77]
Many Americans who believed they had built a solid future
for themselves and their children watched their security diminish as banks closed, houses were repossessed, and unemployment swelled. It was truly a time of lost hopes, unfulfilled dreams, and a lack of confidence. When Franklin Delano
Roosevelt became president in 1933, he introduced the New
Deal, a program designed to lift Americans from the depths
of the Depression and get them back on the road to prosperity. Based on a code of relief, recovery, and reform,
Roosevelt's New Deal stressed that man-made problems had
man-made solutions; thus, through hard work, Americans
could alleviate their social ills. From the first day of his
presidency, when he told Americans "the only thing we have
to fear is fear itself," Roosevelt gave the people reason for
optimism and confidence.[78] Further, he made constant reference to the need for action.[79]

Shirley Temple's films also portray a problematic world
in which children are left parentless, men dote on little
girls, and a child has to confront the president in order to
get things accomplished. Frequently an orphan, the Shirley
Temple character must take care of herself because, quite
simply, the adults around her are ineffectual. In fact, she
looks after them as well, identifying their problems--ones
they are often too blind to see--and quickly and effectively
solving them. By the end of her films, the world is set
right, thanks to the optimism and decisive actions of a little
girl; thus, in her own way, she has followed Roosevelt's
dictum and achieved for herself, and those around her, a
bright and secure future.

In the second half of the 1930s, eighty-five million
Americans--more than half of the population--attended the

movies weekly, and Shirley Temple was the top box-office attraction.[80] She embodied Americans' hope in the power of youth to right wrongs and ensure a better world. Shirley's message was that the child, who stands at the center of the family, is basically innocent and utilizes this virtue to achieve good in the world. Despite the problems of the present, the family would endure. The solution to Depression strife could not be found far away but rather internally, within the home. It was the good-hearted, responsible, active child--not money --that held the ultimate hope for the future.

The fact that 1930s' Americans flocked to the movies to see an innocent child right the world around her takes on further significance in terms of prevailing attitudes toward childhood. In the 1920s, children were highly valued, as demonstrated by the social reforms that were taking place in child welfare; this interest in children continued during the Depression. In 1930, the third White House Conference on Child Health and Protection was held, which culminated in the writing of the Children's Charter providing the rights of every child in America, regardless of sex, race, or financial status, to health, education, and safety; legislation in the remainder of the decade called for the carrying out of these measures. Consistent with New Deal programs of the Depression era, the institutionalization of childhood was stepped up, largely in response to human needs and values. Parks, schools, playgrounds, and libraries were built for children, creating for them, in a sense, a world of their own. Children were also making gains as an audience for entertainment. In the 1930s, as the radio became an essential fixture in American homes, children enjoyed Little Orphan Annie, Buck Rogers, Jack Armstrong, Flash Gordon, Dick Tracy, and Terry and the Pirates--all radio shows specifically designed for a young audience. And at the movies, several children's literary classics, among them, Alice in Wonderland (1933), Little Women (1933), Little Lord Fauntleroy (1936), Treasure Island (1934), and The Wizard of Oz (1939), were adapted for the screen.

However, at the same time that children seemed to be highly valued and making cultural gains, many were severely mistreated, victims of the Depression. As Milton Meltzer notes, "The deepest wounds of the Depression were borne by children. Years of poverty, hunger, and disillusionment piled a weight of suffering on shoulders too young to bear

it."[81] Throughout the country, undernourishment was common, and infants and children, in the growing years when
good food, decent shelter, and a sense of security are of
greatest importance, faced famine and homelessness.[82] Further, in several states, consumption of milk dropped drastic-
ally, and health officials everywhere reported that child welfare and public nursing were frequently the first services to
suffer when city and state budgets were cut.[83] By 1930, at
least a third of the children reported out of school were
working in factories, canneries, or sweatshops--anyplace
they could get work to supplement the family income--and
were often the victims of long hours, poor wages, and un-
healthy working conditions.[84] Some of those who could not
find work near their homes simply took to the road to avoid
being burdens on their impoverished families, so that by
1932 the United States Children's Bureau reported that a
quarter of a million youths were roaming the country--
hopping freight trains, bumming food, and living among
hoboes.[85] It is not surprising to note that during the difficult Depression years, the birthrate per thousand population also dropped, from 18.9 in 1929 to 17.4 in 1932 and
16.5 in 1933, the last figure reflecting largely the dismal
economic conditions of the previous year.[86] Parents were
presumably reluctant to bring into the world innocent children for whom they could not properly provide.

    These statistics suggest an interesting contradiction:
At precisely the time when Americans professed to be taking
an interest in the institution of childhood, many real children
were living in misery. In view of this, the exalted on-screen
image of Shirley Temple suggests a societal conflict. On one
hand, it represents Depression Americans' hope that youth
will bring about a better world; thus, a brighter future lies
ahead for themselves and their children. On the other hand,
it reflects a subconscious guilt. In her movies, Shirley Temple is the epitome of the happy, well-adjusted child--one who,
when confronted with problems, simply exclaims, "Oh, my
goodness!" and sets the situation right. Her affirmation of
the happy childhood may have better enabled Americans to
believe that, even though their own children were making
sacrifices, they were nevertheless content and optimistic. In
a sense, Americans' embracing of Shirley Temple suggests
their love for children at a time when they were most unable
to treat their own children generously.

Depression America remained charmed by children and
what they represent. In view of this attraction, it is not
surprising that Shirley Temple was not the only child film
performer to attain great stature in the 1930s. In 1937,
Jane Withers, Shirley Temple's foil in Bright Eyes, appeared
in the sixth spot on the annual list of the top ten box-office
stars; the following year, she occupied eighth place.[87] Her
character in Bright Eyes, as the bratty, loud, mischievous
kid, was reflective of a great many of her screen roles.
Norman Zierold notes the contrast between the Temple and
Withers screen images:

> Where Shirley was the model child, incredibly
> bright, unbelievably pretty and gifted, ever obedient
> --the sum of what most parents would have liked
> their dream child to be--Jane was much closer to
> the real thing, the noisy, brawling youngster ac-
> tually making a mess of the living room before de-
> parting, strictly against orders, for some neighbor-
> hood gangland mayhem.[88]

Despite the striking differences in their filmic portrayals,
both Shirley and Jane attracted large numbers of movie fans
to the theatres, thus attesting to the fact that several images
of children may be popular at the same time. Jane, who made
forty-seven pictures before retiring from the film screen in
1947,[89] was reminiscent of the mischievous, rambunctious
Our Gang kids, who continued to draw an enthusiastic audience. As in the Our Gang series, the focus in Jane's films
was on humor, usually generated by the terrible fixes she
encountered and her tomboyish ferocity in getting herself
out of them;[90] a Jane Withers film, in the Mary Pickford and
Our Gang vein, almost always included a good tussle.[91]
Nevertheless, Jane, with her chopped-off, dark brown bangs,
wild eyes, and thick, chubby body, was ultimately as much
of a fix-it as angelic little Shirley. Norman Zierold notes
that many of Jane's roles were first offered to Shirley and
rejected by her governing council, a fact that accounts for
the similarity in plot structure between the two girls' films:

> Like Shirley, Jane did an enormous amount of good
> on screen. Like Shirley, she could reform wayward
> characters, like the smuggler in Always in Trouble
> or manage to bring together troubled lovers, as in
> Paddy O'Day. Like Shirley, she was often lost or

orphaned, but for those who were kind to her, she
could accomplish near miracles; in 45 Fathers she
saved her wealthy benefactor from marrying a gold-
digging socialite, and in Pepper, she turned grouchy
millionaire Irvin S. Cobb into a reasonably likable
old codger.[92]

In some ways, Depression America's embracing of the Jane
Withers character is even more revealing of its attitudes toward children than its acceptance of Shirley Temple. On
screen, Jane Withers showed that children need not be perfect and obedient to bring about good in the world. Their
ranting and raving, kicking and screaming are merely indicative of childish mischief; underneath it, they still have
hearts of gold.

    Just as little girls on the American movie screen
earned the admiration of Depression audiences, so did little
boys make their mark. In 1936, United Artists released Little Lord Fauntleroy, a filmic adaptation of Frances Hodgson
Burnett's 1886 literary classic. (Mary Pickford had starred
in a silent version in 1921.) The film starred Freddie Bartholomew, a slender, dark-haired young actor who was born
in London in 1924. Freddie's main attraction to Depression
audiences was his British air, his sense of politeness, compassion, and decorum. As Herald Tribune writer Ruth Woodbury Sedgwick wrote,

> Freddie is one of those boys who, until this last
> generation, were typical of English boyhood, that
> boyhood which first made England, and then went
> out and made an empire. You cannot define their
> quality without pilfering from the language of old
> ballads: they were manly, gentle, brave, true,
> full of honor and love of God.[93]

In Little Lord Fauntleroy, Freddie Bartholomew plays the
male version of Shirley Temple's little-miss-fix-it role. Upon
the death of his father, Ceddie Errol (Bartholomew), a young
Brooklyn boy, receives word that, because his paternal grandfather, the British Earl of Dorincourt, has no other living
relatives, Ceddie is to become his successor and heir. So,
after saying goodbye to his good friends in Brooklyn--
especially Mr. Hobbs, the grocer, and Dick, the shoeshiner
(played by another popular young actor, Mickey Rooney[94])--

Ceddie and his mother, whom he affectionately calls Dearest,
journey to England. There Ceddie is given the title of Lord
Fauntleroy and groomed to be the next Earl of Dorincourt.
The story takes on a further complication as Ceddie's beloved Dearest, whom the Earl of Dorincourt has never met
but nevertheless despises, is housed in a nearby residence
but forbidden to set foot into Dorincourt Castle where her
son and his grandfather live. During his stay at the castle,
little Lord Fauntleroy touches the heart of his cruel, tyran-
nical, old grandfather and proves himself to be fair, peaceful, intelligent, and compassionate--characteristics of the
perfect earl. In the process of his own education, Lord
Fauntleroy, through his love for the Earl of Dorincourt, in-
spires the old codger to be kind and repentant. Near the
film's end, a woman emerges who claims that she was married briefly to the Earl's oldest son and that, therefore, her
gangly, unimaginative son is the real Lord Fauntleroy; she
even produces a birth certificate to prove it. Her hoax is
discovered by none other than Dick and Mr. Hobbs, Ceddie's
pals from Brooklyn, and the boy is reinstated as Lord Fauntleroy. At the celebration of his tenth birthday, Lord Fauntleroy receives the greatest gift of all--his grandfather has
begged Dearest's forgiveness for his cruel behavior and in-
vited her to come and live permanently at Dorincourt Castle.

This film underlines the versatility of children. With
tremendous ease, Ceddie of Brooklyn becomes Lord Fauntleroy of Dorincourt Castle. Equally comfortable in both en-
vironments, he transcends the commoner and the aristocrat,
the poor and the wealthy. No matter where he is, he maintains his elemental integrity and basic values; he is caring,
loving, and generous. Further, the child bridges generations. Despite his grandfather's years, Lord Fauntleroy
shows deeper wisdom and understanding; thus, it is he who
teaches the old man the meaning of love and acceptance. In
Depression America, when family problems caused by financial
tensions were not uncommon, the story of the super-child,
Little Lord Fauntleroy, was openly embraced. His portrayal
suggests the moral superiority of children. Just as England
had an optimistic future to look forward to with Lord Fauntleroy waiting in the wings to be its next earl, so too did Depression America find hope in the knowledge that good children anywhere have the power to make a better world.

Many Freddie Bartholomew films, including David

Copperfield (1935), Anna Karenina (1935), and Kidnapped
(1938), were adaptations of literary classics. His most popular film, however, was Captains Courageous, the sixth-
biggest money-maker of the 1936-1937 cinema season.95 In
this picture, Freddie plays the reverse of his role in Little
Lord Fauntleroy. Bartholomew plays Harvey Cheyne, the
spoiled, self-centered son of a busy millionaire; his mother,
who might have been able to give him more time and attention, had died a few years before. Because of his father's
money, Harvey thinks he is important; thus, he brags, lies,
threatens, and bribes to get his way. When his father
learns that Harvey is not liked at school, he resolves to become more of a father in order to make his son the fair, upright individual that he has the potential to be. Mr. Cheyne
takes Harvey on a ship, where, after trying to impress some
boys he meets by consuming several sodas in a row, Harvey
becomes ill and falls overboard. He is rescued by a kind
fisherman, Manuel, played by Spencer Tracy, who teaches
him in time the importance of hard work, cooperation, friendship, and humility. Further, he shows him the value of
those intangible beauties--nature, music--that money cannot
buy. By the end of the film, Harvey's admiration for the
poor-but-contented fisherman is undaunted, and Manuel has
transformed Harvey into the sort of boy that his father always wanted him to be. At that point, Manuel is involved
in a sea accident and dies, and Harvey, who has matured
through his experiences at sea, feels a great loss. Reunited
with his father, who vows not to let his business interfere
with his time with his son, Harvey begins life anew as a
wiser, more just young man.

As Shirley Temple's films affirm Depression America's
values, so does Captains Courageous. Under the tutelage of
Manuel, Harvey learns to be hardworking, cooperative, brave,
and caring. This film also addresses the issue of family relationships, a topic of paramount concern in Depression America, when financial difficulties could lead to familial discord.
Because Harvey's father is so obsessed with his business and
assorted money-making ventures, he is blind to Harvey's
problems and needs. It takes an outsider, Manuel, to recognize and correct Harvey's basic inabilities. Once he does
this, Harvey and his father can be restored to one another.
Thus, the family endures and even becomes stronger. Of
particular interest in Captains Courageous is Manuel--and
Harvey's undaunted admiration for him. Americans often

choose as their heroes individuals who are rugged, stalwart,
independent, honest, uneducated but intuitive; Manuel is no
exception. The boy's search for a hero--someone other than
his father--has become a common theme in American films.
Captains Courageous is one of the forerunners of this trend.

Another child star to gain fame during the 1930s was
Jackie Cooper, who, like Freddie Bartholomew, was frequently on an on-screen search for the perfect hero. In The
Champ (1931), he plays the admiring son of a down-and-out
boxer, and he prefers to live in poverty with "The Champ"
than in wealth with his affluent mother. This film emphasizes
the importance of familial love over money and the regenerative quality that a child's love can have on a downtrodden
adult. In a sentimental climax, "The Champ" dies, thereby
leaving his son, the stronger generation of the future, to
carry on; in him, there lies hope for success.

In the notable Jackie Cooper film Treasure Island
(1934), another example of the cinematic adaptation trend
popular in America in the 1930s, Jim Hawkins (Cooper) finds
disappointment in his choice of hero. Treasure Island is the
consummate boyhood story. It focuses first on a boy's love
for adventure, as young Jim, a kitchen boy, sails off with a
band of sailors to search for buried treasure. Second, it
emphasizes a boy's deep trust in those he admires and his
subsequent vulnerability. In this filmic retelling of Robert
Louis Stevenson's classic tale, the key element is Jim's innocence, further enhanced by the halo-like backlighting that
surrounds his face throughout the film. Like so many film
children, Jim has no father; thus, he is, in a sense, seek-
ing a strong, paternal figure, whom he thinks he finds in
Long John Silver, a fiery, cantankerous pirate who joins the
crew. Jim grows to admire the old man, only to discover
later that he has slowly been killing off honest members of
the crew in hope of making off with the entire treasure for
himself and a few treacherous mates. After Jim finds out
Long John Silver's evil motives, he still cannot hate or abandon him. In the film's end scene, Jim frees the incarcerated
pirate, believing he will finally go straight. Even when Jim
discovers that Long John Silver is stealing money and the
embarrassed pirate tries to give it back, Jim urges him to
keep it so he will not starve. In Treasure Island, Jim is
the quintessential good child: he is brave, innocent, trusting, and, most importantly, very much in need of an adult's
acceptance and love.

In 1939, The Wizard of Oz, a capstone film of the entire Depression period, was released by MGM; it has since
become one of America's most familiar and best-loved films.
MGM originally wanted Shirley Temple to play the starring
role; however, Twentieth Century-Fox refused to lend her
out for the big-budget musical, hoping instead to tap her
talents for itself.96 Thus, the role went to Judy Garland,
who, at seventeen years of age, was a bit too tall and buxom
for the part of the preadolescent Dorothy. (She was required to wear a harness during filming to appear flatter.)
Nevertheless, her singing voice, clear and resonant, helped
to make her performance, and the film itself, memorable.
The Wizard of Oz coalesces many of the major themes of the
Depression era, most significantly the need for action in order to achieve success and the value of home and family.
The film is also an accurate reflection of Americans' traditional belief in the potential of children.

Judy Garland's Dorothy is in all ways an innocent child.
This is first delineated by her appearance. Her hair in pig-
tails, she runs playfully around her Uncle Henry and Aunt
Em's Kansas farm with her little black dog, Toto, scampering
at her heels. Her childish innocence is further established
by her personality. She is friendly and joking but becomes
passionately angry when she senses injustice. Within the
film, she encounters a crisis: a cruel neighbor, Miss Gulch,
comes and takes Toto away. When the dog escapes and returns, Dorothy's first reaction is a spontaneous, childish
one--she runs away. As she attempts to return, she encounters another crisis, a powerful tornado which carries
her and Toto off to another world--the land of Oz. Like
other film children, Dorothy is able to adjust to her new
surroundings. She fits in, is versatile, yet she insists on
returning home. At the suggestion of Glinda, the Good
Witch, Dorothy sets out to see the Wizard of Oz, whom she
believes will grant her wish. Her faith underscores a common image of children in film: They believe in miracles, in
heroes. They have a great optimism that everything will
turn out all right. As Dorothy makes her way to the Wizard,
she encounters the Scarecrow, Tin Man, and Lion, who desire a brain, a heart, and courage, respectively. Through
friendship and cooperation, they reach the Wizard's castle,
and meet his stringent tests. Interestingly, though, although
Dorothy is just a child, she leads her trio of friends, acting
most decisively and rising to the occasion even when she is
afraid; ultimately, it is she who actually kills the Wicked

Witch as well as scolds the Wizard when she learns he is a
hoax. Thus, Dorothy is not unlike the typical, independent,
brave, and self-assertive fix-it child so common in American
films. At the film's end, the Wizard shows the Scarecrow,
Tin Man, and Lion that he cannot grant their wishes, for
the solutions to their problems are internal; he can only
provide them with worldly symbols. Such is also the case
with Dorothy. In order to return to Kansas, she need only
affirm her love of home; thus, she learns to rely on herself
--not wizards, magic, heroes, or dreams--to solve her problems. As Harvey R. Greenberg ends his assessment of
Dorothy, "The Yellow Brick Road ... points the way down
the rest of her days, into a future brimming with promise."[97]

Perhaps this message is the most pertinent of all to
Depression audiences. Confronted with a crisis, Dorothy
proves herself to be brave, just, and resourceful, quite
able to solve her own dilemma as well as aid others along
the way. Further, she remains appreciative of her home
and family. With children like Dorothy at the center of each
American home, the family--and indeed the future--stands
secure. The optimistic, self-reliant child will endure.

World War II America

As Depression America melded into wartime America, changes
occurred in the fabric of the nation's culture. During most
of the 1930s, both the public and the government paid little
attention to foreign affairs.[98] However, with the outbreak
of war in Europe, interest shifted: Americans became more
aware of other people and other lands. Further, America's
entrance into World War II, following the Japanese attack on
Pearl Harbor in December, 1941, marked an end to New
Deal policy. A wartime economy made for more jobs--
especially in factories that manufactured tanks, airplanes,
and ships--as well as for increases in both work hours and
wages. The Depression over, Americans bonded together
for a common cause--to win the war.

During the Depression, children, both on and off the
movie screen, had given Americans a sense of optimism.[99]
Thus, it is not surprising that as America thrust its way
out of the Depression, confidence in children continued. In
1940, children under fifteen comprised approximately 21 per-

cent of the total population of the United States, 8.3 percent
fewer than in 1930.[100] The decline in birthrate seems attributable to the economic circumstances in the previous decade;
other social factors suggest that children remained highly
valued and their welfare a major concern. During the Depression, people seemed concerned that children's basic sur-
vival needs, food, clothing, and shelter, should be met; as
the economy improved, their needs were broadened. For
example, the 1940 White House Conference on Children in a
Democracy designated as its main concern the need to call
attention to the inequality in opportunities available to children in rural areas, among the unemployed, and in low income, migrant groups.[101] Its proposal declared, "What we
might wish to do for ... a future President, we must be
ready to do for every child."[102] In essence, this statement
affirms the prevalent notion that each child is entitled to,
quite simply, a happy childhood--one that provides him or
her with the basis for a fulfilling and productive life.

     The right to a happy childhood is a dearly held
American belief. Adults, in their consideration of childhood,
look in two directions: first, to their own personal childhoods and second, to the childhoods of their offspring or of
other youngsters that they have come to know well. Indeed,
remembrance of one's own childhood becomes a basis for de-
fining childhood in general, and adults have always had a
tendency to look back on their early years with a sense of
nostalgia and tenderness. In the popular conception, the
years of childhood innocence are happy ones, characterized
by simplicity, spontaneity, and beauty; they are the best
years of one's life. Childhood's pains--feelings of insecurity,
doubt, and loneliness--are acknowledged but become muted
with time. Thus, the bad of childhood frequently gets lost
in a magical memory of a special time that was. This idea
of the nostalgia of childhood became a major theme in several
popular films of the early 1940s.

     In 1947, Orson Welles released Citizen Kane, which has
become a classic of American filmmaking. Although in this
film the child figure, young Charles Foster Kane, appears
on the screen only briefly, the film's central theme concerns
the beauty of childhood innocence. In the movie's opening
scene, seventy-six-year-old Kane, whose rise to success,
wealth, and power epitomizes the American dream, lies on
his deathbed in his exotic mansion, Xanadu, and utters his

last word--"Rosebud." A reporter, trying to discover the
meaning of the word and thereby unlock the key to Kane's
life, seeks out all of those who knew Kane intimately during
his rise to public prominence--and finds no clue. In the
film's final sequence, Kane's personal belongings are dis-
persed, and, unnoticed by everyone, his favorite childhood
toy, an old sled with the name "Rosebud" printed across it,
is tossed into a blazing furnace and slowly consumed by the
flames. As Higham and Greenberg point out, in Citizen Kane
"Everything American society considers worth striving for--
success, riches, power--is shown as empty, sterile, and
meaningless."[103] Thus, Kane's happiest, most inspirational
moments are of his own modest childhood, a time of quiet innocence and simplicity, before he entered the complex, often
disappointing, adult world of money, business, women, and
politics. In designing Citizen Kane, Orson Welles set up
childhood innocence and adulthood experience as two distinct
entities, the former glorified at the expense of the latter.
What is important here is not so much which is superior, but
rather the fact that childhood innocence stands alongside success and material wealth as an inherent value in American
society.

Just as Citizen Kane points to the positive connotation
associated with childhood innocence in 1940s American films,
so do a host of movies that feature an adult's looking back-
ward to his or her childhood and trying to recapture the
essence of a lost past. This was the case in the popular
1945 film A Tree Grows in Brooklyn, which ranked as the
thirtieth-biggest money-maker in the 1944-1945 season.[104]
Adapted from Betty Smith's nostalgic novel bearing the same
name, the film featured child stars Peggy Ann Garner (whose
performance as Francie Nolan won her an Academy Award for
outstanding child actress) and Ted ("Pudge") Donaldson, who
played her younger brother Neeley. A Tree Grows in Brooklyn,
although not a first-person narrative, is seen primarily from
Francie's point of view and chronicles the childhood of a
young girl of Irish descent who lives in poverty in the
Brooklyn tenements at the turn of the century. Crucial to
this film is its tone: While the basic facts of Francie's childhood are dismal--her alcoholic father, lack of proper food
and clothing, and poor, crowded living conditions--her treatment of them reflects tenderness and beauty. This becomes
clear in her emphasis. For example, she focuses not on her
father's chronic drinking but his kindness, sense of humor,

and gift of music. Moving into an even smaller tenement,
she is overwhelmed by the fact that the previous tenant has
left a lovely piano--not by the apartment's smallness and in-
convenience. In essence, Francie's childhood innocence allows her to meet each new experience, be it good or bad,
with sensitivity and wonder. Because of her youth, she has
not yet become desensitized to life's hardships and simple
pleasures. Instead, she feels, and these acute feelings capture the essence of childhood innocence. The film's final
scene marks a rite of passage: After Francie and Neeley
receive their grammar-school diplomas, they reflect upon the
childhood world that they sense they are leaving. Briefly,
they remember the tragedies of their impoverished youth,
but these memories are quickly snuffed out by reminiscences
of the fun they had. As A Tree Grows in Brooklyn so
beautifully shows, children, because of their lack of experience, discover intriguing novelties in their day-to-day
existence--their minds are open and impressionable. These
discoveries make childhood an exciting, enjoyable time, one
that adults may look back on with tender nostalgia.

Another popular 1940s film that looks back at childhood
is How Green Was My Valley (1941), directed by John Ford
and starring another personality from the child-star era,
young Roddy McDowall. The sixth-biggest box-office success of the 1941-1942 movie season[105] and winner of eight
Academy Awards, How Green Was My Valley also treats childhood with a hint of nostalgia. In this film, Huw (McDowall),
the youngest of the Morgan family, is forced as a young
adult to leave the small Welsh mining town of his childhood.
Doing so, he remembers his happy past--when the valley's
landscape was healthy and green and its economy thriving
and his family was close-knit, spirited, and hopeful. Huw
then chronicles in poignant detail the events that have led
to his leaving the valley: the deaths of his brothers and
ultimately his father in mining accidents and the changing
business operations at the mine, leading to a dismal community economy. As J. A. Place writes, "The present of How
Green Was My Valley is Ford's idealized past, seen through
the memory of a boy who lost it before he was able to possess it."[106] In this film, Huw recalls the beauty of his
childhood, especially his admiration for his father and brothers and his desire to someday be a part of their adult world
and carry on the traditions of his family. As a young man,
he learns that the idyllic world and hopeful future that

he perceived as a child were false; it is obvious that the
valley has changed since his youth and he no longer has a
secure place there. Although the film does not end on an
optimistic note, it is important that Huw is leaving the valley to start anew; youth will carry on despite the hardships
of the generations before.

Concurrent with the theme of childhood nostalgia in
movies of the early 1940s was an emphasis on the child's experience as a factor in shaping personality. In 1942, United
Artists released The Jungle Book, adapted for the screen
from Rudyard Kipling's 1894 literary classic. Directed by
Zoltan Korda, the film starred Sabu, who gave a memorable
performance as the Indian boy who wanders away from his
crib and into the jungle, to be raised by wild wolves for
twelve years before happening, once again, on the village
of his youth. Although The Jungle Book did not become a
blockbuster at the box office, the film is important in its
reflection of two 1940s themes. First, it is a tale of a child
of nature, one who was raised without constraints, without
secrets--hence, in total freedom. This idea is reminiscent
of Margaret Mead's The Coming of Age in Samoa, an anthro-
pological study of adolescent girls in a South Sea Island culture; first read by anthropologists and scientists after its
publication in 1928, the book had reached the popular domain
by the 1940s. Second, The Jungle Book points to the theory
that the child enters the world as a blank slate and gains
all knowledge from experience. This doctrine--known as the
tabula rasa theory--had been studied by behavioral psychologists for several years before becoming of interest to the
general American public. In The Jungle Book, when the wolf-
child returns to his village, he barks, walks on all fours,
and is afraid of fire. Further, and more importantly, because he has been raised in nature, he is fully innocent; he
does not know greed or treachery--vices that he sees in
others upon his entrance into the civilized adult world.
Thus, the story supports the belief that children come into
the world as innocents, to be molded then into products of
their experience and environment; further, it affirms that
one can never change what one is. Hence, the wolf-child
returns to the jungle to be among those like him.

A product of nature, The Jungle Book's wolf-child is
innocent and good. Another popular film of the early 1940s,
Hitler's Children (1942), the eleventh-biggest money-maker

of 1942-1943,[107] foretells the horror of children exposed to
a very different sort of environment. Children appear on
the screen only rarely in this film, but its main message unquestionably regards them. Propagandistic in nature, Hitler's Children, directed by Edward Dymtryk, commences with
a scene featuring a group of schoolchildren huddled around
a bonfire; as they chant their beliefs--"I consecrate my life
to Hitler. I am ready to die for Hitler"--the camera focuses
on the Nazi flag. The blatant indoctrination of the Nazi
school is immediately contrasted with the freedom of a neigh-
boring American school. The rest of the film traces the lives
of two youths--a Nazi boy, Karl, and an American girl, Anna
--who meet as students attending adjoining schools. Eventually, the Nazi Party destroys both of them. Of note in
Hitler's Children is the Nazi order to have all women who are
unfit to have children--those who are weak or have anti-Nazi
ideologies--sterilized. The film brings to bear the Nazi belief in heredity as a means of determining a child's personality and potential. However, it also points to the impact of
a child's experience on his or her development. Anna, with
her traditional American hope in the future, refuses to bring
a baby into the Nazi world, realizing it will only be corrupted.
After exposing the atrocities of Nazi Germany, Hitler's Children ends on a chilling note. The Führer affirms his belief:
"The future belongs to youth. The youth belongs to the
future." To this, the film's narrator, an American schoolteacher, asks, "Can we stop Hitler's children before it is
too late?" In essence, just as The Jungle Book suggests
that a child reared in nature will be innocent and just,
Hitler's Children paints a horrible picture of the world of
tomorrow if children continue to be born into a Nazi environment. Thus, children's early experiences determine
their later personalities; collectively, these films speak to
an optimism or pessimism in the future.

Children, especially the heralded children of nature,
have frequently been associated with animals, and this con-
nection emerged as another major theme in American films of
the 1940s. In 1944, however, child psychologist James H. S.
Bossard acknowledged the long-standing relationship between
children and animals by citing the importance of animals in
the socialization of children.[108] In the same year, MGM,
also responding to the popularity of the child/animal theme,
released National Velvet, the nineteenth-biggest money-making
film of the 1944-1945 cinema season.[109] Much of the film's

appeal also had to do with its two youthful stars, Elizabeth
Taylor and Mickey Rooney. Like several other wartime films,
National Velvet, adapted from the 1930 novel by Enid Bagnold, looks with a hint of nostalgia to the beauty of childhood innocence. The main theme of this film is childhood
obsession manifested by a girl's love for her horse and her
dream that her horse will be able to win the Grand National,
England's most prestigious racing event. This film, set in
England in the late 1920s, tells the story of the maturation
of two youths, Velvet Brown (Taylor) and Mi Taylor (Rooney). As the film opens, Mi, carrying a satchel with all of
his worldly belongings tucked inside, strolls down an open
road on a summer day. Thus, his character is established:
He is a happy-go-lucky rogue headed nowhere in particular.
Along the way he meets Velvet on her way home from her
last day of school. Immediately, her character is established
as well. A lover of horses, she encounters a runaway steed
and steps out to stop it. Almost magically, as if tamed by
her touch, the horse calms. Within her family, Velvet is not
the only one with a kinship to living things. Her younger
brother, Donald, keeps insects in a jar; presumably, because
he is the youngest in the family, he does this to show authority and exert control over something. Velvet's older sister,
Dwina, keeps canaries.

     The main crux of the story of National Velvet is the
significance of youthful folly. In an intricate turn of events,
Velvet learns that Mi, whom she has brought home for dinner,
is the son of a man, now deceased, who coached Velvet's
mother to be the first woman to swim the English Channel.
With Mi's help and direction and the prize money her mother
has been keeping for many years for the right purpose,
Velvet believes--like her mother did many years before--that
what seems impossible can be accomplished by one who has
dreams. Thus, Velvet is convinced that her wild horse can
win the Grand National. Further, she becomes determined
to ride it in the race herself, even though girls are barred
from the competition. As the film concludes, Velvet, disguised as a boy jockey brilliantly races her horse in the big
event. As she crosses the finish line, the winner of the
race, she falls off her horse from exhaustion, and doctors
discover her true identity. Thus, her triumph is disquali-
fied. Nevertheless, Velvet is recognized and has scored for
herself a personal victory. In the course of the story, two
items remain of note. First, Mi is transformed, through the

Browns' trust, from an errant rogue into a responsible young
man, another example of the prevailing notion of the impact
of one's experience on a developing personality. Secondly,
Velvet has demonstrated her unsquelchable optimism in her
abilities and in the future. Preparing for the race, she fantasizes, "He'll be an enchanted horse with invisible wings if
I ride him." Hence, she will stop at nothing to achieve her
dream. Ultimately, her fall leads to her disqualification; nevertheless, Velvet's personal goals are met. She has shown
her self-reliance and determination; her future seems bright
and secure.

Just as National Velvet speaks to the notion of childhood obsession and dreams, another popular film of the same
years, Meet Me in St. Louis, focuses on childhood fears;
both of these approaches are reflective of a steadily increasing awareness of child psychology in America. Directed by
Vincente Minnelli, Meet Me in St. Louis stars Judy Garland,
five years after The Wizard of Oz, as a spirited teenager
and Margaret O'Brien as the little sister; the latter won an
Oscar for her captivating performance. Set in St. Louis in
1903, on the brink of the great World's Fair, Meet Me in
St. Louis begins as a typical slice-of-life picture, capturing
in amusing detail the day-to-day bustle in a family with five
children. The youngest of the family, Tootie (O'Brien), is
notable for her charm and grand imagination. Popular in
the town, she rides in the ice truck with the iceman, telling
him all about her doll's funeral. In a particularly entertaining scene, Tootie, who yearns to be a part of the adult
world by staying up late, comes downstairs late at night and
wants to sing with her grown-up sisters. She and her sister (Garland) dance the cakewalk as their audience of friends
marvel at the child's cuteness; she is then sent off to bed.
In time, the family's idyllic everyday routine is shattered:
The father receives a promotion that threatens to uproot the
family from St. Louis and move them to New York. All of
the family members, except for father, are disturbed and
somewhat afraid of the new life that awaits them in a faraway place. Tootie, however, acts. In a dramatic scene,
she charges out into the snow and brutally destroys the
snow-people she had created. If she cannot take them with
her, she wants no one else to have them either. Robin
Wood interprets the scene thusly:

The snow-people, dressed in adult coats, hats, and

> scarves, are fairly obvious parent figures; Mr.
> Smith watches impotently from an upstairs window
> (as if from a box at the theatre) as Tootie hacks
> down with a shovel effigies of the father who is
> going against the wishes of his family and the
> mother who passively submits to this outrage. At
> the end of the scene the father, deeply shaken,
> goes quietly downstairs (standing aside while the
> sobbing Tootie is led back to bed), then ab-
> ruptly summons the whole family to the living-room
> and announces that they are staying in St. Louis
> after all.[110]

Thus, Tootie, although her means are drastic, proves to be
the catalyst, the fix-it child who teaches her father what is
important in life and what is not. In this way, she works
within the fix-it tradition set by so many filmic children before her. The ending of Meet Me in St. Louis smacks of
the same message as Judy Garland's The Wizard of Oz.
While attending the much anticipated World's Fair, Tootie's
sister affirms that "all that we want is under our nose."
Thus, thanks to Tootie's actions, the family has realized
the importance of home, family, and a sense of place.

Collectively, popular American films produced prior
to the end of World War II suggest the nation's interest in
and affection for children. In early silent films, released at
the same time that child welfare was becoming an important
issue, children were frequently placed in dangerous situations while their parents plotted their rescue. This dual
image of the child as vulnerable and the parent as protector
underscores a strongly held belief in parental responsibility.
At the same time that this image was popular, children on
screen attained larger, more diversified roles--ones, however,
that were usually played by adult performers made to appear
like children. As audiences became more accustomed to seeing child characters in the movies, real children landed major
film roles, thus giving rise to the child-star era, which
ranged approximately from 1925 to 1945. During this time,
children on screen became strikingly commonplace, and a
generous number of child performers reached pinnacles of
success as major box-office attractions. In many cases,
their popularity dwindled upon adolescence, an attestation
to the fact that audiences were not as much taken with a
particular child's talent as they were with his or her childish image.

Inherent in the screen images of children in the first half-century of movies in America is the quality of innocence. Albeit a bit mischievous, children remain happy and good, and frequently they utilize their intrinsic goodness in order to solve adults' problems and right the world around them. Independent and honest, children in prewar films suggest a belief in the happiness of childhood and the potential of youth. Without qualification, they symbolize an optimistic hope in the future.

Notes

1. Eric Barnouw, Documentary: A History of the Non-Fiction Film (New York: Oxford Univ. Press, 1974), p. 8.

2. Lewis Jacobs, The Rise of the American Film: A Critical History (New York: Teacher's College Press, 1939), p. 37.

3. Jacobs, p. 39.

4. Jacobs, p. 41.

5. Jacobs, p. 101.

6. Garth Jowett, "The First Motion Picture Audiences," in Movies as Artifacts, ed. Michael T. Marsden, John G. Nachbar, and Sam L. Grogg (Chicago: Nelson-Hall, 1982), p. 21.

7. Jowett, p. 21.

8. Jacobs, p. 76.

9. Robert H. Bremner, ed., Children and Youth in America: A Documentary History, Vol. II (Cambridge: Harvard Univ. Press, 1971), p. 1525.

10. Jacobs, p. 76.

11. Bremner, p. 1525.

12. Bremner, p. 1525.

13. Bremner, p. 1525.

14. Bremner, p. 1526.

15. John Sommerville, The Rise and Fall of Childhood, Sage Library of Social Research, No. 140 (Beverly Hills: Sage, 1982), p. 159.

16. Sommerville, p. 211.

17. Jacobs, p. 250.

18. Jacobs, p. 251.

19. Jacobs, p. 251.

20. Frederick Lewis Allen, Only Yesterday: An Informal

History of the Nineteen-Twenties (New York: Harper and Row, 1931), p. 159.

21.   John W. Caughey and Ernest R. May, A History of the United States (Chicago: Rand McNally, 1964), p. 499.

22.   Allen, pp. 93-94.

23.   Allen, p. 93.

24.   Allen, p. 163.

25.   Cobbett Steinberg, Reel Facts: The Movie Book of Records, updated ed. (New York: Vintage Books, 1982), p. 46.

26.   Jacobs, p. 388.

27.   Like many other stars of the silent screen, Gish began her acting career in childhood, first on the stage and then under the direction of D. W. Griffith in the movies. In some of her early films, she played the role of the innocent child.   More frequently, though, she was cast as a young woman--frequently a mother--who, in the Victorian tradition, embodied the virtues of goodness, piety, and innocence.

28.   Edward Wagenknecht, The Movies in the Age of Innocence (Norman, Oklahoma: Univ. of Oklahoma Press, 1962), pp. 121-122.

29.   Wagenknecht, p. 226.

30.   Wagenknecht, p. 234.

31.   Diana Serra Cary, Hollywood's Children: An Inside Account of the Child Star Era (Boston: Houghton Mifflin, 1979), p. 115.

32.   Wagenknecht, p. 225.

33.   Cary, p. 34.

34.   William K. Everson, American Silent Film (New York: Oxford Univ. Press, 1978), p. 369.

35.   Cary, p. 33.

36.   Cary, p. 43.

37.   Raymond Lee, The Films of Mary Pickford (New York: A. S. Barnes, 1970), p. 20.

38.   Wagenknecht, p. 143.

39.   Cary, p. 159.

40.   Cary, p. 204.

41.   Cary, p. 52.

42.   As quoted in Norman Zierold, The Child Stars (New York: Coward-McCann, 1965), p. 12.

43.   Walter Kerr, The Silent Clowns (New York: Knopf, 1979), p. 171.

44.   John Bodnar, Roger Simon, and Michael P. Weber, Lives of Their Own (Urbana: Univ. of Illinois Press, 1982), p. 98.

45. Kerr, p. 173.
46. Cary, pp. 58-59.
47. Barbara Kaye Greenleaf, Children Through the Ages: A History of Childhood (New York: McGraw-Hill, 1978), p. 123.
48. Bremner, p. 1525.
49. Bremner, p. 1525.
50. Bremner, p. 1525.
51. Zierold, p. 23.
52. Zierold, p. 20.
53. As quoted in Leonard Maltin and Richard W. Bann, Our Gang: The Life and Times of the Little Rascals (New York: Crown, 1977), p. 18.
54. Maltin and Bann, p. 18.
55. Maltin and Bann, p. 18.
56. Frederick Lewis Allen, Since Yesterday: The Nineteen-Thirties in America (New York: Harper and Row, 1940), p. 135.
57. As quoted in Zierold, p. 57.
58. Zierold, p. 57.
59. Zierold, p. 58.
60. Zierold, p. 58.
61. As quoted in Robert Windeler, The Films of Shirley Temple (Secaucus, N.J.: Citadel, 1981), p. 16.
62. Windeler, p. 13.
63. Zierold, p. 67.
64. Zierold, p. 77.
65. Windeler, p. 20.
66. As quoted in Windeler, p. 20.
67. Steinberg, p. 57.
68. Zierold, p. 72.
69. "Temple, Shirley," Current Biography, 1945 ed., p. 598.
70. See Eugene Rosow, Born to Lose: The Gangster Film in America (New York: Oxford Univ. Press, 1978) for a similar argument. Rosow holds that part of the reason for the popularity of gangster films in the 1930s was because of the underworld success stories they told.
    During the Depression, Horatio Alger books, another form of the success tale, were widely read.
71. Windeler, p. 13.
72. "Black, Shirley Temple," Current Biography, 1970 ed., p. 37.
73. Edward Edelson, Great Kids of the Movies (Garden City, N.Y.: Doubleday, 1979), p. 12.
74. As quoted in Zierold, p. 75.

75. Zierold, p. 75.

76. As quoted in Zierold, p. 16.

77. Milton Meltzer, Brother Can You Spare a Dime? (New York: New American Library, 1969), p. 97.

78. Allen, Since Yesterday, p. 104.

79. Allen, Since Yesterday, p. 105.

80. Allen, Since Yesterday, p. 280.

81. Meltzer, p. 42.

82. Meltzer, p. 43.

83. Meltzer, p. 43.

84. Meltzer, pp. 46-47.

85. Meltzer, p. 49.

86. Allen, Since Yesterday, p. 134.

87. Steinberg, p. 57.

88. Zierold, pp. 98-99.

89. More recently Withers had played Josephine, the Plumber, on television commercials for Comet cleanser.

90. Zierold, p. 100.

91. Zierold, p. 99.

92. Zierold, p. 100.

93. As quoted in Zierold, p. 188.

94. Mickey Rooney, who was born in 1922, was a top box-office attraction from 1938 to 1943. Thus, he is well known for his teen roles, especially his long-running Andy Hardy series which was popular in America in the 1930s and 1940s. Prior to the age of twelve, however, Mickey had performed in seventy-eight comedies in the Mickey McGuire series, as well as thirty-one feature films.

95. Steinberg, p. 17.

96. This may have been a misjudgment. At eleven years of age, Shirley Temple was losing her babyish charm, and her screen popularity was waning. Exposure in MGM's lavish production of The Wizard of Oz might have boosted her career at a time when she needed it most. In 1940, Twentieth Century-Fox cast her in the leading role in The Blue Bird, which dealt with the same theme as The Wizard of Oz--that the answer to one's happiness is not in some faraway, exotic place but rather right at home, but the picture was Shirley's first to lose money.

97. Harvey R. Greenberg, M.D., The Movies on Your Mind (New York: Dutton, 1975), p. 30.

98. Caughey and May, p. 571.

99. See Cary, p. 207. She notes that during the Depression, some parents tried to conceal the family's financial

plight from the children; however, most children, when confronted with the awful truth, responded with confidence and hope that their elders found inspiring.

100. Bremner, vol. III, p. 1989.
101. Bremner, vol. III, p. 1989.
102. Bremner, vol. III, p. 1989.
103. Charles Higham and Joel Greenberg, Hollywood in the Forties (New York: A. S. Barnes, 1968), p. 109.
104. Steinberg, p. 19.
105. Steinberg, p. 18.
106. J. A. Place, The Non-Fiction Films of John Ford (Secaucus, N.J.: Citadel Press, 1979), p. 171.
107. Steinberg, p. 18.
108. See James H. S. Bossard, "The Mental Hygiene of Owning a Dog," Mental Hygiene (July, 1944), pp. 408-13.
109. Steinberg, p. 166.
110. Robin Wood, Personal Views: Explorations in Film (London: Gordon Fraser, 1976), p. 166. Wood points out that Meet Me in St. Louis, in which Tootie symbolically kills parent-figures, anticipates the Terrible Child of the Seventies horror film.

Chapter 4

IMAGES OF CHILDREN IN POST-WORLD WAR II FILMS:
NEW VARIATIONS

Postwar America, the Baby Boom, and the Grasp for Stability

Prior to the end of World War II, Americans knew of nothing destructive or powerful enough to threaten the future--one aptly symbolized by the image of childhood. On August 6, 1945, however, an event occurred that would have deep ramifications on the American futuristic vision. On this day, the United States dropped an atomic bomb on the Japanese city of Hiroshima, followed three days later by another on Nagasaki, a major seaport. The following day, August tenth, Japan surrendered, thus bringing World War II to an end. According to Henry L. Stimson, secretary of war during World War II, the two bombs the United States dropped on Hiroshima and Nagasaki were the only ones the country had ready, at a time when the rate of production was very slow.[1] Thus, the atomic bomb was as much a psychological weapon as it was a destructive one.[2] Dr. Karl Compton, a war department staff member, affirmed the bomb's psychological effect: "It was not one atomic bomb or two, which brought surrender, it was the experience of what an atomic bomb will actually do to a community, plus the dread of many more, that was effective."[3]

The psychological impact of the nuclear bomb reached far beyond the Japanese emperor who ordered a surrender. Knowledge of the bomb's powerful potential for destruction also had a decided effect on Americans. Along with America's entrance into the atomic age came the realization that humankind can destroy itself and its world. The day after the bombing of Hiroshima, the New York Herald Tribune described the bomb as "weird, incredible and somehow disturbing," so that "one forgets the effect on Japan or on the course of the war as one senses the foundations of one's own universe trembling."[4] Combined with this widespread uneasiness came two very real assumptions. As Jonathan Schell stresses, if a full-scale nuclear war were waged, not only would the human species be eradicated but, in addition, unborn generations would never have the chance to exist:

> ... in extinction by nuclear arms the number of untimely deaths would reach the limit for any one catastrophe: everyone in the world would die. But although the untimely death of everyone in the world would in itself constitute an unimaginably huge loss, it would bring with it a separate, distinct loss that would be in a sense ever huger--the cancellation of all future generations of human beings.[5]

Thus, America, a country that always had its eyes set on the future, was now threatened with the possibility of no future at all. Further, as Schell notes,

> By threatening to cancel the future generations, the nuclear peril not only throws all our activities that count on their existence into disorder but also disturbs our relationship with past generations. We need the assurance that there will be a future if we are to take on the burden of mastering a past--a past that really does become the proverbial "dead past," an unbearable weight of millenia of corpses and dust, if there is not promise of a future. Without confidence that we will be followed by future generations, to whom we can hand on what we have received from the past, it becomes intolerably depressing to enter the tombs of the dead to gather what they have left behind; yet without that treasure our life is impoverished. The present is a fulcrum on which the future and the past lie balanced, and if the future is lost to us, then the past must fall away too.[6]

In essence, the realization of the atomic bomb had a subtle effect on Americans' attitudes toward both the future and the past. Not surprisingly, then, the popular image of the child, which had long symbolized the continuation of past generations

and hope for future ones, slowly began to take on new connotations.

Also of note in a consideration of the psychological effects of the atomic bomb on American culture is the concept
of blame. Who would be responsible for the obliteration of
humankind if nuclear war were to occur? The answer, quite
clearly, was ourselves. As Robert Jay Lifton and Richard
Falk write, "For with the two American atomic bombings in
1945 there came into the world a special image: that of ex-
terminating ourselves as a species with our own technology."[7] The idea of progress had always been at the heart
of America's belief in the future. Born into a world of developing technology, children--good, innocent, and just--
held the key to a bright future and a better world. However, atomic power, if not used judiciously would not create
a better world; instead, it could cause ultimate destruction.
Technological morality became a key issue. Voicing the fear
of many Americans, General Omar Bradley remarked, "Ours
is a world of nuclear giants and ethical infants."[8]

These realizations characterized post-World War II
America, thus affecting the nation's psychological fabric.
Further, after defeating a common enemy, the United States
and the Soviet Union began a "cold war" period, and Americans, who had always before been optimistic and triumphant,
became guarded and uneasy. Assessing the prevailing mood
of the 1940s, Chester E. Eisinger writes,

> It was one of fear, terror, uncertainty, and vio-
> lence, mingled with sad satisfaction and a sense of
> relief at victory. The period is dominated by the
> war and what followed the war--the bomb and the
> split between the East and West. The very meta-
> phors of the time reflect the treacherous, harsh
> mood: the "stab in the back" when Italy attacked
> France; the "iron curtain" dropped between the
> Communist and the Western worlds; the "cold war."
> All give the sense of a refractory world, resistant
> to man's hope for a good life.[9]

This attitude marked a significant change from pre-World
War II America, when, despite hard times, hope for a better
life in the future continued to be a strong, motivating force.
Thus, post-World War II America carried with it a note of

pessimism, a feeling counter to the traditional American spirit. This, however, was only one of the developments that characterized the nation's postwar image.

In addition to changes in the nation's cultural psychology, post-World War II America saw another important social development: a rise in the number of working women. At the wartime peak in July, 1944, 19 million women were employed, an overwhelming increase of 47 percent over the March, 1940, level.[10] In his study of changing women's roles from 1920 to 1970, William Chafe identified World War II as a "watershed event for American women" because it disrupted "traditional patterns of life" in real and lasting ways.[11] The war had legitimized working outside the home for women, married as well as single; and, with the end of the war, some women chose to keep their jobs.[12] Others gave them up, preferring to become full-time wives and mothers. As Joyce M. Baker reflects, "At the war's end, men were eager to return to their homes, families, and civilian jobs--and women were equally anxious to resume their traditional roles."[13] Many women, however, were not given the opportunity to choose between keeping or resigning their jobs: Female workers, especially those in manufacturing, lost their jobs as business and industry attempted to make room for returning servicemen. In the words of Landon Y. Jones, women "were expected to pull off their overalls, tie up their aprons, and begin tidying up the kitchen."[14] Of these, presumably some, being of the same mind as their counterparts who quit of their own accord, were pleased to return home; others were not. Speaking for her fellow workers, wartime crane operator Frankie Cooper asserted that with every war, women go off to work: "World War II, it was exactly the same thing, but the women were different in World War II: they didn't want to go back home...."[15] Thus, women in the 1940s had demonstrated their patriotism by joining the work force and, by doing so, proved their determination and capabilities. This influx of women into the work force accelerated the twentieth-century movement toward equality for women, one which in the years to come would be met with both acceptance and opposition.[16]

Following the war, men returned home to their wives, sweethearts, and a healthy economy. In 1946, 2.2 million couples, twice as many as in any year before the war, affirmed their marriage vows and set a nuptial record that was

not equaled for 33 years.[17] Not surprisingly, following the
great marriage boom came an even more impressive baby
boom. Its statistics were staggering:

> In May 1946, exactly nine months after V-J Day,
> births in the United States jumped from February's
> low of 206,387 to 233,452. In June they swelled to
> 242,302. In October births had spurted to 339,499
> and were running at a record rate. By the end of
> the year, the cry of the baby was heard across the
> land. An all-time high of 3.4 million babies had
> been born in the United States--one every nine
> seconds--20 percent more than in 1945. Every
> known measure of fertility had soared dramatically
> as the overall population made its biggest one-year
> gain in history to a total of 143 million.[18]

And the boom continued. More than 3.8 million babies ar-
rived in 1947, setting another record.[19] In 1957, the boom's
peak year, more than 4.3 million babies were born, and from
1954 to 1964, the final year of the great baby binge, at
least 4 million babies were born annually.[20] All told, the
baby boom lasted from 1946 to 1964 and produced 76,441,000
Americans--an astonishing one third of our present population.[21] It was more than a brief surge in the birthrate following the GIs' return home after the war. Although it began that way, the boom did not end in the 1950s as it did in
Europe.[22] Instead, the American baby boom was a cultural
phenomenon, one that grew out of a thriving economy, a reaffirmation of traditional roles and family values, and, presumably, an interest in children.

However, it also seems to reflect other deeply embedded
cultural concerns. There is traditionally a rise in the birthrate after any war as men return home, marry, and raise
families. On a psychological level, people have a tendency
to affirm life by having children after being exposed to the
death and destruction of war. World War II, though, was no
ordinary war, ending as it did with the atomic bomb's total
annihilation of two Japanese cities, and its capability to do
even greater long-range damage. America's phenomenal baby
boom, along with a general grasp for stability that characterized the postwar years, may have been a continued psychological response to the realization of the bomb's devastating impact.

Owing to the baby boom, child rearing in the latter half of the 1940s became a topic of concern. In 1946, the year the baby boom commenced, Dr. Benjamin Spock published the first edition of The Common Sense Book of Baby and Child Care, which became an immediate success; by 1952, it had sold over four million copies. Edited and re-titled simply Baby and Child Care,[23] the book has since sold over thirty million copies and become the greatest best-seller in America after the Bible. In the late 1940s and the decade that followed, parents espoused the Spock method of child rearing, one characterized by relative permissiveness. According to Spock, children know best what they need and want, and parents should simply follow their lead in order to socialize them into the family.[24] Further, Spock told parents to enjoy their babies: Every baby needs "to be smiled at, talked to, played with, fondled--gently and lovingly--just as much as he needs vitamins and calories ...."[25] In short, Spock believed that parent-child affection was important and enjoyable for both parties. In a section titled "The Working Mother," Spock emphasized that children, especially young ones, need a steady, loving person to care for them and concluded:

> If a mother realizes clearly how vital this kind of care is to a small child, it may make it easier for her to decide that the extra money she might earn, or the satisfaction she might receive from an outside job, is not so important after all.[26]

Thus, Spock reinforced a prevalent belief that a woman's place is in the home.

The family was adjusting to post-World War II America, and so was the movie industry. During the war, Hollywood had done a booming business. As Arthur Knight notes,

> The war itself created a tremendous need for entertainment, a need to escape from the daily headlines of battles fought on distant fronts and from the daily anxieties about friends and loved ones who might be fighting those battles. And, apart from radio (with its disconcerting propensity for broadcasting bad news every hour on the hour), movies provided the cheapest and most readily available escape route.[27]

Since gas rationing had prohibited people's driving for pleasure and the government had restricted the production of many commodities, working Americans had money (for the first time since the Depression) and nowhere to spend it.[28] Hence, seeing movies at the neighborhood theatre became a popular pastime. Between 1941 and 1946, the income of the Hollywood studios more than doubled, rising from $809,000,000 to $1,692,000,000, and approximately 95,000,000 Americans attended the movies weekly.[29] In 1946, the peak year for movie attendance, nearly three fourths of the potential audience made their way to the box office each week.[30] This story, however, was soon to change. By 1948, television was proving to be a formidable threat to the thriving movie industry, making its most significant impact on falling box-office receipts in 1949 and 1950.[31] At first, the movie industry tried its best to ignore television, but dwindling profits soon made that impossible. By 1949, producer Samuel Goldwyn admitted that the industry was in trouble. "It is a certainty," he declared, "that people will be unwilling to pay to see poor pictures when they can stay home and see something which is, at least, no worse."[32]

At the same time that television was beginning to gain momentum, the film industry's studio system, which had served it so well since its silent days, began to break down. In the late 1940s and early 1950s, the Supreme Court determined that movie studios that controlled their own distribution offices and theatre chains were operating a monopoly. Thus, by government order, they were required to give up one of the branches of their holdings, and, one by one, they gave up their theatre chains. With movie production costs continually rising, the movie studios soon felt no pressure to provide independent theatres with a new picture each week; thus, movie production was significantly slowed down.[33] When this happened, studios realized that it was not to their advantage to keep actors, writers, directors, and technicians on long-term contracts but rather to hire them on a per-picture basis. This was a significant deviation from the way the movie industry had been run in the past.

Still other changes characterized postwar America. A strong economy, continuing urbanization, and the rapid development of suburbs made for new life-styles. As more people had money, as well as clear ideas on how to spend it, consumerism became more widespread and sophisticated. In addition, postwar America saw the rising importance of, and interplay between, the various media. All of these interrelated phenomena provided the cultural backdrop for postwar America, a time caught between past traditions and a rapidly modernizing, changing world.

Following World War II, the portrayal of children in American films slowly began to change. Although children endowed with goodness and innocence continued to be the norm, some new images of children emerged--ones that would have been unthinkable in the previous decades. In addition, the conclusion of the child-star era, which had begun around 1925, coincided with the end of the war. Part of the reason for the decline of child stars lies with the breakdown of the studio system in the late 1940s and early 1950s;[34] studios believed that it was no longer in their best interest to incur the expense of placing a child performer under a long-term contract. At the same time, the advent of television seemed to have an effect on the content of films, and on the demand for children in them. Before television, many family-oriented films starring children scored great successes at the box office. With television, however, this type of drama could be seen in the home; thus, adults, expecting more, went to movies less.[35] The filmmakers responded with more adult themes and, consequently, fewer children on the screen. Interestingly, at a time when Americans were having babies in record numbers, children in the movies became less prevalent--a direct contrast to the Depression era when, due to economic hard times, the birthrate dropped, but children on the screen flourished. On the surface, this suggests that the Depression moviegoers embraced children on the screen because they had fewer children of their own, while postwar Americans, obsessed with the real things, were less attracted to their celluloid counterparts. It also reflects a rejection of the sentimental, often simplistic plots that children were usually cast in. In essence, postwar audiences were becoming more sophisticated viewers, and they expected movies to meet their higher expectations.

Margaret O'Brien, who made her mark in Meet Me in St. Louis (1944), proved to represent the last vestige of the child-star era. In 1945, she starred in Our Vines Have Tender Grapes (also featuring another child star, Jackie "Butch" Jenkins), for which she won the prestigious Film Daily Critics Award, and was ranked ninth on the annual list of the

top ten box-office stars.[36] The following year, she performed a classic role as a fix-it child in Bad Bascomb, in
which she transforms a bandit, played by Wallace Beery,[37]
through her innocence and trust; she also appeared in Three
Wise Fools. In 1946, O'Brien rose to distinction as the eighth
most popular box-office attraction;[38] it was her last year to
make the chart. Prior to the end of World War II, children--
the likes of Jackie Coogan, Shirley Temple, Jane Withers,
Mickey Rooney, and Judy Garland--were prizes at the box
office. After the war, however, their widespread appeal declined; it would be a full three decades before another child
performer, Tatum O'Neal, would become a major box-office
success, and her popularity was short-lived--a single year
on the charts.[39]

      In some ways, Margaret O'Brien represents a key fig-
ure in the understanding of the end of the child-star era
and, culturally, the emergence of new attitudes toward children. From the beginning, O'Brien's roles showed greater
range than those played by earlier child stars. Her first
film, Journey for Margaret (1942), deviated from the overly
sentimental, simplistic Shirley Temple sagas of the Depression. Set against a backdrop of war, it tells the story of
two orphan waifs adopted by a war correspondent. Unlike
earlier child-star vehicles, this film does not dwell on the
elements of a happy childhood. Instead, its child portrayals
are more balanced and its tone serious and searching.[40]
Later, in Meet Me in St. Louis, O'Brien played a traditional
fix-it character, but one with an interesting twist: She
solves her and her family's problems by throwing fits, by
initiating an odd form of symbolic violence against her parents. Indeed, this imaginative performance ushers in a new
image of children, one inconsistent with the sunshine and
light portrayals of earlier screen children. Also of note is
Margaret O'Brien's role as Beth in MGM's 1949 version of
Little Women, directed by Mervyn LeRoy. In this film,
which also starred June Allyson as Jo, Elizabeth Taylor as
Amy, Janet Leigh as Meg, and Peter Lawford as Laurie,
O'Brien's Beth seems to be a typical childhood portrayal:
She is the good-hearted but timid baby of the family. However, this characterization, too, has an interesting variation.
In other versions of Little Women, Amy, the sister who even-
tually marries the wealthy neighbor, Laurie, and thus assures herself of a hopeful future, is the youngest; in this
version, however, the youngest is Beth, who dies of scarlet

fever. Thus, Beth's role marks a fitting end to O'Brien's film career as well as to the demise of the child-star phenomenon of pre-World War II America. As Beth, O'Brien is the epitome of childhood fragility; in the end, she, the youngest--traditionally the one in whom the greatest hope for the future lies--languishes on screen. Her passing unintentionally symbolizes the vulnerability of child stars in post-World War II America and the disenchantment that audiences found with them, thereby resulting in less demand for their services.

Although children lost their box-office appeal in the latter half of the 1940s, they were sometimes featured with popular adult performers. In 1945, Bing Crosby, then rated the top box-office star,[41] made The Bells of St. Mary's, costarring Ingrid Bergman; both were nominated for Academy Awards for their performances. Directed by Leo McCarey, who also was nominated for an Oscar, The Bells of St. Mary's tells the story of a priest, Father O'Malley (Crosby), and a Mother Superior, Sister Mary Benedict (Bergman), who devise a clever strategy to convince a wealthy benefactor to donate his newly constructed building to the children of St. Mary's parish so that they may have a fitting school. Although the plot unquestionably involves the educational welfare of children, they receive little screen time; primarily they are backdrops for the continuing interaction between Crosby and Bergman. Nevertheless, the film suggests some important cultural attitudes toward childhood.

In The Bells of St. Mary's, children are portrayed as innocents, a carry-over from pre-World War II tradition. An underlying belief is that children, because they are inherently good, deserve the best; thus, the priest and nuns try to secure the finest possible school for them. This attitude reflects a belief prevalent in postwar America. Parents of baby-boom children had among them an unwritten rule that their children were special; nothing was too good for them.[42] The Bells of St. Mary's speaks to this notion. Further, the children in this film are very much in need of adult guidance, help, and affection. Shirley Temple would have warmed the heart of the rich, old codger herself in order to get him to make a gift of his building, but such is not the case in The Bells of St. Mary's; instead, the adults do all the work. In one particularly amusing scene, Mother Superior takes it upon herself to teach a little boy who has been beaten up by the class bully how to box, thus suggesting that the child needs adult instruction and supervision to make it in the world. Lacking intuition and skill, he cannot succeed on his own.

Lastly, of note in The Bells of St. Mary's is the impact of a broken home on a child, an issue rarely addressed previously in popular movies. In this film, Mrs. Gallagher, whose husband deserted her many years before, pleads with Father O'Malley to allow her daughter, Patsy (Joan Carroll), to board at St. Mary's because she feels that she is a bad influence on the child. As the film ends, Father O'Malley has tracked down the errant husband and reunited the couple; however, Patsy does not know this. After seeing her mother with a man and not realizing he is her father, Patsy suspects the worse. She lets her grades at St. Mary's drop, believing that if she fails her exams, she will be able to stay within the secure walls of the school for another year. Eventually, all loose ends are tied: Patsy graduates and joins her happy parents. Nevertheless, she has suffered because of her father's abandonment and her mother's difficulty in coping with the situation.

The Yearling (1946) was another popular film to bill a child performer with a top money-making star. In this film, blond-haired, gangly built, eleven-year-old Claude Jarman, Jr. played the son of Gregory Peck. Already a notable movie personality at the time of the film's release, Peck was elevated to the eighth-biggest box-office draw the following year.[43] The Yearling which became a top money-maker during both the 1946 and 1947 cinema seasons,[44] was directed by Clarence Brown, who previously had directed Elizabeth Taylor and Mickey Rooney in another popular MGM child-animal film, National Velvet (1945). The success of The Yearling attests to the fact that postwar film audiences were still attracted to the image of the innocent child.

The Yearling, which is set in the rural past--Lake George, Florida in 1878--is an ode to old-fashioned American virtues and the bucolic life. It tells the story of eleven-year-old Jody (Jarman) and his relationship with his Pa (Peck), Ma (Jane Wyman), and pet deer. As the film begins Jody's character is likened to that of his Pa: Both are easygoing, affectionate, and fond of nature. Noting their similarity, Pa remarks, "Us menfolk have to stick together."

His affirmation takes on greater significance when the mother
is introduced. Unlike her gentle, caring husband, Ma is
stern and unemotional with her only child. One day, as
Jody watches her standing beside the gravestones of his
three siblings, he intuits the reason: Ma is reluctant to
love him too much because she fears she will someday lose
him, too. The fragility of childhood is further underscored
when Jody's kindhearted, crippled friend, Fodderwing--also
a lover of nature--dies of disease. In essence, the film suggests that innocent children who are closest to nature are
most vulnerable to tragedy. Too trusting, they cannot control their fate.

One day, as Jody and his father are out in the woods,
Pa is bitten by a poisonous snake. In order to get an animal's fresh heart and liver to draw out the venom, he kills
a doe, thus leaving her young fawn to fend for itself in the
forest. Days later, as Pa is recovering, Jody remembers
the abandoned fawn and, fearing it will starve, asks if he
can bring it home and raise it. His father and, reluctantly,
his mother agree, and Jody gets himself a pet yearling,
which he names Flag. In the months that follow, Jody and
Flag become inseparable companions as they play games and
romp through the glen. Thus, Jody and the fawn are paral-
leled; both are young and carefree.

Almost from the start, though, Flag is a nuisance and
eventually becomes a threat to the family's livelihood. After
a particularly devastating rainstorm, Pa is optimistic about
replanting the crops and beginning anew; however, Flag destroys their plans for the future by devouring crop after
crop, despite every barrier that the family can erect. Finally, Pa tells Jody that Flag must be shot, and the child leads
his beloved pet into the woods. Unable to shoot, Jody frees
the fawn and returns home. Flag follows, and Ma, trying to
scare it away with a gunshot, accidentally wounds it, and
Jody must kill his pet to take it out of its misery. After
doing so, the boy runs away, and when he returns a day
later, he is a more mature and responsible person. As Pa
remarks, "He's not a yearling anymore." Now that Jody has
grown up and proved himself, Ma is no longer worried about
his childish vulnerability; thus, for the first time, she is
able to treat him with tenderness and affection.

The Yearling, with its straightforward plot and crisp

characterizations, reflects some important values of postwar
America. First, it affirms the family. During World War II,
many parents had to endure the loss of sons, not unlike Ma's
plight in The Yearling. The film speaks to the fact that,
despite death, the family will prevail. Further, it establishes
traditional roles; Ma as the conscientious housewife (who must
learn, as Benjamin Spock espoused, to be loving with her
child) and Pa as the optimist and provider. Because Jody is
so closely tied to him throughout the film, it is suggested
that he will follow in Pa's footsteps; thus, the future of the
family farm remains secure. In its portrayal of childlike innocence and the optimism of youth, The Yearling greatly resembles its prewar counterparts. What is interesting, however, is a new focus that was emerging in child/animal films.
In National Velvet, for example, the emphasis is on childhood
obsession and the potency of a child's dreams. In The Yearling, it is on the adjustment problems a child encounters as
he or she nears adolescence. At the beginning of the film,
Jody is lonely and confused; by the end, he has become self-
reliant and has defined his goals for the future.

This trend is further represented in another child-
animal film of the same year, Black Beauty (1946), released
by Twentieth Century-Fox and directed by Max Nosseck. In
this film, Ann, the protagonist, is a headstrong adolescent
whose father gives her a colt of her own to train so that she
will be better able to understand his own methods of disci-
plining her. (Like so many other filmic children, Ann has
no mother; hers died several years before.) The crux of
the film's plot involves Ann's problems growing up, her love
for an older man, and the role her beloved horse plays in
her life. Ultimately, it is the mutual concern that she and
her future husband feel for the horse, Black Beauty, that
unites them. This experience enables Ann to make the difficult transition from an impetuous, impatient child to a well-
mannered, caring, and disciplined young woman. Although
Black Beauty was not a postwar blockbuster, it nevertheless
reflects the movies' growing interest in the uncertain identity
and adjustment problems of youth, a trend that, not surprisingly, was being carried out in the culture at large.

Postwar America took an interest in the problems that
children undergo as they enter adolescence. In 1950, the
White House Mid-Century Conference on Children and Youth
was held, taking as its theme "How to provide each child

The success of Jackie Coogan in Charlie Chaplin's <u>The Kid</u> (1921) set the stage for the child-star era.

Top: Mary Pickford takes on one of her many little-girl roles in
Pollyanna (1920).
Bottom: On screen, Mary Pickford was always ready for a good tus-
sle, as seen here in Little Annie Rooney (1925).

Top: Shirley Temple with Jane Withers in <u>Bright Eyes</u> (1934), the first film written expressly for the Temple persona.
Bottom: In <u>Treasure Island</u> (1934), Jim Hawkins, played by Jackie Cooper, finds disappointment in his choice of hero.

Top: Fix-it Shirley Temple demonstrates her musical ability with Bill ("Bojangles") Robinson in <u>The Littlest Rebel</u> (1935).
Bottom: Freddie Bartholomew and Mickey Rooney share a glum moment in <u>Little Lord Fauntleroy</u> (1936).

Judy Garland realizes that there is no place like her Kansas home in
The Wizard of Oz (1939).

Top: John Ford directed Roddy McDowall in <u>How Green Was My Valley</u> (1941), a young man's nostalgic account of his childhood in a small Welsh mining town and a way of life that has been lost.

Bottom: Margaret O'Brien and Billy Severn play orphan waifs who are adopted by a war correspondent and his wife in <u>Journey for Margaret</u> (1942).

Top: <u>The Jungle Book</u> (1942) stars Sabu as an Indian boy who wanders into the jungle and is raised by wild wolves; twelve years
  later, he happens upon his native village.
Bottom: Margaret O'Brien delights onlookers as she performs the
  cakewalk with Judy Garland in <u>Meet Me in St. Louis</u> (1944).

Top: Elizabeth Taylor and Mickey Rooney star in a classic child-
      animal film, <u>National Velvet</u> (1944).
Bottom: Peggy Ann Garner and Ted ("Pudge") Donaldson star in
       <u>A Tree Grows in Brooklyn</u> (1945), a sensitive account of growing
       up in poverty in the Brooklyn tenements at the turn of the century.

Top: Natalie Wood is instrumental in uniting her divorced mother
with a new husband in Miracle on 34th Street (1947).
Bottom: Cheaper by the Dozen (1950) addresses a 1950s phenomenon:
the growing family.

Top: In <u>Shane</u> (1953), the story is told from the point of view of
a young boy (Brandon De Wilde), who regards a gunfighter (in
fringed buckskins) as the perfect hero.
Bottom: The fix-it child prevails in the 1960s, as evidenced by
Hayley Mills in the Walt Disney classic <u>Pollyanna</u> (1960).

Top: Patty McCormack breaks new ground with her portrayal of the monster child in The Bad Seed (1956).

Bottom: Martin Stephens in Village of the Damned (1960) plays a monster child who can control his environment and does so without pity or a sense of right and wrong.

Top: In the climactic scene from <u>The Miracle Worker</u> (1962), deaf,
    dumb, and blind Helen Keller, played by Patty Duke, learns that
    the word "water" stands for the thing.
Bottom: Mary Bedham and Phillip Alford learn the meaning of preju-
    dice in <u>To Kill a Mockingbird</u> (1962).

In <u>True Grit</u> (1969), Kim Darby hires John Wayne to help her avenge her father's death.

The fix-it child takes on new dimensions in the 1970s as Tatum
O'Neal plays smoking, swindling Addie Loggins in Paper Moon
(1973).

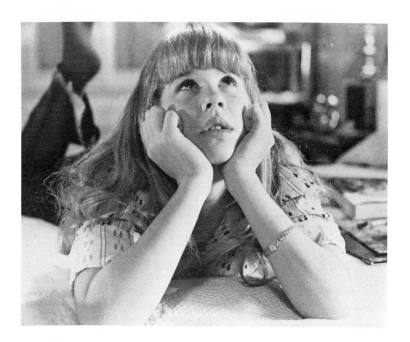

Top: Linda Blair plays the quintessential monster child--an object of demonic possession--in <u>The Exorcist</u> (1973).
Bottom: In <u>The Omen</u> (1976), Harvey Stephens, although seemingly innocent, appears as the Antichrist.

Top: Kramer vs. Kramer (1980) addresses the theme of family dis-
    integration. Following his parents' divorce, young Billy Kramer,
    played by Justin Henry, learns that his father is willing to go
    through a heated custody battle in order to keep him.
Bottom: Henry Thomas, Drew Barrymore, and Robert MacNaughton
    gaze in wonder at their new extraterrestrial friend in Steven Spiel-
    berg's E.T. (1982).

with a fair chance for a healthy personality."[45] Of note in
the title of this conference is the distinction between children
and youth. Although G. Stanley Hall had published a psychological study called Adolescence in 1904, it was not until
the 1940s that the general public identified adolescence as a
stage different from childhood. This change in awareness
was no doubt partly attributable to the onset of puberty at
an earlier age and the media's coverage of teens' pronounced
problems with their psychological and sexual development.
By the end of the 1940s, youth had been identified as a turbulent time, one that required special attention.

     As with other issues of concern, Hollywood acknowl-
edged America's worries about the problems of youth. In
essence, the movies responded with the same standard formula they had found effective in the past: Youth would
prevail and thus, the future would remain secure. This
idea was further established by a reaffirmation of traditional
family values and the ongoing, rejuvenescent, and serene
qualities of nature, as exemplified by animals and a rural
setting.

     Despite the maintenance of well-proven images of chil-
dren and families in postwar American films, some new portrayals were emerging during this transitional and crucial
historical period. Miracle on 34th Street, although not a big
money-maker when it was released by Twentieth Century-Fox
in 1947, has become a movie classic. Directed by George
Seaton and featuring child star Natalie Wood, the film broke
some new ground in the area of filmic characterizations, and
set trends for what was to come later. The mother in this
film, Mrs. Walker, is a career woman in New York City, divorced when her little girl, Suzy, was just a baby. In previous films, a single-parent household was certainly not uncommon; however, because divorce was not socially accepted,
the absent parent was almost always dead. Following World
War II, the divorce rate in America increased, a result of
wartime knots that had been hastily tied. At the same time,
movie censorship eased up.[46] Thus it became permissible to
portray a divorced, urban, single-parent businesswoman on
the screen. Also of note is the image of Suzy. Unlike so
many of her nature-oriented, innocent filmic predecessors,
Suzy is the prototype of the precocious, sophisticated-
youngster image that would achieve its height of popularity
decades later in the 1970s and 1980s. On the surface, Suzy's

childhood innocence was short-lived. Throughout her early
years, her mother taught her to be critical, questioning, and
factually motivated; thus, her childhood beliefs in fairy tales,
miracles, and dreams have been masked and repressed. It
takes the help of a self-professed Santa Claus to uncover
the childish optimism that lies within her.

Despite the differences in characterization from earlier
films, Miracle on 34th Street essentially fits the mold of a
child-as-fix-it tale. This is not surprising. Following World
War II, traditional movie genres, such as the family drama,
underwent several innovations in order to add novelty to a
familiar form. Although Suzy is not the ordinary "little miss
fix-it," she nevertheless provides her mother with a new
husband and a new home; in addition, she is instrumental in
her mother's change of heart. By the end of the film, both
mother and daughter believe in the wonder of Santa Claus,
the Christmas spirit, and the importance of believing in
dreams. Further, just as The Yearling and National Velvet
are hymns to the rural life, Miracle on 34th Street praises
suburbia, a growing phenomenon in postwar America as cities continued supplying jobs and a thriving economy made it
possible for many Americans to afford automobiles and com-
mute to work. By the film's conclusion, Suzy has achieved
the post-World War II American dream: a beautiful house in
the suburbs, complete with a swing set in the backyard.
Although Mrs. Walker starts out as an urban divorcee, by
the end of the film she is well on her way to becoming a
suburban matron. This seems to suit Suzy just fine, echo-
ing the widespread belief that suburban children are happy
children.

By 1950, owing to the surging birthrate, 14,582,000
babies had been born into postwar America.[47] Still, because
the birthrate had dwindled so low during the Depression
years, the percentage of the United States population under
twenty years of age was a scant 34 percent, smaller than at
any time in the twentieth century.[48] As Americans could
see, though, this low percentage was rapidly changing.
Throughout the 1950s, as couples continued having children,
the five- to thirteen-year-old age group grew by an additional one million children each year.[49] Not surprisingly,
then, as families were growing, a movie to make it big in
1950 was one that focused on a growing family--Cheaper
by the Dozen. Rated as the fourth-biggest money-making

film of 1950,[50] this comedy, directed by Walter Lang and
starring Clifton Webb and Myrna Loy, is the story of Frank
Gilbreth, an occupational psychologist who attempts to run
his wife and twelve children with the same efficiency, discipline, and order that he prescribes for major corporations.
Despite his martinet qualities--he summons his children with
a whistle and commands them to "fall in, fall in" as though
they are an army regiment--he is a kindhearted, loving man.
The film, which was adapted from a popular book of the
same name written by two of the older Gilbreth children,
clearly belongs to the father and his time-saving, idiosyn-
cratic, humorous, but ultimately caring ways. The children
in the film, especially the younger ones, are not well developed; they are merely props for establishing the father's
character. The key to Cheaper by the Dozen is a topic of
interest to the growing numbers of postwar parents: father-
ly admiration. Made prior to the real impact of television,
at which time children learned via the video screen that, although father might know best, he has his share of uncer-
tainties and doubts as well[51]--Cheaper by the Dozen speaks
to the traditional notion that parents are doing a fine job of
raising their children, an affirmation that postwar audiences
no doubt found comforting. At the end of Cheaper by the
Dozen, when the father dies of a sudden heart attack, it is
clear that he has left his wife and children a moral legacy
and that they will continue to carry on his beliefs and traditions.

    The popularity of Cheaper by the Dozen takes on even
greater significance when considered with the postwar baby
boom. Although the film is set in the 1920s, it says more
about 1950, the year it was released, than the time it portrays. As Landon Y. Jones notes, before and during the
baby-boom years in America, something called the Procreation Ethic took hold in America; briefly, its tenets were that
first, it was preferable to marry; second, it was preferable
to be a parent; and third, it was preferable not to have an
"only" child.[52] As the Procreation Ethic became widely accepted, more and more couples had children, and large families were not uncommon or criticized.[53] Cheaper by the Dozen
functions, in a sense, as a parody of the Procreation Ethic.
Although few couples were having twelve children, almost all
were having at least two--and more were not unusual.[54]
Thus, the portrayal of the Gilbreth clan struck a chord
among postwar moviegoers. Like the Gilbreths, Americans

everywhere were having children. In view of the Procreation Ethic, a particular scene in Cheaper by the Dozen becomes hilariously funny. A woman from the birth-control
league, told by a mischievous neighbor that the Gilbreths
are sympathetic to her cause, comes to visit the couple,
only to leave in a state of shock when she learns of their
own rejection of birth control. Clearly, in most suburbs in
postwar America, a birth-control-league representative would
have been met with a similar lack of concern.[55] In addition
to its hitting on the Procreation Ethic that characterized
America, Cheaper by the Dozen's Gilbreth family hinted, in
a microcosm, at what was happening nationally. In one humorous scene, eleven of the Gilbreth children--and their
father--have their tonsils removed on the same day, a situation unmistakably reflective of the crowded hospital situation
as America's early baby-boom children hit the peak years
for tonsillectomies. In essence, children were everywhere in
the Gilbreth household, at just the same time in which they
were beginning to overtake the population of America.

In 1951, United Artists released Kim, a filmic adaptation of Rudyard Kipling's literary classic, which became the
eleventh-biggest box-office attraction of the year.[56] Directed
by Victor Saville, the film starred Errol Flynn, in one of his
typical swashbuckler roles, and child performer Dean Stockwell, who, although he never reached the levels of fame as
did some of his postwar predecessors, nevertheless made some
notable acting contributions. The appeal of Kim is not difficult to understand: It is filled with adventure, intrigue, and
excitement, words frequently used to describe Errol Flynn
movies. Further, its setting, India in 1885, smacks of exot-
icism and romance; even the opening credits are superimposed
on the splendor of the Taj Mahal. Kim is also notable for its
portrayal of a child figure, one very consistent with the
American ideal. At the onset of the film, Kim is described
as an orphan waif, a product of the gutter. He lives by
his wits and is willing to risk his life for a copper coin or a
good friend. In essence, Kim is the classic good child, one
who is--in the Mary Pickford and Shirley Temple tradition--
loyal, intuitive, and determined. It is not surprising, then,
that Kim is an American; however, he is disguised as an
Indian to avoid having to go to school, a requirement for all
Western children. Kim fits the mold of the popular American
trickster figure. In addition to sporting a disguise when it
is to his advantage, he does what he can to secure food. In

one particularly amusing scene, when a woman refuses to
feed him and his friend, a poor holy man, Kim surreptitious-
ly places a burr inside the woman's baby's blanket, thus
causing the child to cry when the prickly object presses
against its tender skin. When the woman cannot stop the
infant's wailing, Kim calls for the holy man to bless the
child. As he does, Kim, unnoticed, removed the burr.
The child is stilled, and the thankful mother rewards both
Kim and the holy man with food. Hence, Kim has acted by
his wits, and, in the process, played fix-it for both himself
and his friend.

Also essential to Kim's filmic portrayal is his deep respect for those adults he admires. In the course of the film,
Kim befriends Red Beard (Flynn) and works hard for him as
a secret-message delivery boy. Later he entrusts a holy
man who is searching for the River of the Arrow, the place
that frees man from the ties and fears of earth. Kim, who
is on a quest of his own--for, as his father told him before
he died, a red bull on a green field--goes with the holy man,
making sure that he has food along the way. Kim is in awe
of both of these men and takes some risks in order to please
them. Ultimately, though, his prime responsibility is to his
father. The red bull on a green field, as he finds out, is
the flag of his father's military regiment, one that Kim vows
to join. In essence, the key to the story is very much akin
to American ideals: a boy's quest to follow in his father's
footsteps, Kim's urge to join the Red Bull. This pursuit,
however, is tempered by the holy man's dying plea. He
tells Kim to don his Western clothes and to return to school
rather than to follow those who feet lead to violence. Going
to school, the old man assures the lad, will lead to a better
world.

No doubt, this message had meaning for 1950s audiences. In 1950, the war in Korea broke out. Shortly thereafter, as the Cold War with Russia persisted, school children
in America endured frequent bomb drills. Although Americans realized they were living in an unsafe world, they continued having a record number of children. In response to
the tensions of living in a nuclear world, people seemed to
be internalizing more and more into family and children as a
means of grasping for stability. While Kim's world is not
one of bombs, it is, nevertheless, one of war. Thus, the
belief that violence is not inevitable, that education of the

young can prevent it in the future, seemed to be a hope
that 1950s Americans shared.

Postwar America frequently looked to literature for
filmic material, as The Yearling, Cheaper by the Dozen, and
Kim suggest. Another popular film to fit this trend was
Columbia's The Member of the Wedding (1952), based on Carson McCullers' novel published in 1946 and her play produced
four years later. Directed by Fred Zinnemann and starring
Julie Harris, Ethel Waters, and Brandon De Wilde, the film
is notable for its portrayal of the intensity, trauma, and confusion of a child entering adolescence. In essence, it takes
a theme introduced in The Yearling, and Black Beauty to its
logical emotional end. This celluloid image of the coming of
adolescence becomes even more striking when compared with
that of another character in the film, a seven-year-old boy.

The Member of the Wedding, set in a small, lazy
Southern town in summer, tells a story of adolescent loneliness, obsession, and confusion. It features Frankie Addams
(Harris), a tall, scrawny twelve-year-old with chopped-off
brown hair. Frankie's main problem is that she is not part
of a group: Her mother died when she was born, her father
has little time for her, and the other girls in the neighborhood have not included her in their club. She has only two
people to confide in: Berenice, her kindhearted, motherly
black cook, and John Henry, her seven-year-old cousin who
lives next door. To them, Frankie voices her dream: She
is tired of being just an "I" person and is ready to belong
to a "we." When she finds out that her older brother Jarvis, a twenty-one-year-old soldier, is planning to marry his
nineteen-year-old sweetheart, Janice, Frankie thinks she has
found "the we of me." Enraptured by the idea of the wedding, Frankie vows to leave her own flawed, lonely existence
by going off with Jarvis and Janice. In essence, Frankie is
caught up in a fairy-tale ideal of marriage, seeing it as a
magic carpet to a perfect world. American society has always touted the glories of marriage, and Frankie's adolescent behavior shows how such a conception can be internalized and believed.

The rest of the film chronicles Frankie's obsessions,
emotions, and moods as she fantasizes to Berenice and John
Henry her plans of leaving with the newlyweds and the
glamour of their future life together. Berenice tries to

dissuade Frankie from her foolish obsession, but Frankie ig-
nores her advice. On the day of the wedding, Jarvis and
Janice refuse to take Frankie with them, and, her hopes
dashed, Frankie runs away, only to be terrified and confused when a drunken serviceman makes a pass at her in a
bar. When she returns home, she finds her father and
Berenice caring for John Henry, who has become very ill.
In the film's final scene, John Henry has died, Frankie has
found a new friend, and she and her father are getting
ready to move. Frankie tells Berenice that she will be back
to visit her, but the knowing old woman realizes she will
have other things to do. Thus, as Frankie leaves--now having found "the we of me"--Berenice hums softly to herself;
now she is the lonely one, left with only sad memories.

Of note in The Member of the Wedding is the contrast
between the turbulence of adolescence and the innocence of
childhood, as exemplified by Frankie and John Henry. Early
in the film, Frankie becomes annoyed and impatient with John
Henry when he takes the jacks and queens from a deck of
playing cards so that he can cut out the pictures. Later,
John Henry asks if he can really have a doll that Frankie
has promised him. A child, he is associated with toys while
Frankie rejects them. The doll, as it turns out, was a gift
to Frankie from her brother Jarvis, and Frankie is insulted
that he thinks her young enough for a doll. Thus, Frankie's
problem is not only the anger and frustration she feels inside
but also the way in which she is perceived.

John Henry's childhood innocence is further established
in other ways. Unknowledgeable as to what is proper and im-
proper in adult conversation, he makes blunders. For example, when Frankie says that because of her tallness and short,
cropped hair she sometimes feels like a freak, John Henry
remembers how cute he thought the freaks at the fair were.
Berenice counters with her opinion that they gave her the
creeps, to which John Henry asks innocently, "Does Frankie
give you the creeps?" Angry, Frankie chases him out of the
house with a fly swatter. In another scene, John Henry
demonstrates his childish curiosity. When Berenice suggests
that Frankie forget about the wedding and get a beau her
own age, like Barney next door, Frankie will not hear of it.
She claims that she has seen Barney and another girl in town
go behind the barn where no one can see them, probably to
smoke. John Henry, however, has made it a point to see

them, and he reveals, "They don't smoke." Thus, Frankie, who claims to be so grown-up and knowledgeable about life, does not have the insight of little, innocent John Henry, who has looked and seen. John Henry's personage is further established by his enjoyment of dressing up. Not caring what anyone thinks of him, he romps around the house in a girl's ballet outfit that Frankie gave him; later, he models Berenice's shoes, hat, and purse. For John Henry, dressing up is simply fun, not a hope for a more glamorous lifestyle. He is an individual, one not concerned--unlike Frankie --with being part of a larger group, with finding "the we of me." John Henry is ultimately characterized by his childish ignorance of death. As the neighborhood girls cut through Frankie's yard, she proclaims, "I hope they die." To this, John Henry asks, "What is die?" In essence, he is a total innocent, knowing nothing of life's tragedies. This makes his own death at the end of the film even more poignant. Frankie, on the other hand, is knowledgeable; however, in her day-to-day misery, she has become numb to reality and feeling. Thus, her adolescent fantasy is contrasted with John Henry's innocence.

Reflective of a growing trend in postwar American films, The Member of the Wedding ends on an ambiguous note, one suggestive of a fragmented world. Frankie presents a darker view of adolescence, one clearly contrasted with childhood. Although she has satisfied her need to belong to a group, one senses that the future is not fully secure; her problem was solved through finding a friend, not through coming to terms with herself and her values. Further, John Henry, the innocent child, has died; thus, the classic American hope of the child inheriting a secure future is dashed. Instead, in a fragmented world, the child emerges as vulnerable. Throughout Berenice's life, people have come and gone. Now, once again, she is alone as her friends and memories disperse; her mood is one of resignation.

In 1953, Paramount Studios released Shane, which ranked as the third-biggest money-maker of the year; by 1981, it was still the ninth most profitable Western of all time.[57] The film starred Van Heflin, Jean Arthur, and Alan Ladd, who that year was rated the fourth-biggest box-office star.[58] Ladd alone, however, cannot be fully responsible for the film's success. Child performer Brandon De Wilde, who played John Henry in The Member of the Wedding the

previous year, received equally rave reviews. As New York
Times reviewer Bosley Crowther wrote, "It is Master De Wilde
with his bright face, his clear voice and his resolute boyish
ways who steals the affections of the audience and clinches
'Shane' as a most unusual film."[59] Shane envelops the classic components of the Western: its frontier setting (filmed
in the breathtaking Tetons of Wyoming), its heroic figure,
its traditional Western film iconography (guns, horses), and,
most importantly, its overriding theme--the clash between the
wilderness and civilization as enacted by the cattlemen and
homesteaders on the open range. What makes the film unusual is its perspective: It is seen through the eyes of an impressionable nine-year-old boy who, after the story is over,
wonders if he has imagined the whole thing. This adds to
the dreaminess of his fairy-tale vision, in which he has found
what American children traditionally seek--a perfect hero.

As the film begins, young Joey Starrett acts as an observer of the adult world. While stalking a deer, he sees in
the distance a gallant-looking man clad in fringed buckskins
riding toward the homestead. As the stranger approaches,
he says that he saw the boy watching from afar and adds,
"I like a man who watches things going around. He's going
to make his mark someday." Hence, Joey's watchfulness and
curiosity--both characteristics highly valued in American
children--are recognized and commended.[60] Immediately,
Joey is intrigued by the stranger, someone he intuitively
regards as more heroic than his good, hardworking, but
very domestic father. As Joey admires the stranger's gun,
the Ryker boys charge onto the land. Herein lies the conflict of the film: The Rykers are ambitious cattlemen who
demand that Joey's parents, Joe and Marian Starrett, as well
as the other homesteaders, give up their land and homes so
that the cattle can have free run of the valley. When the
Rykers leave, the stranger introduces himself, "Call me
Shane."

In a short time, Marian and Joe Starrett begin to share
Joey's admiration for Shane, and he agrees to stay on and
help with the work on the farm. On a trip to the general
store for Starrett, Shane attempts to buy a bottle of soda
pop for Joey, and the shopkeeper sends him to the bar in
the back. There he encounters the Rykers, who verbally
harass him. Shane leaves quietly, without mishap. Interestingly, it is for the child's soda pop that he enters this

world of men; thus, the seed is planted for future confrontations in the bar. In a later scene, Shane reenters the bar to return Joey's soda-pop bottle and again meets up with the Rykers. This time, however, a fight ensues. In essence, the soda-pop bottle functions symbolically. On the surface, it is an artifact of childhood, but it becomes a device for getting Shane into the bar--the world of men--where he confronts the Rykers. This proves significant, for it is the child's future--the right to inherit his father's land--that proves to be the basis of the dispute between the cattlemen and the homesteaders. As Starrett later affirms in an attempt to rally the other homesteaders when they are ready to acquiesce to Ryker's demands, "This is farming country, a place to bring up your family. All Ryker wants to grow is beef, not family."

By the end of the film, Joe Starrett respects Shane as a dependable friend, Marian fights her attraction to him as a potential lover, and Joey sees him as the perfect hero, the sort of man he would someday like to become. In the film's climactic scene, Shane comes to the aid of the homesteader family. He learns that Ryker has hired a professional gunfighter to kill Starrett in the bar that evening and insists on going in his place. When Starrett refuses the favor, Shane hits him on the head with the handle of his pistol and knocks him out. Seeing this, Joey is temporarily disappointed in his hero but is quick to accept his mother's explanation that "Shane did what he had to do." The child follows Shane to the bar and watches as Shane fires adroitly at the gunfighter and then at Ryker, killing them both. Seeing the other Ryker brother lurking upstairs, Joey yells to Shane to look out. Shane ducks and, although wounded himself, manages to shoot the culprit dead.

In the film's final scene, Shane tells Joey he will not be returning home with him: "A man has to be what he is, Joey. Can't break the mold. I tried it and it didn't work for me." He goes on to identify himself as a killer: "There's no living with a killing. There's no going back for me. Right or wrong, it's a brand. The brand sticks." Shane is a representative of the past world of gunfighters, one that no longer has a place in the secure future of the homesteaders, of which Joey is a part. Even after Shane has openly proclaimed he is a killer, Joey's faith in him is unmarred. Shane must tell Joey to go home but, unlike Joey's parents,

he always manages to treat the child as an adult. He tells
the boy, "Grow up to be strong and straight and, Joey,
take care of them, both of them." Thus, Shane recognizes
Joey as the strength of the future, of a new breed that will
take the place of the past protectors, the vanishing breed
of gunfighters. Interestingly, throughout the film, just as
Joe and Marian play the role of protector to Joey, so, too,
ultimately, does Shane protect them. In the bar, by fore-
warning Shane of the last gunman, Joey acts as Shane's
protector. Hence, as Shane leaves, he properly designates
Joey as the new protector, a role the innocent child seems
reluctant to accept. As Shane rides off, Joey cries after
him. Finally, resigned, he bids his hero farewell as he
fades off into the distance.

Joey's childhood innocence makes <u>Shane</u> a memorable
film. Throughout the movie, innocence is established in
many ways. In an early scene, Joey demonstrates his ignorance of death. When Joe Starrett tells Shane that if the
Rykers want to move him off his land, they will have to carry him out in a pine box, Joey asks unknowingly, "What do
you mean, Pa?" In other scenes Joey's childish innocence is
emphasized by his association with artifacts of childhood.
Shane, of course, buys him a bottle of soda pop, a device
which leads to the gunfighter's confrontation with the Rykers
in the bar. Later, as Joey watches the ensuing brawl between Shane and the Rykers, the camera crosscuts between
the fight and Joey, who is watching and munching on a peppermint stick, another artifact of childhood. Joey's innocence is further developed by his utter impressionability.
He immediately becomes Shane's captivated audience, seeing
his hero as a wonderful performer. At one point, he asks
Shane to show him how to shoot and even admits that once
when no one was looking, he secretly examined Shane's gun.
This act underscores Joey's total awe of Shane and all artifacts associated with him.

Joey remains outside of the adult world for the whole
of the film but observes everything within it, even developments, such as his mother's and Shane's relationship, that
he does not fully understand. For this reason, his whole
experience takes on a muted, fairy-tale tone. The splendor
of the mountain setting, Shane's rugged buckskin clothing
and shiny gun, and the unity of husband and wife and their
new friend all find their places in this wonderful, simple,

childhood dream, one in which good and evil are clearly delineated and complex tensions become gauzed over in a dream-
like vision. Even at the end, Joey refuses to compromise his
conception of the perfect hero; throughout, he has maintained
total innocence.

Just as The Member of the Wedding ends on a note of
consolation, so does Shane, another example of a growing
trend in films. Shane affirms the importance of family and
traditional roles: the mother as nurturer and stabilizer, the
father as provider, and the child as innocent. However,
while in The Yearling, Joey's father proved to be an adequate role model for his son, Joey's father--although good,
hardworking, and brave--is not sufficient; Joey, therefore,
looks elsewhere. Similarly, Marian Starrett immediately becomes attracted to the glamorous newcomer. In an ideal
world, this would not have occurred. There seems something missing in their seemingly happy, fulfilled existence.
Shane has secured for the homesteaders a right to raise
future generations on their land. One wonders, though if
Joey, who was captivated in his youth by an overwhelming
hero, and Marian, who sensed something adventurously masculine in Shane that she did not find in her own husband,
will ever, as they settle back to a life of domesticity on the
farm, long for a tinge of the grandeur that Shane momentarily brought into their lives.

Perhaps his notion sheds lights on Shane's original
film audience. Americans in the 1950s dedicated themselves
to attaining the bourgeois goals of security and domesticity,[61]
precisely the life-style that the homesteaders fought for in
Shane. Thus, the film affirmed prevailing values. However,
it also suggests a contradiction. Although the Starretts seem
generally happy, with Shane's arrival they sense an excitement and heroism that seems to be lacking in their everyday
lives. Further, it is Shane--the nonconformist--who saves
them from the threat against them, something that the homesteaders cannot achieve themselves. Although he cannot fit
into their mundane, domesticized world, the homesteaders
nevertheless admire him. In essence, the film espouses that
traditional values will prevail, but perhaps with them comes
a loss of that which is exciting and heroic. Thus, the fantasy of Shane may have had as much of an impact on 1950s
audiences as it did on Joey and Marian Starrett.

In 1956, Warner Brothers released The Bad Seed,
which became the seventeenth-biggest money-maker of the
year.[62] This movie brought to the surface a darker view of
childhood that seemed slowly to be emerging in American
films, one reflective of fears that were forming in the culture at large. Directed by Mervyn LeRoy, The Bad Seed
was a filmic adaptation of a very successful broadway play,
retaining all of the principal performers from its original
cast. Most striking was child star Patty McCormack, who
won an Academy Award nomination for her performance.
The movie version adhered to the same plot as the play,
except for a crucial change in the ending that was made to
conform to Hollywood conventions.

The Bad Seed tells the story of a young mother,
Christine Penmark (Nancy Kelly), who slowly becomes aware,
while her husband is away on an extended business trip,
that their prim, proper, well-behaved, and extremely affectionate eight-year-old daughter, Rhoda (McCormack), is, in
fact, a cold-blooded murderess. In the course of the film,
the child kills two people: Claude Daigle, a classmate who
wins a penmanship medal that Rhoda feels she deserves, and
LeRoy (Henry Jones), a janitor who, Rhoda believes, has
proof of her guilt in the little boy's death. Further, Christine learns that these are not the only deaths Rhoda is responsible for; she began killing even as a younger child.
The story takes on a further complication as Christine confronts her father--prominent writer and former criminologist
Richard Bravo (Paul Fix), with a harbored suspicion that he
is not her real father, adding that she is afraid of what
Rhoda might have inherited. Bravo is reluctant to admit
anything, but finally Christine discovers the truth: she is
the natural daughter of a cold-blooded murderess, and the
Bravos adopted her when she was a young child. Bravo
denies that Rhoda could have inherited any criminal tenden-
cies, saying that criminal children are always the product of
their environment. Christine, however, is convinced that
she is responsible for bringing into the world a child with
no sense of right or wrong, no guilt--in essence, "a bad
seed." Despite what Rhoda has done, Christine loves her
too much to report her to the authorities; thus, she attempts
to commit a murder-suicide. After giving Rhoda a lethal
dose of sleeping pills, Christine goes to her room and shoots
herself. Ironically, the shot summons the police, who are

able to save the overly sedated child, and Christine, although weak, repentant, and confused, is on the road to recovery as well.

In the film's final scene, one that was not a part of the original stage version, Rhoda ventures outside in an electrical storm in order to recover the penmanship medal that Christine, once she discovered it among Rhoda's belongings, returned to the site of Claude Daigle's death. As she searches for the medal with a metal detector, lightning strikes, and Rhoda is killed; thus, in compliance with the Motion Picture Production Code, the villain gets her just punishment.

The Bad Seed ends with the following message to the audience:

> You have just seen a motion picture whose theme dares to be startlingly different. May we ask that you do not divulge the unusual climax of this story.

Indeed, The Bad Seed proved a real innovation for its time; never before had such an evil image of childhood appeared on the screen. Despite its shocking portrayal, and New York Times reviewer Bosley Crowther's contention that the film tended at times to be "downright droll,"[63] The Bad Seed made its mark as a box-office success, thereby providing the germination of a filmic image that would reach its peak in the 1970s: the child-as-monster.

Although the content of The Bad Seed seemed shocking for its time, the film's popularity in the 1950s is not surprising: Its exaggerated portrait of the seemingly perfect little girl who is really a killer reflected a growing awareness of child delinquency. In 1954, New York Times education publisher Benjamin Fine published a book called 1,000,000 Delinquents, the title of which was based on the estimate that, by 1954, a million youths would get into trouble with the law each year. Fine's prediction proved correct, and by 1956, the year The Bad Seed was released, this figure was surpassed, as well over one million youths came to the attention of police annually, many of them, like Rhoda Penmark, from seemingly good families in middle-class neighborhoods.[64] Most juvenile delinquents committed crimes against property, especially car theft, but startlingly often, they committed

such violent acts as rapes, beatings, and murders.[65] As
Boston Judge John J. Connelly remarked, "We have the
spectacle of an entire city terrorized by one-half of one
percent of its residents. And the terrorists are children."[66] In the 1950s, many social problems were repressed; child delinquency, however, gained national concern.[67] In 1955, for example, the Council of State Governments participated in an Interstate Compact on Juveniles to
establish cooperative efforts to return runaways and delinquent children.[68] Three years later, Congress broadened
welfare provisions of the Social Security Act to provide
funds for the return of runaway children.[69] Even J. Edgar
Hoover acknowledged the problem of juvenile delinquency
and offered a simple solution: parental discipline.[70] Like
many of his contemporaries, Hoover believed that the family,
not society, was responsible for juvenile crime.[71]

In addition to reflecting a national preoccupation with
juvenile delinquency, The Bad Seed popularizes a long-
standing psychological debate regarding the importance of
heredity versus environment. By the time of the film's release, the overwhelming majority of psychologists, convinced
by the behavioral conditioning theories of William James, J. B.
Watson, and B. F. Skinner, agreed that a child's dominant
personality traits were a result of his or her upbringing.
By the 1950s, the general public was immersed in this idea
as the proliferation of child care manuals, including Spock's
Baby and Child Care, professed that children, with the proper stimulation, could become anything that their parents
desired them to be. The Bad Seed, no doubt reflective of a
growing fear of child delinquency, plays havoc with this belief by espousing its opposite: That children, despite a
wholesome, loving, suburban environment are capable of
turning bad because they have inherited the sins of past
generations; thus, the family structure retains the basis for
evil. In The Bad Seed, fear and uneasiness pervade and
lead to a chilling revelation: No one can be trusted, not
even a supposedly innocent child. This message takes on
greater meaning when considered in conjunction with postwar Americans' realization that they were living in a nuclear
world. In the past, the child was always considered the
bearer of a bright future; now, however, this hope is qualified. Saddled with the despicable sins of their progenitors,
children are not fully innocent; they must accept whatever
fate holds for them.

The Bad Seed also raises other issues. In the 1930s.
Shirley Temple's on-screen image was characterized by neat-
ness, intelligence, affection, and self-reliance; in essence,
she portrayed the perfect child. Rhoda in The Bad Seed
seems to share Shirley's virtues. At one point, one of the
Penmarks' neighbors even remarks of Rhoda, "Isn't she perfection!" However, while Shirley's virtues were genuine,
Rhoda's are a fraud, thus reflecting a mistrust of childhood
innocence and a suspicion that children are not as virtuous
as they appear or as Americans would hope them to be. As
John Sommerville notes, "To maintain the ideal of childhood
innocence ... could only result in a constant sense of disappointment with real children."[72] The illusion of childhood
perfection deserves one final consideration. In the 1950s,
child-care manuals told parents that they, too, could raise
perfect super-children. The Bad Seed, with its portrayal of
the child who kills for a penmanship medal, paints in exaggerated terms the dangers of abnormal precociousness and
competition among children, especially if developed without a
strong ethical framework. Further, it points to the one to
blame for a child's misgivings: the parent--the same culprit
that 1950s' society frequently blamed for its child delinquents.
In The Bad Seed, Christine Penmark believes that she is to
blame for her child's tendency to kill. At the point at which
she is faced with this awful realization, her husband is absent, thereby suggesting a fragmented world, one in which a
father cannot hold his family together.

In 1958, Paramount Pictures released Houseboat, which
became the seventeenth-biggest money-maker of the year,[73]
largely due to the popularity of its two starring performers,
Cary Grant and Sophia Loren. The plot of Houseboat, reflective of the growing trend of family fragmentation in films
featuring children, is a simple one. Tom Winston (Grant)
arrives at the home of his sister-in-law Carolyn (Martha
Hyer) following the death of his wife, with whom he had
been in the midst of divorce proceedings. The reason for
the visit is to decide what is to be done with Tom's three
children, Robert (Charles Herbert), Elizabeth (Mimi Gibson),
and David (Paul Peterson). Carolyn, a young, attractive,
well-to-do woman, has agreed to take the two boys, and her
parents will adopt Elizabeth. In an unexpected moment, Tom
decides that he wants custody of the children himself, and,
despite the fact that he hardly knows them, he packs them
up and takes them to live with him in Washington, D.C.

Immediately, he proves himself unknowledgeable at fathering, especially in his inability to provide understanding and tenderness. David, the youngest child, runs away, to be found by Cinzia Zaccardi (Loren), a gorgeous, spirited Italian woman who had run away from her father, a hard-headed Italian conductor who wants to use her graciousness and beauty to advance his career while she wants to go off and find glamour and romance. Robert takes Cinzia home, the children convince their father to hire her as their maid (even though she will not cook or do laundry), and eventually the whole family ends up living on a dilapidated houseboat. In the end, Carolyn asks Tom to marry her, confessing that she has always loved him, and he agrees, only to discover that he really loves Cinzia. He calls off the engagement and decides to marry Cinzia instead; however, the children, who previously were taken with Cinzia's kindness and sensitivity, turn against her because they feel their father loves her more than them. The wedding takes place, and, despite the children's insistence that they will not attend, they do come. The last scene shows Tom, Cinzia, and the three children, hand-in-hand, as the couple recites their marriage vows.

Houseboat is a vehicle for the romance between Grant and Loren rather than a story focused on children. As Bosley Crowther writes,

> With Miss Loren slinking about the houseboat in various revealing states of decolletage, designed to catch the audience's attention, as well as Mr. Grant's, it is offensive to pretend to be interested in the emotional disturbances of kids.[74]

Nevertheless, the film points to some common trends that were emerging in 1950s films featuring children, ones reflective of issues and attitudes of the time. Houseboat focuses on two main problems: first, the alienation and rebellion of youth, and second, the inability of parents and children to understand one another's needs. In a humorous, lighthearted way, the film brings to bear the issue of child adjustment in an increasingly complex world.

Houseboat tells the story of a broken home. The children of the family, clearly characterized as innocents, suffer adjustment problems prompted by the death of their mother and their move to live with their father, whom they

barely know. Elizabeth cannot sleep at night. She is particularly afraid to be alone during a storm, a fear that Cinzia, but not her father, understands; thus, Cinzia allows
the child to crawl into bed with her so that she feels safe.
Ultimately, this causes a problem when Cinzia and Elizabeth's
father announce their upcoming marriage and Elizabeth asks
if she will be able to sleep with them. A sexual innocent,
she does not understand why she cannot and therefore believes that her father likes Cinzia better than he likes her.
David's problem is somewhat different. As he nears adolescence, he becomes more troubled. Most obvious is his problem of stealing; however, most serious is his identity confusion. He thinks he is mature, but his father will not accept
him as such. In one crucial scene, his father reprimands
him for changing the rope of the houseboat, and the child
replies dejectedly, "I forgot I was a lame brain." In essence, David is torn between adult and child. He believes
he is competent and mature and becomes angry and confused
when he is not perceived that way. Robert, the youngest
child, has by far the most severe problem. As he declares
at the beginning of the film, "I hate everyone in the whole
wide world." He shows his dissatisfaction in two ways:
first, by playing his harmonica and shutting everything else
out, and second, by running away. Robert's turmoil is further compounded by his childlike innocence. He does not,
for example, understand death. At one point, he even asks
if his mother is in a museum like the artifacts they encounter
on their tour of museums in Washington, D.C. Further, he
does not understand his father's affection for Cinzia and refuses to accept her as his mother, affirming that because
his natural mother is dead, he has no mother. At the time
of the wedding, Robert climbs up a tree and refuses to come
down until the last moment when he disrupts the ceremony
with his harmonica rendition of "Here Comes the Bride."

Houseboat brings to bear the problems that children
encounter as a result of a broken home and a parent's im-
pending second marriage. Unlike Shirley Temple, Elizabeth,
David, and Robert are not perfect fix-it children who adjust
to any situation with ease. Although David does find his
father a mate, he, along with his siblings, becomes jealous
when she threatens to take his affection away from them;
thus, their portrayal is more complex, more vulnerable. At
the same time, Tom Winston proves that parents are not infallible; he too becomes confused and makes serious mistakes.

Even Cinzia, who at first seems to be the ideal mother figure, quickly loses ground, and her tenuous relationship with
her own father suggests that neither is she fully competent
at maintaining harmonious family bonds. Just as Houseboat
points to the problems children encounter, so does it suggest
advice on child rearing. Notably, this film was released at
a time when child-care-manual sales were booming in America,
a response to the surging birthrate as well as to parents'
basic insecurities about raising their children.[75] Houseboat
affirms what Spock and other popular child-care specialists
espoused: In the words of Cinzia, "Children should be
raised with kindness and tenderness." Houseboat, like many
other 1950s films featuring children, ends on a note of resignation. At Cinzia's insistence, Tom goes to talk to the
children, asking them to come to the wedding and reminding
them, "You can't be children forever. Things change.
You'll be leaving me someday too." They clasp hands during the ceremony, thus suggesting that they will try to work
together and overcome their differences. However, all of the
jealousies and misunderstandings of the past are not fully
resolved and more problems inevitably lie ahead.

On the surface, the 1950s seem to have been years of
security, domestic tranquility, and happy carefree times,
and, in nostalgic looks at the period, this is the aura that
is remembered.[76] However, popular films of the era featuring children tell quite another story. Collectively, they re-
veal a world in which children are confused, searching, misunderstood, or deviant. Further, their fathers are frequently absent or ineffectual; thus, the children must look elsewhere for their heroes and role models. The popularity of
this filmic portrayal is telling, especially when considered
with the social realities of the 1950s. During the baby-
boom years, youth was highly valued, and many parents
made great sacrifices for their children.[77] Millions of women
centered their lives around child rearing, and millions of
men worked at unfulfilling jobs to maintain their families.[78]
To be young was special; therefore youth deserved the very
best.[79] Thus, parents did not seem to mind their sacrifices,
as long as the children were happy and the family secure.
But blockbuster films of the 1950s show children who are not
always happy, well adjusted, and capable of solving each
problem that arises. This filmic image suggests glimmerings
of new attitudes: That parents do not know their children's
needs as well as they think they do, and that children, in

the eyes of adults, are falling short of perfection. In rela-
tion to the world the parents were living in, these ideas
take on further significance. Parents, it seems, had high
hopes for their children and believed that by lavishing them
with attention and material goods, they could ensure offspring who were happy, kind, and successful. In a complex
world, child rearing appeared to be one area in which people
had control over the results. However, dominant images of
children in films suggest a disappointment; parents may not
have been getting what they expected.

The Disney Films

The popularity of Walt Disney live-action feature films in the
1950s and 1960s attests to the fact that, amid the emerging
monster children and youngsters traumatized by family and
growing pains, old-fashioned childhood innocence--a Disney
trademark--still appealed to movie audiences. Between 1950
and 1969, several Disney live-action films became blockbust-
ers at the box office. These include Old Yeller (1958), The
Shaggy Dog (1959), The Swiss Family Robinson (1960), Toby
Tyler (1960), The Absent-Minded Professor (1961), Babes in
Toyland (1961), The Parent Trap (1961), Mary Poppins
(1964), That Darn Cat (1965), and The Love Bug (1969).
In addition, Disney Studios produced numerous other live-
action features which, although not major box-office successes, nevertheless captured a particular audience. Among
them are Treasure Island (1950), The Story of Robin Hood
(1952), The Sword and the Rose (1953), Rob Roy, The Highland Rogue (1954), Pollyanna (1960), Three Lives of Thomasina (1964), and The Happiest Millionaire, (1967). To be
sure, Disney began work on live-action features prior to the
1950s. The Three Caballeros and Fun and Fancy Free, released in the 1940s, used live-action footage, and Song of
the South (1946) became the first Disney feature to use a
full cast of actors to tell a fictional story.[80] It was not until the success of Old Yeller, which grossed $8,000,000 in
domestic showing alone, that Disney realized that if his studio was to thrive, he would have to concentrate on live-
action features and keep expensive animation to a minimum.[81]
Just as Disney understood the economics of the movie industry, he also knew his audience. By 1960, owing to the baby
boom, children under fifteen comprised 31.1 percent of the
total United States population.[82] Disney films, traditionally

marked by wholesomeness and traditional values, were designed to appeal especially to children and also to their parents; in essence, Walt Disney was one of the first to tap the
baby boomers as a large consumer audience.[83] Studies have
shown that children like to watch other children on screen
and sometimes see them as role models.[84] Disney instinc-
tively sensed this and therefore included wholesome youthful
characters, in either starring or supporting roles, in most
of his live-action films. Without exception, these images of
children were marked by the same innocence and charm reflective of children in prewar films. Interestingly, though,
many of Disney's more developed child portrayals appear in
films set in the past, reflective of a simpler time when childlike innocence and unlimited hope for the future undaunting-
ly prevailed.

Since 1940, Disney Studios have been responsible for
nearly one fifth of all film adaptations of children's literature.[85] Old Yeller, Disney's first live-action blockbuster,
fits into this category. Adapted from the book of the same
name by Fred Gipson (who co-authored the screenplay with
William Tunberg), Old Yeller is a classic story of a boy and
his dog. Directed by Robert Stevenson, the film contains
two popular components of the then-developing Disney live-
action formula: an animal and adventure. Set in Texas in
1869, Old Yeller begins as Jim Coates (Fess Parker), leaves
on a three-month cattle drive to earn money for his family
and designates his fifteen-year-old son Travis (Tommy Kirk)
to take care of the farm, his mother (Dorothy McGuire), and
his younger brother, Arliss (Kevin Corcoran). One day Arliss brings home a big, yellow, stray mongrel, much to his
brother's dismay. When the dog, which Arliss names Old
Yeller, chases a mule on the farm (resulting in a broken
fence) and drinks out of the family's drinking water, Travis
threatens to shoot it, but his mother says, for the sake of
Arliss, not to harm the dog. In time, Old Yeller proves
himself to be not only a good watchdog but also a fine family friend, thus winning even Travis' admiration.

The climax of Old Yeller occurs when Travis takes the
dog with him on a hunting trip to trap some wild pigs. Trying to rope the pigs from above while sitting in a tree,
Travis loses his balance and falls into the thick of the pack,
and Old Yeller comes to the rescue by fighting off the mean-
tempered animals. Travis is injured, Old Yeller is almost

killed, but both boy and dog survive. In the skirmish,
however, Yeller contracts rabies, and Travis must eventually
shoot him. After doing so, Travis is distraught, but he ultimately finds one of Yeller's feisty little pups, and, because
it reminds him of Yeller himself, vows to raise the pup as
his own.

Although the focus in Old Yeller is on Travis, the
older brother, little Arliss is a significant character as well.
The role is played by Kevin Corcoran, who became popular
among the small-fry set through his movies for Disney and
his television appearances on the "Mickey Mouse Club Show."
In Old Yeller, Corcoran's Arliss epitomizes childhood innocence. Like most Disney children, he is dependent on his
family and ignorant of the adult world. As his father leaves
for the cattle drive in order to earn money, Arliss asks innocently, "What's money?" Arliss is oblivious to his father's
explanation and excitedly explains that he wants to go on the
cattle drive, too. In essence, he demonstrates a boy's desire
for adventure and a lack of understanding of the danger and
responsibility involved. Later, Arliss also proves his innocence of death. When Old Rose, the family cow, contracts
rabies and must be shot (a foreshadowing of Yeller's fate),
Arliss asks questions: "Where will the cow go? Is the cow
up in heaven? Are there cows in heaven for the angels to
milk? Is heaven as far away as Dad is?" The child does not
understand realities of the adult world.

He is, however, in tune with nature, and for this reason it is not surprising that it is he who introduces the family to Old Yeller. Indeed, in addition to adopting the dog,
he also keeps a collection of snakes, horned toads, and other
creatures. Arliss' childlike affection for the dog is one of
the characteristics that makes the film work. A particularly
touching image shows the tyke riding atop Old Yeller as if
the dog were a horse. To the young boy, the pet is a
friend on the isolated, lonely frontier. In one scene, a cowboy (Chuck Connors) comes to retrieve his hunting dog but
Arliss refuses to give up his pet. The cowboy, sensing Arliss' attachment to the dog, accepts a horned toad as a trade
for Old Yeller. Thus, the child's contest for the dog with
the kindly cowboy makes sense; Arliss knows little of adult
decorum, only what he wants--and Old Yeller, he believes, is
his. Because of Arliss' innocence, this scene works beautifully. As Leonard Maltin writes, "The shot of the boy walking

up to the cowboy is shown from the youngster's point of
view, looking up at the very tall man--charming idea that
works perfectly."[86] This technique, which had previously
been used effectively in Shane, emphasizes the child's smallness and vulnerability in the adult world.

Old Yeller ends on a hopeful note as Travis vows to
raise his courageous dog's remaining puppy. It is important
to point out, however, that the ending is not fully a happy
one. Travis realizes that things have changed, that even
though he has Yeller's pup, something precious has been
lost. This sense of loss tempers the impact of a completely
happy ending, thus complying with a continuing trend in
postwar films featuring children.

A year after the success of Old Yeller, Disney released
a curious film called The Shaggy Dog, again utilizing the
talents of Tommy Kirk and Kevin Corcoran, this time teamed
up with Fred MacMurray as their father. This film has little plot. Very simply, a teenage boy named Wilby Daniels
(Kirk) inadvertently carries off a magic ring from a nearby
museum. Under the ring's spell, he changes periodically (he
never knows when) from the boy he is to an oversized sheep
dog, one identical to that owned by his neighbors next door.
While under the spell of the ring, Wilby, in the form of the
dog, learns that his neighbor is an evil foreign spy attempting to steal top-secret government missile plans, and, after
a mad chase, he saves the day.

Both an adventure and an animal story, The Shaggy
Dog adds another usual component of the Disney formula--
humor. This becomes most apparent in the outrageous
scenes in which the boy-turned-dog performs the everyday
acts of humans--such as driving a car or putting on his
pajamas, gargling, and brushing his teeth. Kevin Corcoran,
who plays Wilby's cute little brother, Moochie, also adds a
touch of humor. The emphasis in the film is clearly on Wilby,
the boy/dog, and on his bewildered father, a mail carrier who
has come to despise dogs. Moochie, however, has a significant role: He is the only one who knows about Wilby's recurring transformations. The film would not have the charm-
ing quality that it does were it not for Moochie's innocence.
In a particularly comical scene, Moochie is confused to see a
large sheep dog dressed in his brother's pajamas going to
sleep in his bed. By morning, however, he realizes he has

not had a dream and is perfectly willing to accept that his brother is a dog; thus, he helps to conceal him from his unsuspecting father. Moochie, almost preferring his new shaggy pet to his teenage brother, remains the boy/dog's only confidant, presumably because he is the only one who would believe the story. When Moochie tries to report to his father about Wilby and the spies, he is ignored--in essence, treated like a child. Later, when he and his father are at the police station trying to explain what is transpiring, Moochie tells a tremendous lie, thus making his father look like a fool, in order to get out quickly to rescue Wilby. In The Shaggy Dog, the innocent child--the little brother-- plays the comical role of straight man to a transforming boy/ dog. Seen through his eyes, the antics that appear on screen take on a wondrous, almost magical--rather than stupidly absurd--quality.

In 1960, Kevin Corcoran landed the starring role in another popular Disney live-action feature, Toby Tyler, based on the book by James Otis Kaler. Directed by Charles Barton, this film captures the feel of the circus in turn-of-the-century America. The film begins as young Toby Tyler, dressed in a little cap and big overalls, delightedly looks at a sign announcing the circus's arrival in town. His childish enthusiasm is soon dampened when he realizes that he does not have any money to buy a ticket. Harry Tupper, the head concessionaire, invites Toby to join the circus and work for him, but the child remembers that he must return to his poor Uncle Daniel and Aunt Olive who need his help on the farm. He accepts Tupper's free pass to the circus and returns home, only to be scolded severely by his uncle because of his neglect of his chores. Aunt Olive tries to calm her outraged husband, but Uncle Daniel cruelly berates the boy, calling him a millstone around their necks. Later that night, Toby runs away from home and joins the circus as a concessionaire. There, although he is continuously mistreated by Mr. Tupper, he makes many sincere friends: Ben Cotter, the strong man; Sam Treat, a kindly clown; Mademoiselle Jeanette, a little girl who does a horseback-riding routine; and especially Mr. Stubbs, a mischievous chimpanzee. One day, when Mademoiselle Jeanette's horseback-riding partner is injured, she suggests that Toby replace him, and, even though the boy has had little riding experience, he accepts the challenge, works hard, and, despite many frustrations, masters the routine. By the end of the film, Toby has not

only proven himself to be an important member of the circus
community but also won the respect of his Uncle Daniel, who
offers Toby a heartfelt apology for the unkind things he
said to him. To add to the happy ending, Toby joins Mademoiselle Jeanette in a horseback-riding routine while Uncle
Daniel and Aunt Olive look on with pride at their talented,
much-loved little nephew.

The success of Toby Tyler affirms the 1960s audience's
belief in traditional American values. Toby represents the
classic innocent child. Like Arliss in Old Yeller, he does
not understand money. While working as a concessionaire,
he receives a slug, which he does not recognize, and Mr.
Tupper docks his pay. Later, Toby tells Mr. Tupper that
he does not understand why some customers have told him
to keep the change, and Tupper explains that they are tips
that go to the head concessionaire. In Toby's case, however, if the child promises to say nothing to anyone, he will
split with him half and half; thus, he keeps ten cents and
gives Toby five. The innocent child, then, is vulnerable to
the older man's treachery. In addition to being ignorant of
economic matters, Toby demonstrates his elemental innocence
in other ways. He is excitable and adventurous, reflecting
every child's dream of running off with the circus and becoming the star of the show. In tune with nature, he becomes a chimp's best friend. He is also kind and loving to
adults, even his cruel uncle whom he freely forgives and
wants to help. Interestingly, Toby Tyler is one of the few
Disney films in which a child's relationship with his family
is not central; Toby leaves his aunt and uncle near the beginning of the film, and they return again only shortly before the final fadeout. Toby has, however, joined a new
family of sorts--his circus companions who teach him the
value of friendship. Even though Toby is not portrayed in
the context of a nuclear family, he nevertheless plays the
traditional dependent-child role as Ben Cotter and Sam Treat
look out for him, thereby acting as his protectors.

In the circus, Toby is part of an all-male world, with
the single exception of another child, Mademoiselle Jeanette;
thus he has no maternal influence, no traditional family.
Nevertheless, the importance of a nuclear family is espoused.
At the beginning of the film, Toby is a runaway, a common
childhood image in postwar films, one reflective of an increasingly more complex and fragmented world in which

parents and children have difficulty coping with and understanding one another.[87] By the end of the film, parent-
figures and child have resolved their differences, each accepting the other. However, it is the adults who come to
this realization rather than the child, unlike in such prewar
classics as The Wizard of Oz and The Blue Bird, in which
the child discovers that there is no place like home. This
suggests a confusion in roles and values, one reflective of
1960s trends in child rearing. As parents, following the
advice of Dr. Spock and various child psychologists, began
following the leads of their children, trying to gain their
acceptance and become their friends rather than their disciplinarians, roles became muted. As one childhood historian
observed, "Today parents worry more over whether their
children will like them whereas their earlier fear was a lack
of respect."[88] In Toby Tyler, the child carries the lead.
In the end, however, basic family values remain triumphant.
Toby Tyler also reiterates the importance of hard work, a
quality nicely contrasted with the prevailing circus mood of
frivolity and excitement. Seen through the child Toby's
eyes, the circus is a place where all worlds--fun and hard
work, family and friends, honesty and dishonesty--converge,
and the final outcome is a happy one.

Following Toby Tyler, Walt Disney Studios released
several more films featuring children. Even in Disney films,
however, children seemed to be losing popularity. A month
after Toby Tyler's very successful release, Pollyanna, a remake of the 1920 Mary Pickford picture, hit American movie
screens, touting an all-star cast and introducing the superbly talented child actress Hayley Mills in the title role. Although the film received generally good reviews, especially
for its ability to evoke the nostalgic charm of New England
in 1912, it did not do especially well at the box office, taking in a gross of $3,750,000--far short of Disney's $6,000,000
goal.[89] What had worked in the 1920s--the story of a spirited fix-it child playing "the glad game" and espousing sunshine and happiness everywhere she went--did not flourish
in a more pessimistic decade. Of particular note, however,
is the ending of Disney's Pollyanna, again reflective of a
different world. In the Pickford version, the determined
child sheds her crutches and walks, and, in an additional
scene is shown several years later in a happy scene with
her husband and several children. In contrast, the more
recent Disney version lacks such optimism: The film ends

with the villagers gathered around Pollyanna to wish her well
as she leaves on a train headed for Baltimore, where she
will undergo an operation designed to cure her crippledness.
The feeling is that all will turn out fine, but there is no
guarantee.

Popular films of the 1960s suggest a societal conflict
between embracing the traditional view of childhood innocence and rejecting it in favor of newer, less optimistic
images. In another related filmic trend, children appear in
movies presumably about children; however, their roles turn
out to be minor ones. In Disney's Mary Poppins, the biggest
box-office attraction of 1965,[90] Julie Andrews and Dick Van
Dyke play the lead roles in a film about a magical nanny who
converges upon a proper British household in 1910 and stays
just long enough to teach its family members to love, understand, and appreciate one another. In essence, Mary Poppins speaks to a 1960s concern, the need for family unity
and compassion in a fragmented, work-oriented world, by
portraying a banker, appropriately named Mr. Banks, who
comes to realize that his family and children are more important than business. The film also reflects the 1960s growing
interest in the women's movement--as indicated by Mrs. Banks'
spirited rousings as a leading lady suffragette--and the fear
that women, too, are spending too much time away from their
children. Although the theme of Mary Poppins is clearly the
importance of children and family, the Banks children, Jane
and Michael, do not have extensive on-screen presence. At
the beginning of the film, Mr. and Mrs. Banks are in an up-
roar because the children have run away, a particularly common image in postwar films featuring children. Later, Jane
and Michael sing a song requesting the perfect nanny. However, after the arrival of Mary Poppins, their screen time
becomes secondary to hers and that of her chimney-sweep
friend, Bert. Even when Jane and Michael are on screen,
they rarely govern the action; instead, they passively react
to what is going on around them, especially to the amusing
antics of Mary Poppins and Bert. Whereas Shirley Temple
would have shaped up her father herself and taught him the
power of a child's love, Jane and Michael need an outsider
to do it. This reflects a qualification of the prewar belief
that children can indeed fix everything; it also suggests
that on-screen children do not generate the audience interest they once did. In essence, while the frequency and
domination of children's on-screen images decline, childhood

continues to be a filmic issue. This again holds true in another 1965 blockbuster film, The Sound of Music, produced
by Twentieth Century-Fox and also starring Julie Andrews.
In this film, the focus is on the father who runs his family
like a regiment (not unlike Mr. Gilbreth in Cheaper by the
Dozen or Mr. Banks in Mary Poppins). The children essentially provide cute, textural props that, for the most part,
are not well developed; the theme of family, along with romantic love and political freedom, prevails.

The 1960s and the End of the Baby Boom

By the 1960s, several new images of children in American
films had taken hold. Alongside the traditional innocents
and cheery fix-its stood emerging monsters; precocious,
mature little geniuses; emotionally scarred or confused children; and passive tykes. These new images reflected a
growing ambiguity toward children and their ability to solve
the world's problems and ensure a promising future. It appears that attitudes toward the future were changing, and,
because children had always been associated with the better
world of tomorrow, attitudes toward them were destined to
change as well. By the 1960s, combined with the fear of
nuclear devastation, America's reasons for pessimism intensified. All told, in a few short years, Americans were bom-
barded with threats from all sides--the Cuban Missile Crisis;
the assassinations of a president, a presidential hopeful,
and a noted civil-rights leader; and the Vietnam war, the
first time United States military involvement in a major war
was not perceived by the public as clearly in the right.
Added to these, on the home front, crime in America was
increasing by leaps and bounds, a result of the baby-boom
generation's entrance into the crime-committing years.[91]
Indeed, if postwar Americans believed they were living in
an unsafe world in the 1940s, two decades later, this feeling was augmented.

All of these issues helped to shape attitudes toward
children--and variations in their screen images. In addition
to a pervading pessimism, however, two other social phenomena had a direct bearing on changing views toward children.
By the 1960s, children seemed different from those of decades before. The first generation to grow up with television
--their private "window on the world"--they gained early

access to sexual, social, and political information, thereby
making them less ignorant, and perhaps less innocent as
well.[92] In addition, more and more women, many of them
mothers, joined the job market. Between 1965 and 1970,
the number of women working increased faster than it ever
had--almost four percent a year.[93] Children have been traditionally associated with the realm of women, who are their
nurturers and caretakers. As roles of and attitudes toward
women changed, children were affected as well.

Also, by 1964, the baby boom that had characterized
postwar America had ended. In 1965, just as the first co-
horts of baby-boom women entered their prime years of
childbearing, the birthrate dropped below four million for
the first time in twelve years, and over the next fifteen
years, fertility dropped to the lowest levels in American
history.[94] As Landon Jones notes, "The Procreation Ethic
had been abandoned."[95] And for some, it was none too
soon. As early as the mid 1950s, some people began to
worry about the effects of overpopulation, a condition that
intensified in 1967 when America's population reached an
all-time high of two hundred million.[96] In 1968, Paul Ehrlich published The Population Bomb,[97] outlining the horrors
of large families and consequent overcrowding; the book became a best-seller. The following year, Ehrlich became one
of the founders of Zero Population Growth. Attitudes toward
children, it seemed, were in flux, and it is not surprising
that several images of children gained popularity on the
motion-picture screen. Many of the new variations of childhood portrayals that had slowly begun developing after
World War II had fully emerged.

Some filmmakers, like Disney, colored their portrayals
of children with a natural innocence. In 1963, Universal
released To Kill a Mockingbird, directed by Robert Mulligan;
it became the eighth-biggest money-making film of the
year.[98] Adapted from the best-selling novel by Harper Lee,
To Kill a Mockingbird is structured around the narrative of
Jean Louise Finch, nicknamed Scout (Mary Bedham), who recalls the summer of 1932 when she was six years old and
living in a small town in Maycomb County, Alabama, with her
widowed father, Atticus (Gregory Peck), and her ten-year-
old brother, Jem (Phillip Alford). Atticus is an attorney
who takes on a case which no one else in the racially preju-
diced little town would touch: He defends a black man, Tom

Robinson (Brock Peters), who is falsely accused of raping a
young white woman, Mayella Ewell (Collin Wilcox). At the
trial, Tom Robinson loses, despite overwhelming evidence of
his innocence. Nevertheless, Scout and Jem stand by their
father, whom they have come to admire as a man of intelligence, understanding, honor, and integrity. Despite the
townspeople's growing hostility towards Atticus, he believes
the trial was unjust and plans to appeal the decision; however, he never gets a chance to do so. Panicking, Tom
Robinson tries to run away and is shot dead. Even after
the case has been laid to rest, Mayella's father, Bob Ewell
(James Anderson), continues to hold a grudge, and on a
Halloween night, he attacks Scout and Jem. They are mysteriously saved, however, by Boo Radley (Robert Duvall), a
retarded neighbor whom they had previously feared and often ridiculed. In essence, they learn that Boo had secretly
been their guardian angel, watching over them and leaving
toys for them. Thus, their prejudice of him, which stemmed,
like all other prejudice, from ignorance, was as unfounded as
the town's unjust feelings against a black man.

    In many ways, the portrayal of childhood innocence in
To Kill a Mockingbird resembles that in Shane. Both Scout
Finch and Joey Starrett are observers of, not participants
in, the adult world, and the stories they tell are enhanced
by their childlike charm and spirit. In Shane, Joey is characterized as a child through his association with artifacts of
childhood such as a peppermint stick and soda-pop bottle.
In a similar way, Scout and Jem are immersed in a world of
toys and play. Although Scout is a rambunctious tomboy,
she clutches a cuddly stuffed animal as she sleeps. Jem
finds small toys left for him in the knot of a tree. Together
the children play tricks on their neighbor, roll down the hill
in a tire, and dress up for Halloween. Even when not involved in a game, they adopt a playing stance; in one particularly effective shot, Scout is perched in a rocking chair
on the porch. Rather than sitting upright, however, she is
upside down with her feet draped over the chair's back;
thus, the chair functions as another toy. Also, just as Joey
Starrett slowly learns about death in Shane, Scout comes to
know what poverty is. At the beginning of the film, she
asks her father, "Are we poor?" Although living in the
midst of the Depression, they clearly are not; Atticus is not
a wealthy lawyer, but he does provide his children with a
comfortable home, good meals, and even a housekeeper.

Later, Scout learns what it is to be poor when an impoverished farmer, Mr. Cunningham, leaves hickory nuts on the
porch in payment for Atticus' legal services and when his
son, who eats dinner with the Finches one evening, is so
taken with the sweetness of molasses (which his family cannot afford) that he spreads it over all his food.

In To Kill a Mockingbird, the child's world, represented
by games and toys and a lack of understanding of money, is
clearly one of innocence, and this is where the film's power
lies. While Shane focused on Joey Starrett's personal past
and admiration of a hero, To Kill a Mockingbird revolves
around a larger social issue--racism--and a child's view of
its impact on a community. Scout is the perfect narrator.
As a child, she has no racial prejudices or preconceptions
and thus is able to view a black man's unfair trial for rape,
and its consequences, as an objective observer. As with
all films, To Kill a Mockingbird says more about the year it
was released, 1962, than about the year it portrays, 1932.
During the Depression, racial desegregation was not a hot
social issue, but in the 1960s, it was--especially in its relationship to children. In 1954, in the landmark case of Brown
vs. the Board of Education, the United States Supreme Court
unanimously reversed the doctrine of "separate but equal"
and ruled that legal separation on the basis of race violates
the Fourteenth Amendment; further in a separate ruling,
lower courts were ordered to use "all deliberate speed" to
admit black children to public schools.[99] The ruling was
met with much opposition. In 1957, Arkansas Governor Orville Faubus attempted to block the Little Rock School Board's
efforts to desegregate schools, a move which the Supreme
Court declared unconstitutional the following year.[100] The
year it was released, To Kill a Mockingbird won the Gary
Cooper Award for Human Values;[101] clearly, it had something to say to contemporary audiences. By bringing together the issues of racism and children, To Kill a Mockingbird indirectly addressed the concern at hand: desegregation. In the film, the children prove their ability to understand and overcome prejudice, a particularly effective message for 1960s audiences, who, after seeing the film, would
perhaps be more aware of prejudice and more accepting of
desegregation.

To Kill a Mockingbird is also significant for what it
says about child-rearing techniques. Atticus Finch, whose

children call him by his first name, encourages individuality
and independence in Scout and Jem, which often meets with
disapproval among his neighbors. For practical purposes,
Atticus can be termed a permissive parent. He allows the
children enough freedom to make discoveries on their own
and does not try to shelter them. Scout and Jem, for example, attend Tom Robinson's trial and later accompany Atticus to the Robinson home to tell his family that Tom has
been shot. When the children misbehave, such as tomboy
Scout's getting into a fight at school, Atticus talks to them
rather than scolds. In essence, he practices the childrearing techniques espoused by Spock; however, he is being met with opposition. This suggests a societal tension:
By the early 1960s, Spock's methods were beginning to be
questioned as many so-called "Spock babies" reached their
troublesome teenage years and were proving to be spoiled
and often rebellious.[102]

Childhood innocence also abounds in the musical Oliver!
Released during the Christmas season of 1968, it went on to
become the eighth-biggest money-maker of 1969;[103] it also
won the 1968 Academy Award for best picture. Because
musicals are most often designed for family entertainment,
it is not unusual for children to appear in them; however,
it is rare for a child to hold the title role, as did nine-
year-old Mark Lester. Adapted from Charles Dickens' classic Oliver Twist and directed by Carol Reed, Oliver!, with
its focus on social consciousness, proved to be an appropriate film for the late 1960s. Set in nineteenth-century England, the film tells the story of a lonely little orphan boy
named Oliver who makes his way out of the poorhouse and
heads to London to seek his fortune. There he meets up
with the Artful Dodger (Jack Wild), a self-assured young
pickpocket who takes Oliver under his wing and introduces
him to Fagin (Ron Moody), the conniving leader of a band
of orphan thieves. Oliver goes off on a pickpocketing mis-
sion with Dodger, and, when the latter steals a wallet and
runs, the novice thief, standing innocently alongside, gets
blamed. The next day in court, a storekeeper testifies that
he saw the incident, and Oliver did not pilfer the wallet.
Feeling sorry for the orphaned lad and wanting to make
amends, Mr. Brownlow (Joseph O'Connor), the wealthy man
who accused him, brings him home to live with him. Fearing that Oliver will tell about the den of thieves, Fagin ar-
ranges to have Oliver kidnapped and returned to him.

Meanwhile, Mr. Brownlow learns that Oliver is the son of his niece, who, after being jilted by her lover, died in a poorhouse after giving birth. In the end, after an exciting rescue scene through the streets of London, Oliver is restored to Mr. Brownlow and thus ends his lonely existence as a poor orphan.

The reason for Oliver!'s appeal certainly had much to do with the film's lavish sets and spirited song-and-dance numbers. More interesting about the movie, though, is its portrayal of the child, like so many other filmic children, a young orphan. Thin, wistful, with big brown eyes, Mark Lester is the perfect Oliver. In the film, the key to the character of Oliver is his total passivity. Except for an early scene in which he deliberately sets off for London, he does not act; instead, he is acted upon. This is different from the majority of children in prewar films who, in addition to being elementally good, were active participants in ensuring their own destinies. By the end of Oliver!, the child is adopted, and his future looks bright; however, he has done nothing to bring about the situation himself. Thus, one cannot see him in the same vein as many of his prewar filmic counterparts who, through their own actions, paved the way to a happy future and a better world. This changing role suggests a growing ambiguity toward children in American culture.

Also significant in Oliver! is its overall theme: a child's need for love. Early in the film, little Oliver sits dejectedly in a dark basement singing "Where is Love?"; by the film's end, he has found it. The message, which has much relevancy to 1960s America, is clear: A child can be properly cared for only in a home, surrounded by loving family, not in an institution. In the 1960s, as more and more mothers went to work, day-care centers were still considered by some to be too institutional and not within the child's best interests, reflecting a prevailing belief that, as Landon Jones writes, "organized group care for the very young was considered a social evil rivaled by only godless Communism."[104] Oliver!, then, espouses a mainstream belief that the child belongs in the home; institutions are not acceptable.

Just as Oliver plays a fairly passive role in the film bearing his name, so, too, do the girls in Father Goose,

the eighth-biggest money-maker of 1965,[105] which starred
Cary Grant and Leslie Caron. In this film, Walter Ekland
(Grant), a scraggly, boozing beachcomber (who used to be
a college professor), is coerced into being a coast-watcher
on a South Pacific island during World War II. Much to his
disenchantment, he meets up with Catherine Freno (Caron),
a prim French schoolteacher, and her seven young charges,
all daughters of diplomatic personnel, who have been
stranded on the island. Immediately, Catherine takes over,
not only moving herself and the girls into Walter's quarters
but also demanding that he change his ruffian behavior. In
the end, after a myriad of wartime traumas, Catherine and
Walter realize that they are in love and they marry. Thus,
the children will be delivered home to their parents while
the newlyweds begin their happily married life.

Reflective of a less active role of children in films, the
girls in Father Goose do very little; they are essentially
props designed to create atmosphere and provide a reason
for Catherine's being on the island. Also, they contrast
superbly with Walter's seedy personality. Of particular interest, though, is the duality of their innocence. Catherine
thinks their youthful minds should be shielded from Walter's
depravity--his drinking and his foul language. However,
the girls are much more savvy to what is going on than she
thinks. Thus, they help Walter hide his booze and seem to
sense the growing relationship between Walter and Catherine
even before they themselves do. This depiction reveals a
contradiction, not unlike one taking place in American culture, that children's own conception of their innocence dif-
fered greatly from what adults believed of them.

The Innocents (1961), released by Twentieth Century-
Fox and directed by Jack Clayton, was not a box-office
blockbuster; nevertheless, the film is significant for its foreshadowing of future images of children in film. Adapted
from Henry James' short novel The Turn of the Screw, the
film utilizes children in a horror genre. In this film, Miss
Giddons, a young governess played by Deborah Kerr, accepts a position to care for two precocious children, Miles
(Martin Stephens) and Flora (Pamela Franklin), on their
wealthy uncle's country estate. During her stay, she comes
to believe that the innocent children are possessed by the
dead spirits of their former governess, promiscuous Miss
Jessel (Clytie Jessop) and her cruel and passionate lover,

Peter Quint (Peter Wyngarde), the former valet. Miss Giddons tries to save their young souls by making them admit that they are being haunted. By the end of the film, the innocence of both children has been destroyed, but it is uncertain who did it. Were the ghosts of the impassioned lovers real or simply fabrications of the imagination of an undersexed, psychotic governess' imagination? Further, were the children destroyed by the spirits or by Miss Giddons herself, who, in trying to preserve their innocence, actually takes it away?

The Innocents is important for its theme--the loss of innocence. In essence, Henry James' darker vision of childhood innocence was beginning to strike a chord in a more modern culture. In her review of The Innocents, Pauline Kael writes that perhaps Miles and Flora "are destroyed by the innocent who now controls them (in her idealism, she may expect children to be so innocent that she regards actual children as corrupt)."[106] By the 1960s, as methods of birth control became more developed and widely accepted, greater numbers of children were planned, and, as John Sommerville notes, family planning "no doubt leads to rising expectations, which can sour the relationships of parents and children."[107] In a subtle way, The Innocents addresses some growing questions of its time. Are we a society that is losing its innocence? Do we expect our children to be better, more innocent than they possibly can be? High parental expectations characterized the American baby boom. Child portrayals like those of Miles and Flora suggest that these expectations were unreasonable, thus leading to disappointments among both parents and children.

Although children's images in American films in this period were undergoing transitions--especially in their depiction of innocence--some old standbys remained; these were not, however, without innovations. Immensely popular, True Grit, the sixth-biggest money-maker of 1969,[108] starring the indomitable John Wayne and Kim Darby, retells the classic tale of the child as fix-it. In this film, tough, determined Mattie Ross (Darby) hires fat, boozing, one-eyed United States deputy Rooster Cogburn (Wayne) to track down the cowhand who murdered her father and bring the scoundrel to justice. Cogburn, who charges Mattie his "children's rate" of $100, is described as a "pitiless man, double tough," and Mattie makes a suitable counterpart to

him. Although a child, she insists on accompanying Cogburn
and a Texas ranger on the manhunt. Taken with her "grit,"
Cogburn marvels, "My God, she reminds me of me!" With
the help of Cogburn and the Texas ranger, Mattie avenges
her father's death. In the midst of the fracas, however,
she is seriously injured when she is jolted by the backfire
of her gun and falls backwards into a snakepit. Cogburn
proceeds to save her life, and, as a result, she is determined to play fix-it one more time. Because Cogburn has
no family, she offers him a plot in her family's graveyard
where, when his time comes, he can "meet eternity." In a
later film, The Cowboys, the twelfth-largest box-office draw
of 1972, Wil Andersen, also played by John Wayne, hires
approximately a dozen young boys to assist him on a long,
treacherous cattle drive. When Andersen is killed along the
way, the boys do what they have to in order to complete
the task, including killing off cattle rustlers. Despite the
danger involved, they get Andersen's cattle to market so
that they can provide his widow with enough money to take
care of herself.

In both True Grit and The Cowboys, the image of
fix-it children is likened to Wayne's tough on-screen persona.
However, unlike the child-as-fix-it films in earlier years,
these end on an ambiguous note: The children get the job
done, but the future remains uncertain. In Mattie Ross'
case, although she organizes the manhunt to avenge her
father's death and even shoots at the culprit, it is not she
but Rooster Cogburn who actually fires the fatal shot; thus,
it seems, fix-it children are losing some of their impact.
Further, in order for the children in True Grit and The
Cowboys to fulfill their functions, they must attempt to kill
(and in The Cowboys they ultimately do kill), which means
giving up their innocence. In prewar films, children could
be fix-its and innocents both, but this seems to be changing. Lastly, True Grit and The Cowboys suggest another
developing trend in films: a preference for older, near
adolescent characters rather than young children.[109] Mattie, for example, shares more characteristics with the independent modern woman than she does with an innocent child,
although, as William R. Meyer observes, her "pouty-lipped
sincerity ... resembles Shirley Temple's best."[110]

In addition to the traditional--albeit varied--images of
children as innocents and fix-its, new dimensions of childhood

were emerging in films of the 1960s--ones like <u>The Innocents</u>
that emphasized a darker view of childhood. In 1962, United
Artists released <u>The Miracle Worker</u>, adapted from William
Gibson's play of the same name, based on <u>The Story of My
Life</u> by Helen Keller. The film, directed by Arthur Penn
and starring Anne Bancroft and Patty Duke, both of whom
won Academy Awards for their performances, creates an image of childhood never before addressed on the screen: the
handicapped child. <u>The Miracle Worker</u> tells the miraculous
story of the young life of Helen Keller (Duke), who is left
deaf, dumb, and blind following an acute illness suffered in
infancy. The film opens with the image--accompanied by no
sound--of a pretty, delicate Christmas ornament crashing to
the ground, thus signifying the loss of hope inherent in
Helen's silent, impermeable world. In time, Annie Sullivan
(Bancroft), a young teacher from Boston who is partially
blind herself, comes to care for Helen and attempts to break
into her shell or, as she says, "disinter the soul." The
task is not an easy one, especially for an inexperienced
teacher. To compound the matter, the severely handicapped
Helen has been very spoiled by her parents, who allow her
to do anything she pleases, including groping for food from
her family members' dinnerplates and lashing out in violent
tantrums. Because her parents have been unable to offer
her guidance and instruction, they simply pity her instead,
and, without discipline, she has become an unruly monster.
Annie Sullivan's confrontation with Helen becomes more of an
ongoing physical battle than a typical cerebral meeting between teacher and student. As the legend goes, Annie Sullivan achieves success in reaching Helen Keller's mind and
soul. In the film's climactic scene, Annie drags Helen to a
water pump to make her fill a pitcher of water that the child
had dumped in one of her rages. At that moment, Helen
realizes that the curious hand symbol that Annie has been
trying to teach her for several months stands for the thing:
water. Further, she makes the transference that other hand
symbols stand for other things: pump, ground, tree, teacher, mother. By the film's end, in addition to knowing the
meaning of language, Helen has overcome the anger and confusion that characterized her silent world; thus, her hostility toward Annie Sullivan is replaced with love, tenderness,
and gratitude.

     The focus in <u>The Miracle Worker</u> is on the intense
physical struggle between Annie and Helen. As Bosley
Crowther notes,

> It is clear that the bold decision the stalwart young
> Annie makes when she arrives at the Southern home
> of the Kellers to try to train their desperately af-
> flicted child is that she must go about it with the
> brute force one would apply to the breaking of a
> head-strong colt.[111]

In this image, the handicapped child is likened to an undis-
ciplined animal; clearly, this contrasts with many earlier
portrayals of children in films that showed the calm, nature-
loving, innocent child who is able to tame even the wildest
of creatures. Interestingly, this depiction of the unruly,
spoiled child comes at a time when Dr. Benjamin Spock's
more permissive methods of child raising were being questioned.[112] In essence, the key to The Miracle Worker is
discipline; without it, a child cannot mature. Also significant in The Miracle Worker is the role of the parents. Following in the trend set by many of their filmic predecessors,
Captain Keller and his wife, Kate, are ineffectual parents; it
takes an outsider--and a young, partially blind, emotionally
scarred one at that--to reach their troubled, misbehaved,
deaf, dumb, and blind daughter. This depiction reflects a
growing feeling of inadequacy among parents.

A final point of importance regarding The Miracle Worker is its portrayal of the handicapped child, one marked by
serious physical and emotional problems and needing, more
than anything, to be respected as a person rather than
simply treated as an unthinking, uncontrollable animal. This
image, too, reflects the history of childhood in America. In
earlier decades, people tried to ignore the realities of physical and mental retardation, pretending such problems did not
exist; instead, child-oriented legislation focused on the right
of all youths to a happy childhood. By the 1960s, however,
it could not be denied that many children suffered severe
physical and psychological disabilities; thus, concern lay with
them. In 1950, the National Association for Retarded Children was formed, and, within the decade, funds were appro-
priated to provide services for young children with amputa-
tions, to treat and rehabilitate juvenile delinquents, and to
print and circulate braille books for blind children.[113] In
1960, the Golden Anniversary White House Conference on
Children and Youth was held; further delineating the differences between children and youth, it focused primarily
on the problems of adolescent alienation. As in the previous

decade, the 1960s saw an effort to help children with special
needs; aid came to orphans, crippled children, delinquents,
abused children, and poor children. (By 1968, the latter
group represented one seventh [10.6 million] of America's
children.[114]) In essence, The Miracle Worker, with its com-
pelling portrait of an exceptional child, popularizes the growing realization that not all children are normal and happy;
some have debilitating problems that require special attention.
Further, as the film suggests, children are not love personi-
fied, spreading brightness and charm everywhere they go.
(Indeed, one of Annie Sullivan's dilemmas is that she does
not love the misbehaved child whom she is trying to teach.)
Children, too, must have special care and the right to ex-
press themselves before they can learn affection.

The Child-As-Monster Film

Helen Keller in The Miracle Worker clearly fits the description of a child monster as she hits, screams, rants and raves
her way across the movie screen. However, there is an ex-
plicable reason for her behavior: She is handicapped and
has not been taught discipline. Not coincidentally, a previous monster child, Rhoda, the little girl in The Bad Seed,
also had a reason, again parent-related: She had inherited
the trait that predisposed her to killing from her mother
whose own mother had been a cold-blooded murderess. The
fact that these explanations exist attests to a cultural belief
that children are innocent.

Children who act like monsters are not fully guilty;
further exploration reveals that their behavior is not really
their fault. Evidence of the widespread acceptance of the
child-as-innocent paradigm also takes on another dimension.
By the 1960s, children portrayed as monsters were used to
achieve a shock effect in films, one that could never work if
movie audiences actually believed in the evilness of children.

Some child-as-monster films took a realistic approach.
In 1962, The Children's Hour, Lillian Hellman's well-known
play, was adapted for the screen and directed by William
Wellman. Starring Shirley MacLaine and Audrey Hepburn,
the film tells the story of two schoolteachers who are accused of being lesbians by a malicious young student (played
by Karen Balkin). The teachers go on trial and, despite a

lack of evidence, are found guilty; thus, their lives are
ruined by a child's lie. In another popular film released
the same year, Lolita, adapted from the best-selling novel
by Vladimir Nabokov, a middle-aged man marries an over-
weight, overbearing widow so that he can be near her sexually provocative adolescent daughter. Although the actress
in the film (Sue Lyon) looks a bit more developed than the
nubile nymphet of Nabokov's book, the message remains the
same: The child is a temptress and thus is not fully innocent. (Interestingly, although a handful of television docu-
dramas have addressed the issue of sexual child abuse, the
movies have not. In Lolita, because the child is as guilty
as the man, interest lies with his devastation after she rejects him, not with any trauma she may have faced.)

In both The Children's Hour and Lolita, the youngsters depicted are normal; although conniving, they have no
extraordinary powers or special gifts. Such is not the case
in an array of films that began in the 1960s and reached
their peak in the 1970s--the horror film featuring the child
as monster. It is important to note that the horror film is
not a recent genre; it has existed nearly as long as the film
medium has. In the 1960s and 1970s, however, the horror
film merged with the family comedy that had achieved its
height of popularity in the 1930s and 1940s, thereby creating a new genre--the family horror film.[115] Children as
aggressors featured prominently in this new genre.

A forerunner of the 1960s trend in monster children
can be found in Village of the Damned, released by MGM in
1960 and directed by Wolf Rilla. Although not a major box-
office success, this film is important for historical reasons:
It features a monster child in a combination family-horror/
science-fiction creation. Village of the Damned opens with a
peaceful scene of the little town of Midwich. The scene cuts
to the home of Gordon Zellaby (George Sanders) and his wife
Anthea (Barbara Shelley) as Gordon tries to call his brother-
in-law to borrow a book. Midway through the call, he falls
into a deep sleep--along with everyone else in the town.
Four hours later, Midwich residents awake, and officials,
relieved that no harm has been done, simply chalk up the
odd phenomenon as an "electric impulse" from another planet.
In a short time, however, the effects of the deep sleep are
discovered: Anthea Zellaby, along with every other women
in Midwich who is capable of childbirth, is pregnant--

regardless of any sexual contact. The fetuses develop rapidly, and when the babies are born, they are all over ten
pounds. They seem normal except for three identifying characteristics: They have strange, glowing eyes, an unknown
hair group, and unusual fingernails. As the children grow,
they exhibit more abnormal traits. At four months of age,
they are as developed as a normal eighteen-month-old baby.
They possess unusual intelligence, the ability to read minds,
and immediate internalized knowledge of information or skills
that any of the other special children learns. Further, and
most disturbingly, by merely flashing their eyes, the children can control their environment, and they do so without
pity or any sense of right and wrong. The situation becomes desperate when the children, headed by the Zellabys'
son, David (Martin Stephens), cause murders and suicides
among several Midwich townspeople who think badly of them.
Midwich residents learn that other children like theirs have
been born in similar occurrences in other parts of the world
and have been destroyed. Midwich must do the same in order to save itself. In the film's final scene, Gordon Zellaby
goes into a classroom, presumably to teach the children about
atomic energy; however, the children are confused when they
read his mind and see that he is thinking only of a brick
wall. Fixating on this image in order to allay their suspi-
cions as to what is really happening, Gordon waits patiently
until the bomb that he has set explodes, thereby destroying
the threatening children and Gordon himself.

In many ways, Village of the Damned is patterned after Invasion of the Body Snatchers (1956), a successful horror film released a few years before that tells the story of
invading giant seed pods that turn a community of sensitive,
feeling individuals into unfeeling, robotlike zombies. Believing that this film captured the then-current themes of conformity, paranoia, and alienation, Stuart Samuels writes,

> Directly or indirectly, Invasion deals with the fear
> of annihilation brought on by the existence of the
> A-bomb, the pervasive feeling of paranoia engen-
> dered by an increasing fear of dehumanization fo-
> cused around an increased massification of American
> life, a deep-seated frustration resulting from an
> ever-widening gap between personal expectation and
> social reality, and a widespread push for conformity
> as an acceptable strategy to deal with the confusion
> and growing insecurity of the period.[116]

These same themes appear in Village of the Damned. However, unlike in Invasion, the focus in Village of the Damned
is on the children: They are the conformists, all looking
and acting alike, emotionless and defensive, and posing a
threat to their families and community. This film is crucial
in providing an understanding into the changing attitudes
toward children as reflected in American films. In prewar
films, children were characterized by their unlimited goodness; in them lay hope for the future and a better world.
Village of the Damned takes this idea to its opposite extreme.
When Gordon first learns of the children's keen intelligence
and special powers, he suggests that their gifts can perhaps
be directed to solve the world's problems. However, his
hope is soon shattered when he realizes that the children--
like Rhoda in The Bad Seed--possess no sense of right and
wrong, guilt, or remorse. Gordon then learns the ultimate
truth: The powers of the children are as unlimited as the
mind and, if not controlled, will be used to wreak unlimited
devastation. Like Invasion of the Body Snatchers, Village
of the Damned carries an indirect statement regarding nuclear war. Indeed, at the end of the film, when the bomb
explodes, Gordon is lecturing the children about atomic power. The message is clear: No hope exists in an immoral
nuclear world; children, then, can become the keys to destruction.

    Although an "electrical impulse" from another planet is
suggested as a reason for the strange phenomena at Midwich,
by the end of Village of the Damned, no definite explanation
has been found. Such is not the case in several other child-
as-monster films in which possession--usually demonic--is
the certain culprit.[117] The first successful family horror
film to exhibit this trend was Rosemary's Baby, the seventh-
biggest money-maker of 1968.[118] Adapted from the best-
selling novel by Ira Levin, this film, directed by Roman
Polanski, chronicles the pregnancy and growing realization
of a young woman, Rosemary Woodhouse (Mia Farrow), that
her husband, Guy (John Cassavetes), has sold their baby
to a witches' coven in return for a successful acting career.
The film comes complete with a demonic conception scene that
Rosemary awakens from, convinced that it was all a dream,
and two kind but eccentric neighbors, Minnie (Ruth Gordon)
and Roman Castevet (Sidney Blackmer), who put Guy up to
the scheme. Rosemary gives birth to her baby, but Guy
tells her it has died. Suspecting the truth, however,

Rosemary persists and finally learns that she has in fact
borne a diabolical child. In the film's final scene, Rosemary
accepts her baby and assumes the responsibility of raising it.

The "image" of the child is not important in Rosemary's
Baby; the Satanic infant, which is born at the end of the
film, is never shown on screen. Instead, the film focuses
on the mother, Rosemary, and her fears during the pregnancy. The most effective horror stories are those that
audiences can relate to, those that bring their own fears
to the surface; this seems to be the appeal of Rosemary's
Baby. The situation is not an uncommon one: A young
woman becomes intensely aware of the changes in her body
as her pregnancy progresses; with every pain or unusual
sign, she worries that something is wrong, something that
may mar her hopes for a healthy, normal child. This is
the fear that envelops Rosemary. When her child is born,
it is healthy; it is, however, evil, the devil incarnate. Like
Village of the Damned, Rosemary's Baby uses the myth of
the bad child to shock: Parents worry about a child's physical normality but never his or her moral sense. Films of
the 1960s seem to espouse that one cannot take a child's
goodness for granted. Traditionally, filmic children have
always been vulnerable; by the late 1960s, they had become vulnerable to becoming evil. The composition of elements in Rosemary's Baby suggests a cultural uneasiness
about having children, one that no doubt increased as the
birthrate in America fell and people began contemplating
alternative life-styles to parenting. A final point of interest regarding Rosemary's Baby hinges on the responsibility
for the child's depravity; as in The Bad Seed, it is a parent who is responsible, in this case the father, who has
sold his child to the devil.

The popularity of Rosemary's Baby led to other films
featuring the demonically possessed child. Most successful
were The Exorcist and The Omen, both of which employ
child performers. The Exorcist, based on the best-selling
novel by William Peter Blatty and directed by William Friedkin, was the second-biggest money-making film of 1973;
when it was reissued two years later, it again did a tremendous business, ranking seventeenth for the year.[119] This
film begins with an eerie scene in Iraq in which a priest
discovers an ancient icon of universal evil. The scene immediately cuts to a modern household in Georgetown where

actress Chris MacNeil (Ellen Burstyn) and her daughter,
Regan, (Linda Blair) discuss plans for celebrating Regan's
twelfth birthday. In the days following her birthday (on
which her estranged father in Europe does not bother to
call), Regan begins to act strangely. In one of the film's
first crucial scenes, the child, dressed in a nightgown,
enters her mother's late-night cast party, tells an astronaut,
"You're going to die up there," and proceeds to urinate on
the floor. Later that night, her bed begins shaking violent-
ly, and the child wonders what is happening to her. Concerned about her daughter, Chris MacNeil takes her to the
hospital where she undergoes several painful tests which fail
to provide a definite diagnosis. In the meantime, Regan's
condition worsens: both her personality and her appearance
grow coarse and ugly; further, the child's language becomes
characterized by rage and obscenities. Then Chris MacNeil
slowly becomes aware, like Christine Penmark in The Bad
Seed, that her daughter has committed a murder: One evening Chris's director, Burke Dennings, was sitting up with
Regan; later he was found dead with his body badly contort-
ed, presumably after having been pushed from Regan's
second-story window.

Unable to do anything more for Regan, the doctors
suggest exorcism, an ancient Catholic ritual used to ward off
demonic possession. Chris dismisses the idea, only to return
home to find her child masturbating with a crucifix. Shouting obscenities, she pushes her mother's face toward her
bloodied vagina. Two priests agree to perform the exorcism;
Father Merrin, an older priest who beheld the token of evil
in Iraq, and Father Karras, a young priest who has begun
to doubt his faith and, very recently, has been trying to
come to grips with severe guilt following the death of his
poor, elderly mother. The grueling exorcism is successful,
but it is not without its costs. Father Merrin suffers a
heart attack and dies, and Father Karras, shouting to the
demon, "Take me! take me!" becomes transformed and throws
himself out of Regan's window onto the street below, where
he dies moments later. Following the traumatic ordeal, the
child, fully restored to her original state, cries in a corner
of her room, and her mother comforts her. In the film's
final scene, as Chris MacNeil and her daughter are leaving
Georgetown, they are visited by another priest. Regan sees
the man's collar, senses something, and kisses his neck.
Her diabolical nightmare over, she remembers nothing.

The Exorcist was the first film employing a juvenile performer to receive an "R" rating; thus, it was technically off limits to child audiences. It was, however, well attended by teenagers, a group of whom Vincent Canby observed at a New York showing:

> The kids especially, several of whom lay in an or-
> chestra aisle near my seat and smoked and talked
> about basketball during those sections of the film
> in which the tormented child on screen was not
> vomiting bile at the priests, masturbating with a
> crucifix, screaming obscenities about the young
> priest's dead mother, or, for fun, turning her head
> 180 degrees to the rear. At those moments the
> kids were spellbound, almost it seems in spite of
> themselves.[120]

The kids were not alone. The above-mentioned scenes, those that generated the most ire and controversy among movie audiences, were the ones that sold the film. Quite explicitly, these scenes depict a demon who has violated the body of a child in a blatantly sexual way. Culturally, sexual contact of any sort is taboo for a child. Thus, this image gives the film its shock value.

Interestingly, though, The Exorcist is not as innova-tive as it might seem: Except for a few shocking images, it is a very conventional film, one that espouses the importance of religion, the responsibilities of motherhood (Molly Haskell has even suggested that the film is a statement against the Women's Movement and that Regan's affliction is her mother's punishment for being a divorced career woman[121]), and the innocence of childhood. Throughout the film, there is a clear line drawn between the child and the devil. Chris says, "That thing upstairs is not my daughter." Later, the words "HELP ME" appear on Regan's stomach, an obvious plea from the child trapped inside the possessed body. In this film, childhood innocence exists, but it has been defiled, thus supporting the traditional image of the vulnerable child. The demon is evil and powerful; the child (not unlike her mother) remains helpless.

Despite these observations, the fact remains that au-diences went to this film to see some disturbing images: first, an innocent child sexually violated by a demon and

second, a demon in a child's body acting as a heartless, pro-
fane aggressor. This duality suggests some interesting cultural tensions. In the years following World War II, as Americans felt threatened by the world around them, attitudes
toward innocence seemed to change. On one level, The Exorcist addresses the vulnerability of innocence: Once social
attitudes toward innocence break down, so do the taboos
against its symbolic representatives--children. However, because innocence is so endemic to the American character, it
can never fully be destroyed; thus, Regan's body is defiled
but the innocent child remains somewhere within. Secondly,
The Exorcist speaks to changing attitudes toward childhood.
As Robin Wood notes, horror films often bring to the surface
repression, and children make up the most repressed--even
most oppressed--segment of the American population.[122]
The Exorcist was released at a time when more attention was
being given to children's rights--not to the protection of
children but rather to their rights for entering into responsible adult life as soon as they are capable.[123] The lashing
out of Regan perhaps suggests that children had been socially oppressed for too long; thus, she makes up for centuries' worth of their being barred from the responsibilities
and freedoms of adult life.

A similar message occurs in The Omen, released by
Twentieth Century-Fox in 1976 as an obvious response to
Warner Brothers' money-making Exorcist. In this film,
Robert Thorn (Gregory Peck), a successful American political figure living in Italy, accepts a baby from a hospital
priest after being told that his own infant was born dead.
Wanting to spare his wife, Kathy (Lee Remick), from grief
for her own dead baby, he does not tell her about the
switch. Soon after, Thorn is appointed as American ambas-
sador to Great Britain so he, Kathy, and their son, Damien,
leave Italy for London. By Damien's fourth birthday, strange
happenings have begun. His nanny hangs herself, and a
coldly competent one appears to replace her. When Kathy
takes Damien to the zoo, the animals run away from the child,
and baboons furiously attack their car as they drive through.
A demented-looking priest keeps trying to talk to Thorn, and
when the latter finally listens, he learns the truth: Damien
is the Antichrist. The priest explains that Kathy is pregnant with a child that Damien will kill in the womb. Then
he will kill her, and once it is certain that he will inherit all
of his father's wealth, he will kill him and establish his

kingdom on earth run by Satan. After the warning, the
priest is killed in a bizarre incident--a spire falls from a
church during a violent storm and impales him. At first
Thorn does not believe the prophecy, but when his wife is
seriously injured in a fall that Damien causes and a photographer provides him with chilling information about the dead
priest's satanic roots, Thorn, accompanied by the photographer, travels to Italy to trace his son's roots. There he
learns that his natural child was killed, and that Damien is,
indeed, the devil. When word arrives from London that
Kathy has been killed, Thorn vows that Damien must die
too, but he cannot murder a child. The photographer declares that he will, only to be decapitated immediately in a
ghastly accident. Convinced of what he must do, Thorn
returns to London, fights off the evil nanny who is an
apostolate of hell, and takes Damien to a church so that he
can murder him and save the world from the devil by sprin-
kling his blood on the altar. As Thorn attempts to stab his
son, the police intervene and shoot him instead. The film's
final scene depicts the funeral of Robert and Kathy Thorn.
Damien has survived, according to the prophecy, and is being
adopted by the President and First Lady of the United States.

Like The Exorcist, The Omen received an "R" rating;
Damien was not a figure intended to be seen by other children. Like many children in more recent films, Damien has
very little on-screen presence; what is said about him takes
on greater importance than what he actually says and does.
He is not a human child; he is a changeling. In this film,
the innocent child becomes the manifestation of an exterior
force, evil. As in The Exorcist, in The Omen, a line exists
between child and the devil. In The Bad Seed, which is in
some ways even more chilling than The Exorcist and The
Omen, a real child does the killing; in the others, it is not
a child at all but rather a demon contained in a child's body.
This, however, causes confusion, especially in The Omen, in
which Damien's parents are not aware of the truth of their
son's identity; this allows him access to his father's domain,
thus leading, unlike in The Exorcist, to the total destruction
of family, church, and government. This idea has cultural
connotations: It suggests a growing loss of trust, a realization that that which appears innocent may be deceptive. This
idea takes on further significance when one considers the
priest's prophecy that the Satanic child will inherit the world
--in essence, that the end of the world will be in the hands

of Satan. As this film became popular, Americans were not
concerned with the end being brought on by the devil; however, they were uneasy with the fact that nuclear war could
bring about ultimate destruction. Damien's deceptive innocence, then, adds to a societal sense of mistrust: Anyone
can be the aggressor. Not surprisingly, The Omen came
only two years after Nixon's resignation following the Watergate scandal, another incident that fostered feelings of mistrust when Americans learned of treachery among individuals
who had attained high political position. Of final note in
The Omen is the role of the father, who unknowingly brings
the Antichrist into his home and refuses to heed warnings
until after it is too late. In The Bad Seed and The Exorcist, the father is absent, and in Rosemary's Baby, he is
responsible for selling his child to the witches' coven.
Thus, Robert Thorn fits the filmic trend of ineffectual
fathers, reflective of a pervading belief in the disintegration of family strength.

While The Exorcist and The Omen were the most successful films featuring possessed children, they were not the
only ones. Both spawned sequels, Exorcist II: The Heretic
in 1977 and Omen II: Damien in 1978. The latter, which
became the twentieth-biggest blockbuster of the year,[124]
encouraged a third film, Omen III: The Final Conflict
(1981). In 1976, Joan Collins starred in The Devil Within
Her, in which she plays a London nightclub performer who
gives birth to a devil-possessed infant after spurning the
amorous advances of a dwarf endowed with supernatural
powers. Before the film's end, the innocent-looking child
kills off his nurses, pediatrician, and parents. In 1977,
Julie Christie starred in The Demon Seed, in which she is
the reluctant target of a sophisticated, evil computer that
wants to perpetuate its kind in human flesh by impregnat-
ing a woman. In addition to demonic possession, children
in 1970s films were the object of other sorts of possession
as well. In The Other, (1972), a ten-year-old boy is possessed by his evil, dead twin brother. In the course of
the film, the surviving child kills off his father, uncle,
cousin, a neighbor woman, and an infant niece (who turns
up pickled in a barrel of wine). He attributes the deaths
to his twin, refusing to acknowledge he is dead. The protagonist of Audrey Rose (1977) does no damage; she, however, is possessed by a past life. As Audrey Rose Hoover,
she died at five years of age in an automobile accident in

Pittsburgh, only to be reborn two minutes later in a hospital in New York where her new parents name her Ivy. The soul of Audrey Rose/Ivy has not endured the proper interval before passing from one body to another; thus, Ivy suffers frightening nightmares and severe identity problems; like Regan in The Exorcist, she is a possessed, suffering child.

In other popular 1970s films, children who are not possessed still manage to wreak havoc everywhere they go. One of the most representative films of this sort is It's Alive, released by Warner Brothers in 1977 and directed by Larry Cohen. In this film, an unusual baby, equipped with claws and teeth, is born in a Los Angeles hospital and immediately proceeds to murder everyone in the delivery room except its mother, before mysteriously escaping through a skylight. Crawling, the infant manages to make its way through the city, planting a large, fatal gash in the neck of anyone who gets in its way. Believing that anything that kills like an animal must be killed like an animal, the police organize a manhunt. The child's father, Frank Davis (John Ryan), who has rejected his mutant baby, wants to be the one to kill it. At the crucial moment, however, Frank cannot murder his offspring. Like his wife, Lenore (Sharon Ferrell), and his other son, Chris (Daniel Holzman), he assumes the role of the child's protector, and someone else fires the fatal shot. As a policeman drives Frank and Lenore home following the death of their baby, they hear over his police radio that another such child has been born in Seattle.

It's Alive takes the child-as-monster trend to its logical ending: Even a newborn infant--one who, as Robin Wood notes, is not possessed by the devil but is merely the product of the environment and the family[125]--can be a deadly killer. The idea of the family structure retaining a basis for evil recalls Rhoda in The Bad Seed. If a child is at the center of the family, and the child is evil, the family is in danger, a theme also expressed in another successful horror film of the 1970s, Halloween (1978), in which a six-year-old boy stabs his teenage sister to death. With its portentous ending, It's Alive suggests that evil is pervasive; in an unsafe world no one is immune, an idea further developed in the film's sequel, It Lives Again (1978).

In the 1930s, Twentieth Century-Fox produced several movies starring Shirley Temple, who danced her way across

the screen--and into the hearts--of Americans. Forty years
later, the same studio gave us The Omen and The Other.
And Warner Brothers, which delighted postwar America with
such wholesome features as Jackie Cooper in Dinky, countered decades later with The Bad Seed, The Exorcist, and
It's Alive. Clearly, American tastes had changed. Children's filmic images, which were once almost sacred, could
now be defiled and tortured any way the director saw fit--
and audiences responded with enthusiasm. There is no
single reason for this variation in direction; however, it
seems to be the result of several factors which began taking
hold in America following World War II and reached a peak
in the 1970s.

As has been stated, postwar America was characterized
by a sense of pessimism brought on by the realization that
Americans were living in a nuclear world, one in which atomic
warfare could annihilate the human species. Thus, an unlimited hope for the future, which had always been at the
core of the American character, was threatened. In the
decades that followed, subsequent happenings--the Cold War,
the Korean War, the Cuban Missile Crisis, the assassination
of a president, the Vietnam War--aggravated Americans' pessimism. By the 1970s, America's unexpected defeat in Vietnam destroyed the myth that America was all-powerful and
always in the right. Equally important, the Watergate
scandal, which resulted in the resignation of a president in
1974, added to a mistrust of American leadership. Collectively, these occurrences destroyed American confidence, and
without it, the future cannot be secure. As Landon Jones
writes,

> Ironically, the loss of confidence in the future was
> strongest among those former activists and reform-
> ers who had once placed so much hope in a better
> world. Their attitude had spread until, by the
> end of the 1970s, more than three out of every
> four Americans agreed with President Carter that
> "the erosion of our confidence in the future is
> threatening to destroy the social and political
> fabric of America."[126]

It seems that Americans, who had always valued innocence
and childlike intuition, sensed a vulnerability. They questioned natural innocence, believing that in a world fraught

with treachery, scandal, mistrust, and disappointment, it
might not exist. Traditionally, children have been the symbols of innocence and confidence in a hopeful future. Therefore, when these values were doubted, evil children became
a filmic manifestation of much larger social and political problems. The child-as-monster syndrome in films of the later
1960s and 1970s points as much to growing pessimism about
the future and about belief in innocence as it does to a societal disenchantment with real children. Not surprisingly,
in the run of child-as-monster films, frequently the real
point is not the evil of children, often the victims of demonic
possession themselves, but rather the ineffectiveness of the
family, church, and state--America's most highly valued
institutions--to guard themselves against deception and im-
pending destruction. These films seem to suggest that the
current state of affairs, best exemplified by the fatherless
or ineffectually fathered family, is not satisfactory; new
leadership is called for.

In addition to a general reevaluation of innocence in
1970s America, attitudes toward children seemed to be changing. John Sommerville explains the change thusly:

> Americans are notorious for looking to their children
> for approval. How our children turn out and what
> they think of us has become the "final judgment" on
> our lives. As a nation, we have always been ori-
> ented toward the future and to new frontiers. So
> long as this is true, we will imagine that the rising
> generation is rendering history's verdict on us. We
> may resent them simply because we expect a harsh
> judgment. But there is no denying that they have
> the power to make us feel we are being left behind.
> Recently, however, we have begun to doubt our na-
> tion's and even the world's future. For several
> centuries industrialization has steadily increased
> economic opportunities and thereby brightened the
> future. But now we are told that industrialization
> is propelling us past the limits of our planet's re-
> sources. Our children now represent a time that
> will only have bigger problems and not a better life.
> This may well make us lose our zest for change.
> We may begin to worry less about what the future
> and our children think of us. Worse than that, we
> may resent the fact that these little citizens of the

> future are already compounding all our problems--
> energy, food, employment, pollution, crowding.
> Babies are the enemy. Not your baby or mine, of
> course. Individually, they are all cute. But to-
> gether they are a menace.[127]

Real children, it seems, had not lived up to the exalted image that Western culture had given them. Further, as Ehrlich had pointed out in 1968, there were too many of them,
thereby creating an overpopulation problem that was destined
to become worse if Americans did not choose to have fewer
children.[128] So for the first time in history, the belief
that children are a nuisance and a burden rather than a
delight became popular. By the 1970s, owing to the baby-
boom generation's hitting its crime-prone years, the crime
rate had continued increasing for two decades. Although
youngsters more often commit crimes against property than
crimes against persons,[129] it is not surprising that this ag-
gressive characteristic was translated into films as murder,
the most serious of offenses. At the same time that this
portrayal was having its heyday on screen, more apartment
complexes posted signs prohibiting children, the Supreme
Court decreed that teachers could spank the little brats in
school, and televisions blared the message, "It's ten o'clock.
Do you know where your children are?"[130] Children, it
appeared, were getting out of hand.

At the same time, another significant cultural phenomenon was occurring. Older baby-boom children were entering their childbearing years at a time when more people were
unemployed in the United States than at any time since the
Depression.[131] These potential parents, who themselves had
been raised at a time when children were highly valued and
parents believed in sacrificing for them, still felt that they
deserved the best of everything; hence, the self-centered
"me generation" was born.[132] In order to achieve their material goals, though, in a difficult economy, a family needed
two breadwinners. These career-oriented individuals, for
the first time in our country's history, regarded children as
a life-style, a choice rather than a given. Consequently,
the birthrate in America dropped. By 1972, the number of
births stood at 2.03 children per family, below replacement
level, the lowest birthrate in twenty-seven years.[133] Not
surprisingly, the nonfiction best-seller list was sprinkled
with titles such as The Baby Trap (1971) by Ellen Peck,

Mother's Day Is Over (1973) by Shirley L. Rode, and The
Case Against Having Children (1971) by Arnold Silverman.[134]
Of course, some women still chose to have children, but they
were less likely than ever to remain full-time housewives. In
the 1970s, nearly one third of married women returned to
their jobs within a year after having a child and nearly half
were in the labor force by the time the child was two years
old.[135] Further, the increase in working married women
with children has been even faster than that of women without children.[136]

    Added to a growth in the number of working mothers
was another crucial social phenomenon--an increase in divorce. Americans were finding out that the happy nuclear
family, as espoused in the movies of the 1930s and 1940s, as
well as in such popular television shows of the 1960s as
Leave It to Beaver, Father Knows Best, and Ozzie and
Harriet, was not coming to pass. By the end of the 1970s,
divorce in America had firmly taken hold. Landon Jones
records some astounding statistics:

> Today divorce is doing what death did one hundred
> years ago in creating one-parent families. It is
> estimated that nearly one-half of all children born
> today will spend a meaningful portion of their lives
> before 18 in single-parent families. Already one
> out of every six children lives with a single parent,
> usually the mother, double the portion in 1950. If
> a child is living with two adults, they are increas-
> ingly less likely to be his or her biological parents.
> One-quarter of all school-age children today do not
> live with their real fathers.[137]

The disintegration of family, then, especially the absent
father, that was so prevalent in child-as-monster films, reflected a much larger social concern--family problems at home.

    The combination of an increase in working mothers and
a rise in the divorce rate may have contributed to a cultural
tension regarding attitudes toward children. On one hand,
the traditional ideal remained. As John Holt notes, children
give adults something they need: "someone to boss, someone
to 'help,' someone to love."[138] The idea of the child as innocent is befitting to the adult ego: It places adults in a
position of authority, making them nurturers and protectors.

On the other hand, as parental lives were made increasingly
more complex through career demands and divorce, some
adults seemed to shun the responsibilities entailed in raising
innocent, dependent, unknowing children. Thus, in the
popular conception, the image of the innocent child was
countered with its opposite--the tough, independent, hard-
nosed kid who already knew all of the adult tricks. Not
surprisingly, many advocates of child rights in the 1970s
took a different direction from those of earlier decades:
Rather than protecting children, they encouraged the lib-
eration of children from laws that protect--and often repress--
them. In Escape from Childhood (1974), child-rights advocate
John Holt stressed that children should become independent
and capable of making their own decisions at an early age.
He enumerated the following rights of children: the right to
vote, work, own property, travel, choose one's own guardian,
receive a guaranteed income, obtain legal and financial responsibility, control one's learning, use drugs, drive, have
sex, and have privacy.[139] Perhaps Regan, Damien, and the
other monster children of the 1970s, representative of society's most oppressed group of individuals, lashed out at the
institutions that had historically repressed them: the family,
the church, and the state.

The dominance of the child-as-monster image in American films of the 1970s may, at first glance, suggest that
Americans hated children, but this is not fully true, although children as a cultural group may not have attracted
public admiration in previous decades. Certainly, demon
children inhabited the screen in the 1970s; however, the
children themselves were often innocent, the vulnerable victims of an evil force. What this filmic image reflects is not
so much hatred of children as a growing inability of adults
to cope with the combined responsibilities of work and family in a world that was becoming increasingly more fragmented
and demanding. Further, this image underscores a societal
tension regarding the changing attitudes toward children. If
Americans really bought into the argument that children are
monsters, the images presented in The Exorcist and The Omen
would not have been so shocking, and much of the popularity
of those films hinged on their shock value. In essence, what
these portrayals reflect is conflict, not abiding acceptance.
On a larger scale, the image of the child as monster reveals
a pervading sense of mistrust and fear of deception. Children have always been symbols of innocence, goodness, and

unlimited hope for the future; if anyone could be trusted, it was they. By the 1970s, the feeling of pessimism and a breakdown of confidence in the future--sentiments that had slowly begun accumulating following the devastation of the atomic bomb during World War II--reached a peak, no doubt a consequence also of the defeat in Vietnam and the Water- gate scandal. No one, it seemed, could be trusted; further, Americans doubted their own abilities to recognize deception until it was too late. Symbolically, then, images of children were affected; they reflected serious conflicts and fears in the fabric of American culture.

In the 1980s, the monster child in film continues to exist but seems to be losing ground. In 1980, Martin Shaker, Gil Rogers, and Gale Garnett starred in The Children, in which schoolchildren exposed to radiation from a nearby nuclear power plant become monsters who murder their par- ents with deadly hugs. This film makes an interesting con- nection: It links nuclear power specifically to children, who then become a threat to their environment. This brings to the surface a subtle, unconscious fear that had characterized America since World War II: In the hands of those who can- not be trusted, nuclear power could devastate the future. The Children, although its general image of childhood was not unlike many of its successful predecessors of the 1970s, did not rate as one of the year's top movies at the box of- fice. The most recent developments in the child-as-monster image have been in films based on novels by Stephen King, the current master of the horror genre. Advertised as a horror story for adults, King's Children of the Corn (1984) features a group of youngsters who systematically kill off all the adults they encounter in order to take over their small, secluded Midwestern town; the film did not do well at the box office. Nor did Firestarter, another Stephen King feature released the same year. This film, like many child- as-monster films before it, combined the image of the monster child with the classic innocent. In it, a little girl named Charlie McGee (Drew Barrymore) has the power to start fires by simply getting angry and fixating her eyes on an object. She wreaks havoc everywhere she goes; however, she is unsure why it happens. Deep down, she remains innocent.

Stephen King may be among the last to contribute to the current child-as-monster filmic trend by bringing it to

its peak, its logical conclusion. As stated previously, the
child-as-monster image flourished in the 1970s because, first,
it proved to be shocking; a dozen films later, children who
kill seem to lose their initial impact. Further, the image
proliferated as a response to growing tensions in the culture
--ones involving home, family, career, future. In the 1970s,
this combination of tensions, previously unexplored, reached
a peak; the paranoia and pessimism of the time resulted in
the child-as-monster image. Although such tensions may not
go away, they stabilize as cultures learn to cope with them.
Thus, new filmic images, relfective of this trend, gain popularity.

The Precocious Imp and Other Images

During the 1970s and continuing into the 1980s, the child as
monster proved to be a dominant image in American films.
However, as in other decades, several conceptions of childhood flourished concurrently. A related image--one whose
seeds were planted years before, immediately following World
War II--also reached a height of popularity in the 1970s and
has remained in the mainstream. This was the precocious
imp, the savvy, know-it-all child who is frequently more
competent than the adults he or she encounters. No doubt,
this image provided a solace to the parents of the growing
numbers of latchkey children; it underscored that the youngsters can take care of themselves. The filmic portrayal of
the precocious child was often combined with other popular
images of children to add still more variations to the postwar
movie screen. Paper Moon combines the tough, precocious-
imp image of the 1970s with the traditional fix-it. Ranked
as the fifth-biggest money-maker of 1973,[140] Paper Moon is
essentially a parody of the early Shirley Temple vehicles.
Set in Depression America, the time Temple made her films,
Paper Moon features the opposite of the innocent, honest
child; she is nine-year-old Addie Loggins, played by Tatum
O'Neal, who won an Oscar for her performance.

Paper Moon, which is short on plot but rich in 1930s
atmosphere, begins as Moses Pray (Ryan O'Neal) drives his
claptrap car up to the funeral of Addie's mother, the prostitute he had been with the night before she died. One of
the women at the funeral asks Moses if he will deliver Addie
to her Aunt Billie, her only known relative, in St. Joseph,

Missouri, and, after a bit of hesitation, he agrees. Immediately, he uses Addie to get $200 from the person responsible
for her mother's fatal accident, and, with the money, he has
his car fixed. Conscious of what he has done, Addie is furi-
ous and demands her $200; thus, the partnership between
Addie and Moses, who, she believes, might be her illegitimate
father (despite his denial), begins. For the rest of the film,
Addie accompanies Moses through rural Kansas and Missouri
and learns his trade: He is a small-time swindler whose
specialty is conning distraught widows into buying lavish,
personalized Bibles that he says their husbands ordered. In
a short time, though, Addie takes over as leader of the duo;
she sets the Bible prices, plans all the moves, and manages
all the money (which she keeps in a cigar box and counts at
night while smoking cigarettes in bed and listening to Jack
Benny or FDR--her real hero--on the radio). In one in-
stance, Addie even directs Moses' love life. When Trixie
Delight, a voluptuous carnival kootch girl, attracts Moses'
attention, Addie gets jealous and insists on sitting in the
front seat of the automobile with Moses while his new flame
sits in back. Treating Addie like an adult, Trixie tries to
reason with her. "Let Trixie with her big tits sit up front,"
she pleads, and goes on to confide to Addie that men do not
stay with her for very long. Addie agrees to being relegated to the back seat momentarily, but, understanding
Trixie's weakness for money and sex, connives a scheme to
get rid of her for good. When Moses finds Trixie in bed
with a lecherous hotel manager--a meeting Addie set up--
the little girl gets back her man. As the film ends, Moses
and Addie reach St. Joseph, and the child is united with
her loving and very well-to-do aunt. But Addie does not
appreciate the luxury; she misses Moses. She runs away
and finds him; he takes her back, and to the sound of
1930s radio music the two drive off together in Moses' rick-
ety old car down an open road.

Smoking, swindling, conniving little Addie is, on the
surface, a far cry from perfect little Shirley Temple, and
her appearance--her chopped-off, dirty-blond hair and ever
present smirk--underscores this difference. However, in
some elemental ways, Addie shares Shirley's virtues. She
is hardworking--a dedicated con artist, quick-witted, and
resourceful. When she and Moses get apprehended for stealing a bootlegger's liquor and selling it back to him, Addie
plans their escape; Moses simply follows her lead. Further,

Addie is sympathetic and just--she will swindle the rich without blinking an eye, but when she confronts the poor, she
shows compassion, even concern; sometimes, instead of conning the latter into buying a Bible, she just gives it away.
Most importantly, Addie is independent, able to take care of
herself. But ultimately she needs love. In the end, she
teaches Moses that, despite difficulties, it is worth going on
and that money is not everything. In essence, she shows
him that, through loving a child, he can come to see life in
a new dimension--and a brighter one at that. This, of
course, was Shirley Temple's message, too. Thus, in the
1970s, amid the filmic monster children, the fix-it still prevailed, although in a radically changed form.

In addition to presenting a parody of the early Shirley
Temple films, Paper Moon is important for other reasons.
First, it enabled nine-year-old Tatum O'Neal to win an Oscar
for Best Supporting Actress, not simply a miniature replica
for a notable child's performance but an official Academy
Award; she won over another child performer, Linda Blair
of The Exorcist, and adults Candy Clark, Madeline Kahn
(who played Trixie Delight in Paper Moon), and Sylvia Sydney. Prior to Paper Moon, however, Tatum had had no previous acting experience; this may, in fact, have contributed
to her success. Reflecting on his own career as a child
performer, Jackie Cooper once said,

> Kids don't act. So-and-so speaks in a particular
> way, this one has a cute smile, that one is a natural
> for sad, underprivileged roles. If they want a cer-
> tain look they hire the child actor who goes with
> it.[141]

This may have been the case with Tatum. According to
Paper Moon director Peter Bogdanovich, she was no professional; he often had to bribe her with candy bars to get her
to memorize her lines, which she did by listening to cassettes
on which Bogdanovich had recited all of her lines--complete
with every inflection and pause needed.[142] Nevertheless,
Bogdanovich considered Tatum the perfect Addie: "What
made her so good was that she wasn't a professional," he
said. "She didn't have any idea of what she looked like.
She was just being natural."[143]

Paper Moon was also responsible for catapulting young

Tatum to stardom, thus making her the first bona-fide child
star since the pre-World War II child-star era. While other
children--among them Claude Jarman, Jr., Brandon De Wilde,
Hayley Mills, Kevin Corcoran, and Patty Duke--made significant contributions to postwar films, they did not become
great money-makers. Tatum, however, drew in the crowds,
and her salary attests to her box-office appeal. She was
paid only $16,000 for Paper Moon, but based on its financial
success, her next feature, The Bad News Bears (1976),
earned her $350,000 and a 9-percent share of the film's
profits.[144] The Bad News Bears grossed an impressive
$22,266,517, making it the fourth-biggest money-maker of
1976[145] and distinguishing Tatum O'Neal as the highest-paid
child star in the history of Hollywood.[146] She also was the
only female named to the 1976 annual list of ten box-office
stars, on which she ranked in eighth place.[147]

In The Bad News Bears, Tatum O'Neal once again
plays the role of a precocious fix-it. In this film, Amanda
Whurlizer (O'Neal) is approached by her mother's former
boyfriend, Morris Buttermaker (Walter Matthau), a down-
and-out little-league baseball coach who urges her to pitch
for his team, the Bears. Amanda reluctantly agrees--after
talking Buttermaker into paying for her ballet lessons and
new blue jeans. With the help of Kelly Leak, a tough but
athletically inclined street kid whom Amanda recruits for the
team, she brings the Bears from last place to within one run
of the championship. Although Buttermaker hopes to win the
big game, he soon learns that some of the team members,
while appreciative of what Amanda and Kelly have done for
the Bears, nevertheless resent their making all the plays;
thus, in crucial moments of the game, Buttermaker puts in
less competent players. In the end, the Bears lose the
championship, but they win for themselves a personal victory as well as the respect of one another and all of the
other teams in their league.

Most of the action of The Bad News Bears takes place
on the baseball diamond or in the dugout; thus, the children
are not shown in the context of the family, as in most other
films, but rather in a peer group. This portrayal is significant, for it points to the formation of a new community, one
that may be able to meet the child's emotional needs better
than the family. In The Bad News Bears, it is within this
new community--one formed through circumstance and chance--

that the children find friendship and acceptance. This idea is further underscored by the role of parents in the film: They are concerned only with winning, not with personal fulfillment. By the end of the film, not only have the children learned their own self-worth but Buttermaker is better off as well. The Bears' surrogate father, he has been transformed by their trust.

In Paper Moon and The Bad News Bears, Tatum O'Neal popularized the precocious-kid image. Further, in both of these films, because she is not part of a traditional, nuclear family, she forms important bonds with others--in Paper Moon with Moses and in The Bad News Bears with Buttermaker and her teammates. Both of these themes were reflected in other films of the time, often with interesting variations. As a child, Jodie Foster did not achieve the box-office success that Tatum O'Neal did; nevertheless, she gave some notable performances, always cast as a precocious youth. In Taxi Driver, the eleventh-biggest money-maker of 1976, she plays the role of a twelve-year-old prostitute whose pimp is slain.[148] The same year, in Bugsy Malone, a satire on gangster movies in which children are cast in seedy adult roles, she is a prettily painted moll. In both of these films, Jodie Foster plays the "adultified" child, one with experience and street sense, who finds community in the underworld.

In other popular films, the image of the precocious child took on further dimensions. The Sailor Who Fell from Grace with the Sea (1976) creates the precocious monster child. In this film, thirteen-year-old Jonathan Osborne (Jonathan Kahn) belongs to a clique of boys led by the Chief (Earl Rhodes), a pretentious, overintellectual, treacherous classmate. When Jonathan's attractive, widowed mother (Sarah Miles) falls in love with a sea captain (Kris Kristofferson) who wants to leave the sea and marry her, the Chief believes that the sailor is violating "the pure and perfect order of the world"; therefore, the boys plot to kill him. A Little Romance (1979) features a twelve-year-old American girl living in Paris (Diane Lane) who has an I.Q. of 167 and reads Heidegger for fun; her equally intelligent French boyfriend (Thelonious Bernard) does not know his I.Q. and, afraid that he would be found out to be a genius, does not want to know it. "Nobody likes smart kids," he asserts. The image of these children blends precocity with innocence. The movie revolves around their attempt to fulfill a romantic, idealistic dream: to kiss in Venice in a gondola under the Bridge of Sighs at sunset while the bells of the city toll. This, an old man tells them, will enable them to love one another forever. In order to fulfill their dream, they link up with the old man (Laurence Olivier), who offers to help them reach Venice; later they learn he is a fraud.

The precocious-child trend has continued into the 1980s. Gloria (1980) paints the portrait of a little boy who is left with a gangster's ex-moll after his whole family is murdered by mobsters; his personality combines childhood innocence with the savvy precocity of a New York City street kid. In Shoot the Moon (1982) and Author! Author (1982), children who are coping with the fragmentation of their families due to divorce advise their once-again-single parents as to the appropriate way to go about conducting their love lives. Little Casey Brodsky in Irreconcilable Differences (1984) finds herself in a very adult situation: She is filing for divorce. Hers, however, is not against the usual spouse but rather against her divorced parents who have become too preoccupied with their respective love lives and careers to spend much time with their daughter. Casey seeks custody with her Mexican maid. In all of these films, the traditional family unit has broken down, thereby causing intelligent, resourceful children to confront difficult situations and form new bonds.

Thus, in the past decade, many youths on the motion picture screen have appeared to be smarter, more worldly, and in some ways less innocent than their earlier filmic counterparts. This cinematic trend can be explained in several ways. It may be in part a response to the biological fact that children are maturing earlier; it has been claimed, for example, that the onset of puberty in females has been falling by about four months per decade for the past one hundred and thirty years.[149] If children are approaching adulthood earlier, it seems likely that films would reflect this image--and this does seem to be the case. By the age of ten, filmic children are likely to be independent know-it-alls; in short, they seem very close to adolescence. Not surprisingly, along with the increase in movies featuring precocious children, there has also been a recent proliferation of films featuring adolescents and teenagers.[150]

Another explanation for the change in cinematic children

hinges on the cultural developments brought about by television. In 1982, Neil Postman published a book with the astonishing title The Disappearance of Childhood, in which he argues that, due to the widespread popularity of television, the distinctions between childhood and adulthood are being obliterated. With the simple flick of a switch, children have access to a body of information that previously they had to learn to read to obtain. As children gain access to this information, the barriers between childhood and adulthood begin to break down. Therefore, as Postman notes, "the idea of childhood is disappearing, and at dazzling speed."[151] Films, as reflectors of culture, exemplify this trend by portraying the "adultification" of children (frequently accompanied by childish adults who follow the youngsters' advice and leads). Such is the case in several recent popular films that "have in common a conception of the child who is in social orientation, language, and interests no different from adults."[152]

In a similar vein, it is interesting to note that by the dawn of the 1980s, the real-life child receiving significant public attention is one who most resembles an adult in terms of his or her intellectual or physical development. Frequently the son or daughter of upwardly mobile young professionals, the child prodigy or "super baby" is one who at an early age is already a computer wiz, an accomplished musician, or a star swimmer.[153] In previous times, parents worried about providing their child with a happy, carefree childhood; today they frequently fear the implications of keeping a child back, apparently believing that a child who is not taught to compete and excel at an early age will quickly fall behind his or her peers.

The precocious-child image in films of the 1970s and 1980s also suggests another cultural phenomenon: the disintegration of family. Frequently not a part of the traditional nuclear family, these streetwise children learn to take care of themselves. They also form relationships with other individuals, sometimes other children, in order to create a new community to take the place of family. The popularity of this image may reflect the growing fragmentation of the classic American family. As the traditional structure breaks down, children become more independent or seek other support groups.

Despite the proliferation of the precocious adult-child, the classic image of the child as innocent in American films has survived. Americans, it seems, are reluctant to totally give up their belief in the innocent child. Still, there have been notable variations in filmic portrayals. Child/animal films, like those that flourished in the 1940s and 1950s, still appeared in the 1970s and 1980s; however, unlike their earlier counterparts, the later films focused more on the animal than on the child. This, no doubt, was in response to the surge in pet ownership that characterized the 1970s, a phenomenon that may have reflected Americans' turning to animals for loyalty because they increasingly mistrusted their children's love.[154] Benji (1974), starring Higgins (the dog), became the third-biggest money-making film of 1975 and the top-grossing child/animal film of the decade.[155] In it, a cute, stray canine rescues two children from kidnappers and wins a place in their family, despite their father's earlier objections to owning a dog. The children, who get very little screen time, are merely plot devices while the courageous dog is the center of attention; much of the movie is filmed from his point of view. In the film's sequel, For the Love of Benji (1977), the children get even less screen time as their talented canine gets caught up in a CIA chase in Athens, Greece. The Black Stallion (1979), a beautifully photographed film produced by Francis Ford Coppola and directed by Carroll Ballard, tells the story of a young boy named Alec Ramsey (Kelly Reno) who is saved by a wild Arabian stallion in a shipwreck and, in time, tames the animal and rides him to victory in a national horse-racing competition. This film, which deals with the traditional themes of a child's taming a wild animal and believing in the impossible, was not among the top box-office successes of 1979; thirty-four years earlier, National Velvet, a film with the same themes and also featuring the same actor, Mickey Rooney, as the splendid horse's trainer, was one of the year's greatest hits. Another child/animal film, International Velvet (1978), a long-delayed sequel to National Velvet (1945), shows a new orientation to its genre. Unlike the original, which featured a twelve-year-old girl and her childhood obsession, the sequel has as its protagonist a bitter sixteen-year-old (Tatum O'Neal) and the more mature theme of teenage adjustment.

Other films--not including animals--that portray childhood

innocence include The Champ (1979), a maudlin remake of
the 1931 classic that starred Jackie Cooper and Wallace Beery,
and Willy Wonka and the Chocolate Factory (1971). In the
latter, Charlie, a poor, kindhearted, unselfish boy, passes
a difficult test of honesty, perseverance, and goodness to
become the heir to a wonderful, giant chocolate factory. Interestingly, of the five children portrayed in the film, only
Charlie is likable; the others are spoiled, selfish brats, a
rather curious feature in a movie designed to be a hit with
child audiences.

Childhood innocence also appears in other films based
on novels by Stephen King. Prior to Children of the Corn,
King achieved success with The Shining (1980) and Cujo
(1982). In both of these, the child characters are innocent
victims, in the former of a deranged father and in the latter
of a rabid dog. Danny Torrence, the child in The Shining
has a special power, extrasensory perception. Unlike power-
possessing children in many 1970s films, he does not use his
maliciously to destroy his family and community. Instead,
his power makes him more of an innocent victim because its
foretelling of the atrocities that will take place serves to in-
tensify the child's fear. This presents a change in direction
from the majority of horror films in the previous decade, in
which the children acted as the aggressors.

The return to child-innocence trends can perhaps best
be seen in Kramer vs. Kramer, the second-biggest blockbuster
of 1980[156] and Academy Award-winning best picture for the
previous year. The certain success of this film suggests that
the child-as-innocent image--which never completely left--is
regaining a strength among movie audiences in the current
decade. In Kramer vs. Kramer, which addresses the impact
of divorce on the American family, Joanna Kramer (Meryl
Streep), an unfulfilled New York housewife, leaves her husband, Ted (Dustin Hoffman), a successful advertising executive, and the couple's seven-year-old son, Billy (Justin Henry), in order to travel to California to resume a career and
"find herself." After coming to grips with her situation, she
returns to claim her little boy, and his father, who has with
great difficulty come to accept the responsibilities of a single
parent, refuses to give him up. A heated court battle over
the child's custody ensues. In the end, the mother wins
legal custody but realizes that she cannot take her son away
from the only home he has ever known.

Kramer vs. Kramer focuses on a very real modern problem in America, the disintegration of family and its toll on
all involved. Billy, assuming the role of the innocent child
who does not understand what is going on around him, feels
alienated. In one scene, he receives a letter from his mother,
who tells him that, although she will not be his mommy in
the home, she will always be his mommy of the heart; feeling
abandoned, he turns up the television set as loud as it will
go in an attempt to block out the world. In another scene,
Ted is delayed after work and becomes the last parent to
pick up his child after a birthday party. Billy, who has
been waiting alone for what seemed like an eternity, again
feels left out and depressed. Thus, he shares emotions usually relegated to adults. However, Billy remains very much
a child. Like other filmic children, he asks his father simply,
"Where's Mommy?" Later, when he encounters his father's
sleep-over girlfriend in the hallway while on his way to the
bathroom in the middle of the night, he implores innocently,
"What's your name?" Lastly, Billy takes on a traditional
filmic role of children: He is a victim, in this case of family
disintegration. In one of the film's most dramatic scenes,
Billy falls from the top of a jungle gym and is injured, thus
underscoring his physical vulnerability; this parallels his
emotional vulnerability at the center of a broken family. For
Billy, as well as for his parents, the future is not secure;
they will survive in their new lives, but difficult adjustments
may be necessary. As Landon Jones notes, films exploring
the consequences of family disintegration flourished in the
1970s and 1980s as the baby-boom generation, the largest
movie consumer audience, reached its thirties and tried to
grapple with the mid-life crisis--which meant balancing family happiness with career goals and personal satisfaction.[157]

At one point in Kramer vs. Kramer, Ted's lawyer,
mindful of the fact that New York law tends to side with
the mother in child-custody cases, tells Ted to go home and
make a list of the pros and cons involved in keeping Billy.
This, he supposes, will enable Ted to determine whether an
arduous legal battle is really worth it. Ted makes his list,
and although the disadvantages of keeping Billy--the time
the child takes up, the worry he causes, the demands he
makes--greatly outnumber the advantages, there is one bene-
fit that outweights all: He loves Billy and wants to be with
him.

By the 1980s, as children continued to be considered
not as a given but as a choice of a particular life-style, it
seems that several couples were devising similar lists regarding the value of children. In the current decade, Americans
reached a new low for babies born per capita--about 16 per
1,000 population.[158] On the surface, this would seem to suggest an increasing devaluation of childhood, that adults seem
to find other activities more rewarding than the rearing of
children. As John Sommerville writes, "As never before, we
are coming to see children as a burden. In our accustomed
fashion we have even managed to put a dollar figure on
this liability: in 1980 terms a child would cost a middle income family $85,000, not including a mother's lost income."[159]
At a time when forty percent of women with preschool children work outside the home, women, it seems, are encouraged to see almost any job outside the home as more chal-
lenging and rewarding than child rearing, though it may be
simply selling clothing or real estate.[160] However, the devaluation of children seems to be a simple answer to a much
more complex question. (In the 1930s, the birthrate dropped
significantly, and no one explained it as a manifestation that
children were being devalued; instead it was a response to
difficult financial times.) Recent films featuring children--
like Kramer vs. Kramer, Gloria, Author! Author! and Shoot
the Moon--do not suggest that children are unimportant but
rather that they are highly valued; all of these movies feature adults who place children as a top priority in their
lives, which, amid a time of personal confusion and disappointment, creates new problems and challenges. Further,
these films paint portraits of children who are often intelligent and in control; however, they are not the bastions of
perfection and happiness that earlier filmic children were.
Instead, this new breed is composed of young, imperfect human beings who, like adults, experience alienation, fear,
disappointment, frustration, and adjustment problems when
confronting new situations. If movies reflect what is happening in society, perhaps fewer children are being born
not because Americans dislike children or devalue them but
because the pervasive complexities of divorce, a strained
economy, and a growing social acceptance of (and in many
cases pressure on) women to pursue careers has led to a
less stable, less optimistic, and ultimately less domestic environment. As Kramer vs. Kramer, Shoot the Moon, Author!
Author!, and Irreconcilable Differences illustrate, happy
children do not easily thrive in such an environment.

The Age of Spielberg

In the current decade, one cannot consider the portrayals of
children in contemporary movies without focusing on the contributions of one particular filmmaker: Steven Spielberg.
He is to filmic children today what Walt Disney was in the
1950s and 1960s; his vision of childhood--one characterized
by innocence--has indeed won for him a wide audience.
Spielberg, the thirty-eight-year-old wonder child of American cinema, one of a new breed of modern sophisticated young
filmmakers, brings with him a clear knowledge of film history,
its past traditions and movements.   His portrayals of children,
which draw upon and innovatively combine many past images,
have been enormously successful, thus establishing Spielberg's
reputation as one of Hollywood's premier directors and producers.

Thanks in part to Spielberg, the child-as-innocent image regained a stronghold in the late 1980s.   In Close Encounters of the Third Kind (1977), which became the combined ninth- and second-biggest money-maker of 1977 and
1978, respectively,[161] director Steven Spielberg, who has
become the new voice of children in film, uses an innocent
child to telegraph the emotions of awe and wonder.   As this
film opens, Barry Guiler (Cary Guffey), a four-year-old
Muncie, Indiana, boy, is awakened by the sound of his toys
coming alive downstairs.   He goes to investigate and discovers that alien visitors have left their mark on the household.
Electronic toys buzz unattended through the house to the
tune of a child's record, and spilled milk and broken bottles
lie on the kitchen floor.   Noting a disturbance, Barry's
mother, Jillian (Melinda Dillon), rushes downstairs and finds
her son in pursuit of the unknown beings.   In essence,
Barry is enchanted by what he has seen and seems to share
with the unknown space creatures some sort of psychic con-
nection.   As Thomas Durwood writes, "The magic of Close
Encounters is the magic of a child.   Spielberg takes the
child's side from time to time: The sense of wonder we feel
is through Barry (perhaps the true hero of the film)."[162]   In
Close Encounters, the audience sometimes sees through Barry's eyes.   Unlike his mother, Barry is not frightened; instead, he is delighted, mesmerized.   Without caution, the
anxious little boy rushes to find his new friends while his
mother follows closely behind.   Then, together, they witness
blinding lights as a succession of dazzling spacecrafts lift

off the ground and rise high above them until they are out
of sight. Again, Barry is happy, filled with wonder. Jillian, on the other hand, feels a great uneasiness. Her years
of experience tell her that such a happening is not normal;
although beautiful, it can also be dangerous.

After the initial sighting of the spacecrafts, Barry and
Jillian's Midwestern home returns to normal--but only for a
short while. The spacecrafts return again, and Barry, not
heeding his mother's frantic warning, rushes out to greet
them. As his mother--the single parent who takes full responsibility for her son's protection--looks on in horror,
Barry is taken into the spacecraft and spirited away. Thus,
the child in Close Encounters performs a function similar to
that of children in decades past: He suggests vulnerability.
Throughout the rest of the film, Jillian embarks on a search
to get Barry back. The child, who like many other recent
filmic children gets very little on-screen time, fulfills another
function: He becomes the object of a search, a plot device
around which the film revolves. Barry's adventure turns
out to be a happy one; he returns to earth unharmed after
having had a wonderful extraterrestrial experience. As he
waves goodbye to his space friends, he remains untainted,
filled with wonder.

Although Barry is missing throughout most of Close
Encounters, much of the action of the film revolves around
his recovery, and he has, therefore, a major role in the
film. However, he is not the only childlike character in
Close Encounters. Roy Neary (Richard Dreyfuss), a telephone repairman, becomes, like Barry, obsessed with the
dazzling spaceships, thereby suggesting that childlike qualities may extend into adulthood. However, Roy's wife and
children do not understand. In one particularly poignant
dinnertime scene, Roy visualizes the shape of Devil's Tower,
the earth headquarters for the spacecrafts, and molds his
mound of mashed potatoes into a similar form. In essence,
he acts like a young child who plays with his or her food
while his own children look on in disbelief, then confusion.
Essentially parent and children have reversed roles, but,
despite the reversals, they fail to understand one another.
One child tries not to notice the carefully whittled structure
on her father's plate; she takes on the adult technique of
ignoring what she does not choose to see. Another child
begins to cry. Ultimately, the children do not feel part of

their parent's world; they feel alienated. The theme of the alienated child that becomes apparent in Close Encounters also makes its way into other popular films of the time, a reflection of the child's response to the widespread familial fragmentation taking place in America.[163]

A similar theme prevails in some of Spielberg's other works, many of which take the child's point of view. In Close Encounters, Spielberg experimeted with the image of the child as a means of telegraphing an emotion--childlike wonder. In his later cinematic creations, Poltergeist (1982) and E.T., The Extraterrestrial (1982), he takes this concept to its logical end. As Poltergeist co-producer Kathleen Kennedy noted in an interview, "The films are totally different in mood. Poltergeist is certainly more of the nightmare, and E.T. is more of the fantasy."[164] In both of these films, children predominate; they are present throughout the duration of the films and are indeed the protagonists. Further, Spielberg treats the child figure with intelligence and sensitivity as he enables the audience to follow the action from a child's perspective.

Poltergeist, written and produced by Spielberg but directed by Tobe Hooper, most famous for the classic horror film The Texas Chainsaw Massacre (1974), focuses on childhood fears. This film begins with the depiction of an upper-middle-class California suburban family, Steve and Diane Freeling (Craig T. Nelson and Jobeth Williams) and their children, who soon discover that a spirit is inhabiting their home. At first, the spirits are great fun. Diane delights in their ability to stack chairs on top of the table and carry little Carol Anne (Heather O'Rourke) across the kitchen floor. Then, for some inexplicable reason, they become evil--intent on destroying the Freeling household and most specifically the children therein. It is interesting to note that there are three Freeling children: Dana (Dominique Dunne) is in her mid-teens; Robbie (Oliver Robins) is several years younger; and the baby of the family is Carol Anne. Dana, who has passed her childhood years and fits the image of the savvy, hip teenager, seems to escape danger; however, Robbie and Carol Anne, like Spielberg's other child characters, are most vulnerable.

Carol Anne is a typical example of the innocent child, one with a higher vision. She first discovers the spirits

lurking in the television set and, like Barry in Close Encounters with the extraterrestrial aliens, tries to communi-
cate with them. As a result of her appeal, she later gets
kidnapped by the spirits, and the rest of the film revolves
around trying to get her back. Indeed, one sees the parallel here to Close Encounters: In both films, a very young
child filled with wonder and curiosity is taken away by an
unknown force, and a mother--assuming the traditional role
of protector--takes risks in her struggle for the child's return. In essence, both Barry and Carol Anne are victims
who need the help of a concerned parent in order to return
home to a normal life.

Just as Carol Anne in Poltergeist is a victim, so is
her older brother, Robbie. While Carol Anne is under the
domination of the spirits, Robbie has trouble in his own bedroom. There, those things that are safe and comforting to
him during the day--the tree outside his window, his toy
clown--become a menace at night. The tree, for example,
extends its arm-like branches through the bedroom window
and grabs the terrified boy, who must be rescued by his
father. The stuffed clown places its arms around Robbie's
neck and tries to strangle him. It is particularly striking
that, while Carol Anne is spirited away, her brother becomes a victim in his own home. Of the three Freeling children, Robbie--the only boy--is the most alienated. As the
middle child, he seems to get neither the attention that Carol
Anne gets nor the respect that Dana gets. His trauma in his
own bedroom is a gross reflection of his sense of isolation.

The Freelings, especially Carol Anne and Robbie, live
through a nightmare. The poltergeists invade their home
and attempt to tear the family--one reflective of any American
family--apart. By the end of the film, the cause of the spirits' revenge is uncovered: The Freeling house, built by
Steve Freeling's greedy real-estate-development firm, is situ-
ated on an old burial ground; thus the dead have been violated and cannot rest in peace. It is only after the Freelings
--the guilty, unseeing father in particular--are able to leave
their house and all of their worldly possessions behind in order to save one another that they become a true family--a
community of loving, caring individuals. Thus, the crisis
draws the Freelings closer together. Although they call on
a professional parapsychologist and exorcist to help them rid
their home of its unwanted guests, the real hero of the film
is the family itself.

The family is of essence in another child-oriented film, E.T., The Extraterrestrial--the biggest money-making film of all time--produced and directed by Steven Spielberg. Unlike Poltergeist, E.T. features a broken home: A father has taken off for Mexico with his new flame, leaving his wife, Mary (Dee Wallace), and their three children--Michael (Robert MacNaughton), Elliot (Henry Thomas), and Gertie (Drew Barrymore)--alone in their suburban home. Indeed, their house could well be in the same neighborhood as the Freelings' in Poltergeist. What Spielberg seems to be saying is that, in suburbia, the houses all look the same; it is the people inside, especially the children, who provide the personality.

As the film begins, Elliot seems to be the loneliest of the children. Like Robbie in Poltergeist, he is approximately ten years old and the middle child of three. His brother, Michael, and his friends still consider Elliot "the kid brother" and do not accept him as one of them. At the same time, Elliot does not feel the kinship to his mother that Gertie, the baby of the family, does. Of all the children, Elliot seems to miss his departed father most. Not unusually, then, in terms of Spielberg films, it is Elliot--the alienated child--to whom E.T., the alien visitor from another galaxy, first appears. Since E.T. is a friendly, gentle creature, the two become friends. As one reviewer notes: "The bond between E.T. and Elliot is the heart of the film. Even though we never find out how old E.T. is, or even if it has a gender-- Elliot insists it's a boy--the two are soul mates."[165] Elliot, it seems, needs someone, and E.T. fits the bill; in a sense, the alien creature becomes the child's surrogate father.

In the film, the audience sees E.T. through Elliot's eyes. Like Barry in Close Encounters and Carol Anne in Poltergeist, Elliot is filled with wonder. One critic writes, "Children, Spielberg seems to be saying, are the predestined welcoming committee for the extra-terrestrials; their innocence and sense of wonder make them spiritually closer to E.T. than to the adults of their world."[166] This disparity between children and adults becomes the true theme of the film. The children see E.T. not as a novelty or even a pet but rather as a friend, a welcomed guest, a special playmate. In a quest to save E.T. from the scientists who want to treat the alien as specimen rather than a being with feelings, Elliot and his siblings and their friends unite to form a new community, one in which Elliot--the previously alienated

child--becomes the leader. As in Spielberg's other films, it
is children who have the greater sensitivity, a higher vision.
They assume responsibility for spiriting E.T. away so that
he can reach his spaceship and do what he has wanted to do
since he was first mistakenly left on earth--return home.

Although E.T. seems to be a warm and open father-
figure to Elliot, he is at the same time childlike. Small and
babyish in his whimperings, he--like Dorothy in The Wizard
of Oz--finds himself in a foreign galaxy and, although amazed
by what he sees, feels insecure. Utmost in his mind, despite
his new friends and his exciting adventures, is going home.
In essence, just as the movie audience sees E.T. through
Elliot's eyes, it also sees our own world through E.T.'s.
Through E.T.'s vision, one filled with childlike innocence,
the film viewer gains insight into the absurdities of American
life. Like some of Spielberg's other characters, E.T. is a
victim in a strange place. By the time E.T. leaves, Elliot
has formed bonds with his siblings and their friends and a
sensitive scientist, all of whom were drawn together out of
concern for the alien's safe return home. Having come to
grips with his father's departure and his own loneliness,
Elliot has gained the maturity, wisdom, and self-confidence
necessary to resume a happy life without E.T. Still, the
film ends on a note of sadness: Elliot has lost a friend.

Spielberg's success in presenting filmic images of children has inspired a new trend in American movies. Annie
(1982), Six Weeks (1982), Raggedy Man (1982), Savannah
Smiles (1983), Without a Trace (1983), Table for Five (1983),
Something Wicked This Way Comes (1983) and The Neverending Story (1984) all hinge on traditional portraits of innocent
children, often with interesting variations. As always, several images of childhood coexist; however, currently, among
the monsters, fix-its, and precocious imps, the innocent
child has a stronghold. Filmic images of children, it seems,
have come full circle. In the early days of silent films,
D. W. Griffith frequently used innocent children as vulnerable victims in melodramatic vehicles. In films today, after
a brief hiatus in which they were demon-possessed aggressors whom no one could harm, they remain vulnerable, both
physically and emotionally. Not coincidentally, this depiction
coincides with a growing awareness of crimes against children,
especially sexual abuse and kidnapping.[167] It also relates to
another social phenomenon--family fragmentation due to divorce

--which frequently victimizes children emotionally.[168] Current films stress the fragility of the traditional family structure and, frequently, the creation of a community that will meet the child's needs better than the family can.

Although Steven Spielberg has repopularized the image of childhood innocence, his filmic portrayals are not one-dimensional--instead they are rich in their variations. In two of Spielberg's most recent films, Indiana Jones and the Temple of Doom (1984) and The Goonies (1985), youngsters who balance on the boundary between childhood and adolescence play predominant roles. Directed by Steven Spielberg, Indiana Jones and the Temple of Doom, which ranked as the second-biggest blockbuster of 1984[169] and the eighth most successful money-maker of all time,[170] continues the story of heroic anthropologist Indiana Jones (Harrison Ford) that was begun in a previous film, Raiders of the Lost Ark (1981). This time, Indiana Jones is in Shanghai, where he is being sought by killers. He escapes, thanks to his trusty sidekick Short Round (Ke Huy Quan), a hip, streetwise youngster whose foot barely reaches the gas pedal but who skillfully maneuvers the getaway car. For the rest of the film, Short Round accompanies Indiana and his new love interest, a night-club girl named Willie (Kate Capshaw), on a myriad of exciting adventures. Eventually, witty and ingenious Short Round helps Indiana and Willie to save the day; together, they recover a stolen sacred rock with magical powers and also a group of children who have been abducted from their small Himalayan village by an evil maharajah and put to work in chain gangs underground. The missing children in the film support the idea of the victimized child as innocent; however, Short Round's portrayal adds dimension. It combines the image of the precocious imp with that of the innocent child who ultimately wants to bring about good in the world.

Although Richard Donner directed The Goonies, Steven Spielberg acted as the film's executive producer, and, as such, it bears his stamp: a certain vision of--and respect for--the entity of childhood. The Goonies, which holds the position of the sixth-biggest blockbuster of 1985,[171] features several children, all with different, distinguishable personalities; in this way, the film resembles the Our Gang comedies of yesteryear. The plot of The Goonies is straightforward and simple: A group of youngsters from a small Oregon town find out that their comfortable suburban neighborhood

is slated to be razed to make room for a golf course, and
their parents do not have the money to stop it. At the same
time, one of the boys discovers a treasure map that points
the way to the underground booty of an abandoned pirate
ship, and he recruits his friends to join in the quest. They
do, and this is where their individual personalities begin to
shine through. Chunk (Jeff Cohen), for example, is the
spirited fat kid whose mind seems to be always on his next
sweet snack; however, he also reveals his inner goodness
by his good nature and compassion for others. Mikey (Sean
Astin) is controlled and responsible; Mouth (Corey Feldman)
is a smart aleck with braces; Brand (Josh Brolin) exhibits
intelligence and maturity; and Data (Ke Huy Quan), perhaps
the most unique of the bunch, is a closet inventor who, at
the appropriate moment, unveils his newest technological
creation. Although not as clearly defined, the girls, Andy
(Kerri Green) and Stef (Martha Plimpton), are ready with
loud screams at the first sign of trouble, thereby spurring
the others to action; their interaction with the boys, both
bellicose and flirting, makes for a well-rounded, believable
neighborhood group. On their quest for the missing fortune, the gang encounters one adventure after another.
They happen upon the hideout of a desperate band of crimi-
nals who follow them through a series of underground tun-
nels hoping to do away with the children and claim the treasure for themselves. Smart and courageous, the neighborhood
group prevails: The kids find and lose the pirate-ship
treasure, all except for a few valuable jewels. These, however, are significant. By the end of the film, the children
have accomplished what the adults could not: They have
secured enough money to save their neighborhood, and, although they are somewhat disappointed that they did not get
more of the precious gems, they are nevertheless satisfied.
Like Short Round in Indiana Jones and the Temple of Doom,
their image combines precocity and innocence. They are
tough talkers--"shit" is the most frequently used word in
their vocabulary--and they show that they are more intelligent and resourceful than all the adults combined. Still,
they maintain a child's sense of adventure and intrigue. It
is only because they believe in the wonder and magic of
buried treasure that they are able to save their homestead.

Filmic portrayals of children--in this current age of
Spielberg--bear slight resemblance to the movie children of
decades past. In many popular films of the 1970s, abnormal

children inhabited a seemingly happy, secure, normal world; 1980s films suggest the opposite: Normal children must cope with an abnormal world. They confront traumas, economic problems, loneliness, alienation, responsibilities, fear, kid-napping, and treachery; sometimes, the situations they face are not dangerous, as in the case of Elliot's discovery of E.T., but still outside the realm of normal everyday events. In essence, children remain innocent, but innocence has a new definition; this may have been one of the legacies of the atomic bomb. In pre-World War II films, inherent in the definition of innocence was an unqualified optimism and a hope in the future. Since then, this hope has steadily di-minished. Although basically good, children, like the future, are fallible;[172] thus, the future remains insecure. Often filmic children are left disappointed, resigned, or confused. In many cases, they may encounter a single triumph, but more problems inevitably lie ahead.

This portrayal is not all bad. Prewar filmic children who happily pranced along--problems melting in their paths--provided overidealized portrayals of childhood; when com-pared with this image, real children fall disappointingly short. Children, ultimately, are both good and bad, and perhaps the Shirley Temples and Freddie Bartholomews of yesteryear simply underscored Americans' guilt in admitting that children are less than perfect. Just as children can be adorable, happy, loving, intelligent, and obedient, they can also be scowling, troubled, confused, mean-tempered, and misbehaved.

This is the message of Steven Spielberg and perhaps his greatest contribution to the developing image of children on the popular American movie screen. In a symbolic way, a recent film, Gremlins (1984), produced by Spielberg and directed by Joe Dante, speaks to the duality of childhood. This film tells the story of an unusual pet that a father buys in Chinatown as a Christmas gift for his teenage son. Called a Mogwai, the strange creature is unmistakably childlike, very small, cute, cuddly, and kind--in essence, the innocent child. It comes with three warnings: Keep it out of sun-light, do not get it wet, and above all, do not feed it after midnight. In time, all of the warnings are violated, the Mogwai multiplies, and the new Mogwais are gruesome, mean, and destructive, to the point of creating mayhem everywhere they go. The Mogwais symbolize the duality of children:

they are the good child and the bad; they are both loved
and resented.

Perhaps this is the direction in which filmic portrayals
of children are headed in the 1980s. The little-miss-fix-it
had her day, as did the monster child. Filmic children today, it seems, are not so one-dimensional. They can be
both good and bad, happy and troubled, realistic and dream-
ing. Inherently innocent, they are vulnerable to, even symbolic of, corruption in American society and changes in the
institution of family. In essence, they bear the mark of an
increasingly complex world.

Notes

1. Henry L. Stimson, "The Decision to Use the Atomic
   Bomb," in The 1940s: Profile of a Nation in Crisis,
   ed. Chester E. Eisinger, Documents in American Civilization Series (New York: Anchor Books, 1969). p. 70.
2. Stimson, p. 70.
3. As quoted in Stimson, p. 70.
4. As quoted in Robert Jay Lifton and Richard Falk, Indefensible Weapons: The Political and Psychological Case
   Against Nuclearism (New York: Basic Books, 1982),
   pp. 57-58. Reprinted from New York Herald Tribune,
   7 August 1945.
5. Jonathan Schell, The Fate of the Earth (New York:
   Avon, 1982), p. 115.
6. Schell, pp. 165-166.
7. Lifton and Falk, p. 57.
8. As quoted in Clyde Kluckhohn, "Mid-Century Manners
   and Morals," in The 1940s: Profile of a Nation in Crisis, ed. Chester E. Eisinger, Documents in American
   Civilization Series (New York: Anchor Books, 1969),
   p. 160.
9. Chester E. Eisinger, ed., The 1940's: Profile of a Nation in Crisis, Documents in American Civilization Series
   (New York: Anchor Books, 1969), pp. xiv-xv.
10. Karen Anderson, Wartime Women: Sex Roles, Family
    Relations, and the Status of Women During World War II,
    Contributions in Women's Studies, No. 20 (Westport,
    Conn.: Greenwood, 1981), p. 4.

11. William H. Chafe, The American Woman: Her Changing Social, Economic and Political Role, 1920-1970 (New York: Oxford Univ. Press, 1972), pp. 195, 246.
12. Anderson notes the following statistics: "Although the postwar employment rate for women was considerably less than the wartime peak, the labor force participation rate of women over the age of sixteen jumped from 28.9 percent to 33.0 percent during the 1940s and continued to rise thereafter," p. 7.
13. M. Joyce Baker, Images of Women in Film: The War Years, 1941-1945. Studies in American History and Culture, No. 21 (Ann Arbor: UMI Research Press, 1980), p. 131. Baker further notes that "the popularity of the housewife-mother figure in films, television programs, magazine short stories, and novels of the post-war period suggested that Americans of both sexes were willing to pay tribute to this role," p. 131.
14. Landon Y. Jones, Great Expectations: America and the Baby Boom Generation (New York: Ballantine, 1980), p. 194.
15. As quoted in Mark Jonathan Harris, Franklin D. Mitchell, Steven J. Schechter, interviewers, "Rosie the Riveter Remembers," American Heritage, Feb.-March 1984, p. 103.
16. Baker, p. 130.
17. Jones, p. 10.
18. Jones, p. 10.
19. Jones, p. 11.
20. Jones, p. 2.
21. Jones, p. 2.
22. Jones, p. 2.
23. Benjamin Spock, Baby and Child Care (New York: Pocket Books, 1946).
24. Spock, p. 19.
25. Spock, p. 19.
26. Spock, p. 460.
27. Arthur Knight, The Liveliest Art (New York: New American Library, 1979), p. 289.
28. Knight, p. 289.
29. Knight, p. 290.
30. Robert Sklar, Movie-Made America: A Cultural History of American Movies (New York: Vintage Books, 1975), p. 269.
31. Sklar, p. 272.
32. Samuel Goldwyn, "Hollywood in the Television Age,"

Hollywood Quarterly, 4 (Winter, 1949), p. 146. Reprinted from New York Times (February 13, 1949).

33. Knight, p. 291.
34. Norman Zierold, The Child Stars (New York: Coward-McCann, 1965), p. 246.
35. Marc Best, Their Hearts Were Young and Gay (South Brunswick, N.J., and New York: A. S. Barnes, 1975), p. 9.
36. Cobbett Steinberg, Reel Facts: The Movie Book of Records, updated ed. (New York: Vintage Books, 1981), p. 58.
37. Wallace Beery, a top box-office attraction, frequently appeared in films with children. He played with Jackie Cooper in The Champ (1931), Treasure Island (1934), and The Bowery (1933) and with Bobs Watson in Wyoming (1940).
38. Steinberg, p. 58.
39. Steinberg, p. 61.
40. Zierold, p. 246.
41. Steinberg, p. 58.
42. Jones, p. 53. On a subconscious level, this attitude may have been related to the impact of the atomic bomb. In a nation that feared what the future might hold, there became a clear emphasis on the present. Thus emerged the give-them-everything-now ethic.
43. Steinberg, p. 58.
44. Steinberg, p. 19.
45. Bremner, Robert H., ed., Children and Youth in America: A Documentary History. Vol. III: 1933-1973 (Cambridge, Mass.: Harvard Univ. Press, 1974), p. 1991.
46. Between 1946 and 1951 the Production Code Administration made slight revisions in the code to accommodate changes in American morals. As divorce became more socially accepted in America, it was no longer taboo on the screen.
47. Jones, p. 396. Reprinted from U.S. Bureau of the Census, Current Population Reports, Series P-25, No. 802, "Estimates of the Population of the United States and Components of Change: 1940 to 1978," U.S. Government Printing Office, Washington, D.C., 1979.
48. Bremner, p. 1991.
49. Jones, p. 42.
50. Steinberg, p. 20.
51. See Neil Postman, The Disappearance of Childhood (New

York: Delacorte, 1982) for a discussion of the insight into adult confusions and crises that children gain from watching popular television.

52. Jones, p. 31.

53. Jones, p. 31.

54. Jones, p. 32. Jones notes that during the baby boom there was not a return to the large American families of the nineteenth century; the biggest change was that almost everyone chose to marry and have at least two children (pp. 31-32). However, see also James S. Bossard and Eleanor Stoker Boll, The Sociology of Child Development, 4th ed. (New York: Harper & Row, 1966). They note that in 1961 an estimated 447,268 babies were born to mothers who had formerly given birth to five or more children, and three years later the Census Bureau reported that 2,165,000 families had five or more children (p. 37).

55. Jones notes that family planning was not an issue during the baby boom as couples married younger than their parents had, preferred to have children, and could afford an unplanned pregnancy if one occurred. The National Fertility Studies conducted by Princeton researchers in 1965 and 1970 reported that nearly 20 percent of all pregnancies in the postwar period were unplanned, thus accounting for over 15 million babies (pp. 32-34).

56. Steinberg, p. 20.

57. Steinberg, pp. 21, 12.

58. Steinberg, p. 59.

59. Bosley Crowther, review of Shane, New York Times, 24 April 1953, p. 30, col. 3.

60. Ann L. Clark, "Childrearing in Matrix America," in Culture and Childrearing, ed. Ann L. Clark (Philadelphia: F. A. Davis, 1981), p. 39.

61. Douglas T. Miller and Marion Nowak, The Fifties: The Way We Really Were (New York: Doubleday, 1977), p. 15.

62. Steinberg, p. 22.

63. Bosley Crowther, review of The Bad Seed, New York Times, 13 Sept. 1956, p. 39. col. 6.

64. Miller and Nowak, pp. 280 and 282.

65. Miller and Nowak, p. 280.

66. As quoted in Newsweek, 9 Nov. 1953, p. 29.

67. Miller and Nowak note that in the 1950s many social problems like poverty, militarism, racism, and sexism

were seldom perceived as national concerns but rather
as problems only to their victims (p. 280).

68. Bremner, p. 1992.
69. Bremner, p. 1993.
70. Miller and Nowak, p. 280.
71. Miller and Nowak, p. 281.
72. John Sommerville, The Rise and Fall of Childhood,
    Sage Library of Social Research, Vol. 140 (Beverly
    Hills: Sage, 1982), p. 204.
73. Steinberg, p. 22.
74. Bosley Crowther, review of Houseboat, New York Times,
    14 Nov. 1958, p. 24, col. 1.
75. Mary Jo Bane, "A Review of Child Care Books," in The
    Rights of Children, Reprint Series No. 9., ed. Harvard
    Educational Review (Cambridge, Mass.: Harvard Educa-
    tional Review, 1974), pp. 364-365.
76. See Jones, Chapter 19, "The Nostalgic Style," pp. 280-
    295.
77. Miller and Nowak, p. 270. See also Jones, Chapter 4,
    "From Spock to Sputnik," pp. 33-69.
78. Miller and Nowak, p. 272.
79. Miller and Nowak, p. 270. See also Jones, Chapter 4,
    "From Spock to Sputnik," pp. 53-69.
80. Christopher Finch, The Art of Walt Disney (New York:
    Harry N. Abrams, 1975), p. 129.
81. Maltin, Leonard, The Disney Films (New York: Crown,
    1973), p. 146.
82. Bremner, p. 1993.
83. Walt Disney has been accused of pandering the child
    audience for his own financial gain. See Frances Clarke
    Sayers and Charles M. Weisenberg, "Walt Disney Ac-
    cused," Horn Book, 40 (December 1965), pp. 602-611.
84. Almeda, Pamela M., "Children's Television and the
    Modeling of Proreading Behaviors," Education and Urban
    Society (November 1977), pp. 55-59.
85. Douglas Street, ed., Children's Novels and the Movies
    (New York: Ungar, 1983), p. xix.
86. Maltin, p. 146.
87. Other popular films showing children who run away in-
    clude The Yearling (1946), Houseboat (1958), Mary
    Poppins (1965), Paper Moon (1973), and Savannah Smiles
    (1983).
88. Sommerville, p. 219.
89. Maltin, p. 172.
90. Steinberg, p. 24.

91. See Jones, Chapter 11, "The Crime Boom," pp. 166-175.

92. See Postman for an extensive discussion of this argument.

93. Jones, p. 178.

94. Jones, pp. 221-222.

95. Jones, p. 222.

96. In 1957, Pittsburgh banker James Neville Land warned about overpopulation, and similar warnings appeared in Fortune and The New York Times (Jones, p. 223).

97. Paul Ehrlich, The Population Bomb (New York: Ballantine, 1968).

98. Steinberg, p. 23.

99. Bremner, pp. 1991-1992.

100. Bremner, pp. 1992-1993.

101. Steinberg, p. 104.

102. Barbara Kaye Greenleaf, Children Through the Ages: A History of Childhood (New York: McGraw Hill, 1978), p. 143. See also Jones, "The Archipelago of Youth," pp. 90-105.

103. Steinberg, p. 25.

104. Jones, p. 245.

105. Steinberg, p. 24.

106. Pauline Kael, I Lost It at the Movies (Boston: Little Brown, 1954), p. 171.

107. Sommerville, p. 14.

108. Steinberg, p. 25.

109. In the 1960s, many films focusing on older youth also became popular. These include Splendor in the Grass (1961), West Side Story (1961), Georgy Girl (1966), To Sir, With Love (1967), Up the Down Staircase (1967), and The Graduate (1968).

110. William R. Meyer, The Making of the Great Westerns (New Rochelle, N.Y.: Arlington House), 1979, p. 383.

111. Bosley Crowther, review of The Miracle Worker, New York Times, 24 May 1962, p. 29, col. 2.

112. Greenleaf, p. 143.

113. Bremner, pp. 1991-1992.

114. Bremner, p. 1997.

115. Robin Wood, Introduction, American Nightmare: Essays on the Horror Film, ed. Andrew Britton, Tony Williams, and Robin Wood (Toronto: Festival of Festivals, 1979), p. 17.

116. Stuart Samuels, "The Age of Conspiracy and Conformity: Invasion of the Body Snatchers," in American

History/American Film, ed. John E. O'Connor and
Martin A. Jackson (New York: Ungar, 1979), p. 217.

117. Robin Wood lists "Satanism, diabolic possession, the
Antichrist" and "The Terrible Child" among the five
dominant motifs in the horror film since the 1960s.
See Wood, p. 17.

118. Steinberg, p. 25.

119. Steinberg, pp. 26-27.

120. Vincent Canby, "Why the Devil Dig 'The Exorcist'?"
New York Times, 13 Jan. 1974, sec. 2, p. 1, col. 6.

121. See Molly Haskell, "Jodie Foster and Tatum O'Neal,"
in The National Society of Film Critics on the Movie
Star, ed. Elisabeth Weis (New York: Viking, 1981),
pp. 227-231.

122. Wood, p. 10.

123. See John Holt, Escape from Childhood (New York:
Dutton, 1974) and J. H. Plumb, "The Great Change in
Children," Horizon, 13, No. 1 (Winter 1971), pp. 4-13.

124. Steinberg, p. 27.

125. Robin Wood, "World of Gods and Monsters," in Ameri-
can Nightmare: Essays on the Horror Film, ed. Andrew
Britton, Richard Lippe, Tony Williams, and Robin Wood
(Toronto: Festival of Festivals, 1979), p. 80.

126. Jones, p. 313.

127. Sommerville, pp. 12-13.

128. See Ehrlich, The Population Bomb.

129. Richette, Lisa Aversa, The Throwaway Children
(Philadelphia: Lippincott, 1969). p. 7.

130. Jones, p. 250.

131. Jones, p. 176. Jones also notes that owing to the
baby-boom generation's influx into the job market in
the late 1960s and early 1970s, at the same time that
unemployment was at a postwar high, more Americans
were employed than at any time in the nation's history;
however, the creation of millions of new jobs was still
not sufficient to fill the needs and financial expectations of baby boomers.

132. See Tom Wolfe, "The Me Decade and the Third Great
Awakening," in Mauve Gloves and Madmen, Clutter and
Vine, and Other Stories (New York: Farrar, Straus,
and Giroux, 1976).

133. Bremner, p. 1999.

134. Marvin R. Koller and Oscar W. Ritchie, Sociology of
Childhood, 2nd ed. (Englewood Cliffs, N.J.: Prentice-
Hall, 1978), p. 112.

135. Jones, p. 243.
136. Jones, p. 243.
137. Jones, p. 242.
138. John Holt, Escape from Childhood (New York: E. P. Dutton, 1974), p. 75.
139. See Holt for extensive elaboration on each of these rights.
140. Steinberg, p. 26.
141. As quoted in Zierold, pp. 229-230.
142. Robert Osborne, Academy Awards 1974 Oscar Annual (Laltabra, Cal.: ESE California, 1974), n. pag.
143. As quoted in Osborne, n. pag.
144. Edward Edelson, Great Kids of the Movies (Garden City, N.Y.: Doubleday, 1979), p. 2.
145. Steinberg, p. 26.
146. Edelson, p. 2.
147. Steinberg, p. 61.
148. Steinberg, p. 27.
149. Postman, p. 121.
150. The Blue Lagoon (1980), Little Darlings (1980), Ordinary People (1980), Fast Times at Ridgemont High (1982), The Karate Kid (1984), Gremlins (1984), and The Goonies (1985) illustrate this trend.
151. Postman, p. xii.
152. Postman, pp. 124-125.
153. For a discussion of this cultural phenomenon, see the cover story "Bringing Up Superbaby," in Newsweek, 28 March 1983, pp. 62-68.
154. Sommerville, p. 12.
155. Steinberg, p. 26.
156. Steinberg, p. 27.
157. Jones, pp. 328-329. Other films reflective of this trend include The Goodbye Girl (1977), An Unmarried Woman (1978), Manhattan (1979), Starting Over (1979), Ordinary People (1980), Author! Author! (1982), Shoot the Moon (1982), Mr. Mom (1983), and Irreconcilable Differences (1984).
158. Sommerville, p. 13.
159. Sommerville, p. 13.
160. Sommerville, pp. 14, 19.
161. Steinberg, p. 27.
162. Thomas Durwood, Close Encounters of the Third Kind: A Document of the Film (Kansas City, Mo: Ariel, 1978), p. 56.
163. Jones, p. 158.

164. As quoted in Mark Kane, "The Anatomy of a Block-buster: Producer Kathy Kennedy on 'E.T.'" Film Journal, 85, No. 14 (14 June 1982), p. 9.

165. Peter Rainer, review of E.T., Mademoiselle, 88 (Sept. 1982), p. 60.

166. Rainer, p. 60.

167. For a discussion of this growing awareness, see the following reports on sexual abuse and kidnapping:
      "A Hidden Epidemic," Newsweek, 14 May 1984, pp. 30-36.
      "Stolen Children," Newsweek, 19 March 1984, pp. 78-86.

168. See "Divorce American Style," Newsweek, 10 January 1983, pp. 42-48.

169. "Big Rental Films of 1984," Variety, 16 January 1985, p. 16.

170. "All-Time Film Rental Champs," Variety, 8 January 1986, p. 26.

171. "Big Rental Films of '85," Variety, 8 January 1986, p. 22.

172. One sees an interesting example of this trend when comparing the prewar film National Velvet (1945) with its 1978 sequel, International Velvet. As National Velvet ended, Velvet Brown, who had scored a personal triumph and remained good-hearted, concerned, and kind, seemed well on her way to a happy, well-adjusted life. In International Velvet, however, a middle-aged Velvet Brown is portrayed as being as confused and unfulfilled as her newly orphaned niece. Indeed, the future had not been secure.

Chapter 5

CONCLUSION

During the twentieth century, the American conception of childhood has undergone several variations, and movies, as reflectors of culture, mirror these changes. Traditionally, two conflicting portrayals of children--the good child and the bad child--have coexisted. The good child is characterized by innocence, honesty, and childlike wonder; in this child lies unlimited hope for a better world. The bad child represents one who is elementally evil and threatens the future. Between these two poles lie numerous variations. At the turn of the century when films were introduced to American society, the idea of the good child dominated in the popular arts; thus, it is this image of childhood that the movies adopted. And it has continued. From Charlie Chaplin's The Kid in 1921 to Steven Spielberg's E.T., sixty-one years later, childhood innocence has remained a crucial component in the filmic portrayals of children. However, through the years childhood innocence has taken on several dimensions.

The early silent melodramas of Edwin S. Porter and D. W. Griffith, which gave children very little screen time but used them as a plot device, focused on the vulnerability of children. Defenseless little ones were kidnapped or placed in physically threatening situations while adults frantically came to their rescue. This image fulfilled two purposes: It involved the audience in the action--first, by inciting the emotion of pity for the poor child and, second, by underscoring the adult role of protector, one with which audience members no doubt identified. As children's filmic roles increased, their images took on greater strength. By the 1920s, films starring children most frequently espoused the glories of childhood innocence, a quality which enabled them to be more loving, sensitive, honest, hopeful, and in tune with nature than their adult counterparts. These films

showed that children--even those who were poor or orphaned
--were intrinsically happy. Undaunted by misfortune, the
resilient little tykes could make the best of any situation.
In the immensely popular filmic vehicles of Mary Pickford in
the 1920s and Shirley Temple in the 1930s, good, self-reliant
fix-it children utilized their innocence to identify, confront,
and solve problems that adults were too blind to see or too
ineffectual to handle. Innocence, then, meant clarity of vision and optimism. These films ended on a happy, positive
note: with capable, good-hearted children at the helm, a
better world of the future was guaranteed.

In the films after World War II, children maintained
their innocence, and similar images of children continued;
however, attitudes towards innocence were slowly but per-
ceptibly changing. Child/animal stories, little-fix-it tales,
and family dramas, which had won a place among prewar
audiences, still prevailed. Yet those films frequently ended
on a note of sadness, one that did not guarantee a happy
future. As always, children overcame obstacles and taught
adults the importance of tenderness and love, but postwar
films slowly began to dispel the idea of a continuously happy
childhood; instead, children were portrayed as lonely,
searching, and often deeply troubled. By the 1970s, a
darker view of childhood, which had begun to form after
World War II, reached a peak. Childhood innocence was
openly defiled in a host of child-as-monster films. Along
with these portrayals came more worldly and precocious
youngsters. Despite their negative implications, both of
these images depended on audience belief in the innocence
of childhood for their impact. In the former, the monster
child was possessed by an evil force, usually the devil;
thus, the vulnerable human child was clearly differentiated
from the demon. In the case of the precocious imps, innocence was broken down into its various components. Addie
in Paper Moon, for example, was a tough street kid clued in
on money and sex; however, she still possessed a child's
innocent belief that people can be trusted and that everything will work out as hoped.

In essence, while prewar films spoke to the clarity of
vision inherent in childhood innocence, postwar films came
to address the implications of its blindness. Following World
War II, as Americans coped with the fact that they were living in a nuclear world, they felt more threatened and

distrustful of their neighbors than at any other time since
the end of the Civil War.[1] Innocence was not enough to
get them through difficult situations and blind optimism simply
made them vulnerable. The implications of the blindness of
innocence were further intensified in the 1960s and 1970s.
A country that looked to its heroes with admiration and respect saw a favorite president gunned down. A country
that believed itself to be infallible and always right was de-
feated in war. Lastly, a country that held its political figures in trust and high esteem saw a president resign in the
face of corruption. American mistrust and loss of confidence
reached a peak at precisely the time when filmic representations of childhood innocence were most defiled.

This is not surprising. Since the nineteenth century,
children, in the popular imagination, have symbolized innocence and a hope for a better world. Popular movies, because they are commercial products designed to appeal to the
tastes of a mass audience, mirror the social milieu. Thus,
they traditionally reflected a pervasive belief in the innocent
child. As social attitudes toward innocence changed, filmic
images of children were destined to change as well.

Childhood innocence may have solved problems for Mary
Pickford and Shirley Temple--as well as provided them with a
secure future--but in a more complicated world, it is not sufficient. In order to survive, one must supplant innocence
with wisdom. Thus, as in the early silent pictures, more
recent films focus on the child's innocence as an emotional
vulnerability. Filmic children, still, for the most part,
charged with goodness and innocence, undergo family, adjustment, and identity problems, and they endure. In the
process, though, they often experience loss or hardship and
thereby gain wisdom. It is this--not innocence--that will get
them through the turmoils of the future, and it does not
come without a price. In more recent films, images of childhood innocence have been tempered and unlimited hope for a
bright future diminished.

It is important to note that social attitudes toward
children obtained from movies are difficult to ascertain from
other sources, often because people are too guilty to admit
to any resentment or neglect of children or simply because
they are unaware of their own true feelings. The idealized
child in popular films of the Depression, for example, reveals

as much about Americans' guilt for being unable to generously provide for their own children as it does about their belief in the child as a hope for a bright future; the former,
however, was not openly admitted. In the following decade,
histories of childhood affirm the measures being taken to
guarantee for every boy and girl a happy childhood. Popular movies, however, tell quite another story: They affirm
that children were frequently unhappy, misunderstood, and
searching. In the same way, the popularity of the 1970s'
child-as-monster films reveals that Americans had difficulty
coping with changes in the family structure and new responsibilities, a problem that few individuals were willing
to concede and that was often masked as a general dislike
of children. In essence, films provide a key to important
social attitudes that are either deeply embedded in the unconscious or that are being repressed.

Throughout the history of twentieth-century American
films featuring children, several other patterns have emerged.
First, boys and girls have been equally represented in popular movies, which suggests that gender discrimination of children in films is not a factor.[2] Little girls, in fact, are most
frequently portrayed as good, self-reliant, and independent
characters; they figure as capable, very much in control fix-
its even more often than their male counterparts. Secondly,
children in films, especially younger ones, are not usually
seen with their friends; instead, they are portrayed in a
family situation. Although two- and three-child families are
not uncommon in popular films, an overwhelming majority of
filmic families have only one child; no doubt, this aids in
characterization, and since it has been the case throughout
the history of American film, it does not reflect the average
number of children born per family at any given time. Also
the mortality rate of parents of filmic children is exceeding-
ly high, and in postwar films, divorce has been common; so
although films espouse the importance of family, many filmic
children do not live in a traditional nuclear family. Instead,
several are orphans, sometimes living with relatives, or are
members of a one-parent household. Not surprisingly, many
film plots involve the creation of a new nuclear family.[3] The
majority of child-centered films portray a middle-class family.
Reflective of the democratic ideal, films featuring poor children treat poverty positively; poor children are happy children. Further, although legal officials dealing with juveniles
report that crime is more common among poor children,[4] this

is not the case in films: Monster children are almost always
the products of upper- or middle-class families. These films,
then, are commenting not on the state of child crime but on
the corruption of mainstream American society.

While the preceding trends will most likely continue in
the future, there will, no doubt, be changes in the portrayals of children on the movie screen. As history has shown,
attitudes toward childhood are never static. Some images of
children in film continue and endure while many do not; further, variations and new images are constantly emerging in
response to changing issues and affairs. By the mid 1980s
it was reported that the birthrate in America--although well
below that of the 1950s--reached the highest level in fifteen
years.[5] Thus, the postwar baby boomers, who back in the
1970s were reported to be giving up childbearing, have be-
latedly come through. With a baby boomlet currently in
progress, one suspects that Americans are not child-haters
as popular opinion seemed to suggest a decade ago; instead,
they have merely learned to cope with some difficult family,
economic, social, and personal dilemmas.

On the basis of this, the following predictions regarding the future of images of children in film seem likely.
First, innocence will continue to be a component in filmic
images of children although it will be qualified. The idea of
the child as an unlimited hope for the future has been dashed;
it will not return. As kidnapping, sexual molestation, and
physical abuse of children continue to be important issues,
children in films will reflect social attitudes by holding roles
as victims. The image of the child as a vulnerable victim is
crucial in that it provides as its counterpart the adult as
protector, a role that moviemakers will never fully abandon
because of its audience appeal. Secondly, the child-as-
monster image will run its course and diminish; this portrayal
depends on shock value for its impact, and, after several
films, becomes trite and loses its effect. Thirdly, the precocious child image will gain even greater momentum as parents continue to herald their "super children" and as wisdom
supplants innocence as a means of preparing for the future.
Fourthly, in order to flourish, the child/animal film will have
to take on new variations. Steven Spielberg's innovative
E.T., which in many ways fit the formula of the classic
child/animal film, succeeded at the box office while many
more traditional vehicles failed. Lastly, although the

child-star era will not return, children have moved into more serious, probing portrayals. In order to develop them, they will get more screen time. Perhaps in this process, children in films will land less stereotyped and more realistic roles.

Children have been so pervasive in films throughout the years that no study could touch upon all of their variations, implications, and nuances. This one modestly attempted to identify the major images of children portrayed in popular American films and explore in a sociocultural context the reasons for their proliferation. Further research is called for in many related areas. An in-depth look at any single image --the fix-it, the monster, the precocious imp--would provide ample material for a book-length study, as would comparative analyses of city versus rural children, rich versus poor children, and boys versus girls in films. Also of interest would be an investigation into how society's attitudes toward sex and money are communicated in filmic portrayals of children. Many children are featured in films specifically designed for child audiences. What are these portrayals telling children in terms of real-life behavior? Are these portrayals suitable for the audience for which they are intended? Also, how are children portrayed in animated films, many of which are created for a child audience? Lastly, children's images in American television and the subtle, far-reaching social effects of the atomic bomb suggest new fields for scholarly endeavor.

In closing, it seems appropriate to point out an obvious fact: Children have no say regarding their own portrayals in film. They do not write the script, direct the scenes, set up the shots, design the costumes, or edit the final product. The only role that they have in films is that of actor, and most often they are simply expected to mimic the director's actions and words, thereby allowing very little of what it feels like to be a child to enter into their performances. This is not likely to change; thus, images of children in film will continue to bear the adult's stamp and perception. Adults prefer to see children as vulnerable because these children need them, thus satiating their own need to protect, to rescue, to guide. Further, adults want to hold on to a somewhat idealized view of childhood, for it represents their own cherished memories. Indeed, whatever the actual events, adults choose to remember their own childhoods as beautiful, simpler times when innocence, to some extent, still prevailed.

Notes

1. John Gunther and Bernard Quint, Days to Remember, America 1945-1955 (New York: Harper and Brothers, 1956), p. 5.
2. See Molly Haskell, From Reverence to Rape: The Treatment of Women in the Movies (New York: Holt, Rinehart, and Winston, 1974) for a discussion of discrimination against women in the movies.
3. For a discussion of this aspect in 1980s films, see Marina Heung, "Why E.T. Must Go Home: The New Family in American Cinema," Journal of Popular Film and Television, 11, no. 2 (1983), pp. 79-85.
4. See Lisa Aversa Richette, The Throwaway Children (Philadelphia: Lippincott, 1969).
5. Fisher, Maria, "The Mother Lode," Forbes, 20 May 1985, p. 229.

BIBLIOGRAPHY

Allen, Frederick Lewis. Only Yesterday: An Informal History of the Nineteen-Twenties. New York: Harper and Row, 1931.

_____. Since Yesterday: The Nineteen-Thirties in America. New York: Harper and Row, 1940.

"All-Time Film Rental Champs." Variety, 8 January 1986, p. 26.

Almeda, Pamela M. "Children's Television and the Modeling of Proreading Behaviors." Education and Urban Society (Nov. 1977), pp. 55-59.

Anderson, Karen. Wartime Women: Sex Roles, Family Relations, and the Status of Women during World War II. Contributions in Women's Studies, No. 20. Westport, Conn: Greenwood Press, 1981.

Baker, M. Joyce. Images of Women in Film: The War Years, 1941-1945. Studies in American History and Culture, No. 21. Ann Arbor: UMI Research Press, 1980.

Barnouw, Eric. Documentary: A History of the Non-Fiction Film. New York: Oxford Univ. Press, 1974.

Basinger, Jeanine. Shirley Temple. New York: Pyramid, 1975.

Bergman, Andrew. We're in the Money: Depression America and Its Films. New York: Harper and Row, 1971.

Best, Marc. Their Hearts Were Young and Gay. New York: A. S. Barnes, 1975.

_____. Those Endearing Young Charms: Child Performers of the Screen. New York: A. S. Barnes, 1971.

"Big Rental Films of 1984." Variety, 16 January 1985, p. 16.

"Big Rental Films of 1985." Variety, 8 January 1986, p. 22.

"Black, Shirley Temple." Current Biography. 1970 ed.

Blumler, Herbert. Movies and Conduct. New York: Macmillan, 1933.

_____, and Philip M. Hauser. Movies, Delinquency, and Crime. New York: Macmillan, 1933.

Bodnar, John; Roger Simon; and Michael P. Weber. Lives of Their Own. Urbana, Ill.: Univ. of Illinois Press, 1982.

Bossard, James S., and Eleanor Stoker Boll. The Sociology of Child Development. 4th ed. New York: Harper and Row, 1966.

Bremner, Robert H., ed. Children and Youth in America; A Documentary History. Vol. II: 1866-1932. Cambridge, Mass.: Harvard Univ. Press, 1974.

"Bringing Up Superbaby." Newsweek, 28 March 1983, pp. 62-68.

Britton, Andrew; Richard Lippe; Tony Williams; and Robin Wood. American Nightmare: Essays on the Horror Film. Toronto: Festival of Festivals, 1979.

Burdick, Loraine. The Shirley Temple Scrapbook. Middle Village, N.Y.: Jonathan David, 1975.

Canby, Henry Seidel, ed. The Works of Thoreau. Boston: Houghton Mifflin, 1937.

Canby, Vincent. "Finding the Way to the Heart of Childhood." New York Times, 17 June 1982, p. 17, col. 1.

_____. "Why the Devil Dig 'The Exorcist'?" New York Times, 13 Jan. 1974, sec. 2, p. 1, col. 6.

Cary, Diana Serra. Hollywood's Children: An Inside Account of the Child Star Era. Boston: Houghton Mifflin, 1979.

Caughey, John W., and Ernest R. May. A History of the
United States. Chicago: Rand McNally, 1964.

Chafe, William H. The American Woman: Her Changing Social, Economic and Political Role, 1920-1970. New York:
Oxford Univ. Press, 1972.

Charters, W. W. Motion Pictures and Youth: A Summary.
New York: Macmillan, 1933.

Clark, Ann L., ed. Culture and Childrearing. Philadelphia:
F. A. Davis, 1981.

Cripps, Thomas. Slow Fade to Black. New York: Oxford
Univ. Press, 1977.

Crowther, Bosley. Review of The Bad Seed. New York
Times, 13 Sept. 1956, p. 39, col. 6.

_____. Review of Houseboat. New York Times, 14 Nov.
1958, p. 24, col. 1.

_____. Review of The Miracle Worker. New York Times,
24 May 1962, p. 29, col. 2.

_____. Review of Shane. New York Times, 24 April
1953, p. 30, col. 3.

David, Lester and Irene. The Shirley Temple Story. New
York: Putnam, 1983.

"Divorce American Style." Newsweek, 10 Jan. 1983, pp. 42-
48.

Dowdy, Andrew. The Films of the Fifties: The American
State of Mind. New York: William Morrow, 1973.

Durwood, Thomas. Close Encounters of the Third Kind: A
Document of the Film. Kansas City, Mo.: Ariel, 1978.

Dysinger, Wendell S., and Christian A. Ruckmick. The Emotional Responses of Children to the Motion Picture Situation. New York: Macmillan, 1933.

Edelson, Edward. Great Kids of the Movies. Garden City,
N.Y.: Doubleday, 1979.

Ehrlich, Paul. The Population Bomb. New York: Ballantine,
  1968.

Eisinger, Chester E., ed. The 1940's: Profile of a Nation
  in Crisis. Documents in American Civilization Series.
  Garden City, N.Y.: Anchor Books, 1969.

Elkin, Frederick, and Gerald Handel. The Child and Society:
  The Process of Socialization. New York: Random House,
  1980.

Emerson, Ralph Waldo. The Complete Writings of Ralph Waldo
  Emerson. Vol. I. New York: William H. Wise & Co.,
  1929.

Finch, Christopher. The Art of Walt Disney. New York:
  Harry N. Abrams, 1975.

Fisher, Maria. "The Mother Lode." Forbes, 20 May 1985,
  p. 229.

Ford, Richard. Children in the Cinema. London: George
  Allen and Unwin, 1939.

Forman, Henry James. Our Movie Made Children. New
  York: Macmillan, 1933.

Gaffrey, Maureen, comp. and ed. More Films Kids Like.
  Chicago: ALA, 1977.

Goldstein, Ruth M., and Edith Zornow. Movies for Kids.
  New York: Ungar, 1973.

_____, and _____. The Screen Image of Youth: Mov-
  ies About Children and Adolescents. Metuchen, N.J.:
  Scarecrow, 1980.

Goldwyn, Samuel. "Hollywood in the Television Age."
  Hollywood Quarterly, 4 (Winter 1949), p. 146.

Greenberg, Harvey R. The Movies on Your Mind. New
  York: Dutton, 1975.

Greenleaf, Barbara Kaye. Children Through the Ages: A
  History of Childhood. New York: McGraw-Hill, 1978.

Grylls, David. Guardians and Angels: Parents and Children in Nineteenth-Century Literature. Boston: Faber and Faber, 1978.

Gunther, John, and Bernard Quint. Days to Remember: America 1945-1955. New York: Harper and Brothers, 1956.

Hareven, Tamara K. "American Families in Transition: Historical Perspectives on Change." In The Development of an American Culture. Ed. Stanley Coben and Lorman Ratner. New York: St. Martin's, 1983, pp. 341-361.

Harris, Mark Jonathan; Franklin D. Mitchell; and Steven J. Schechter, interviewers. "Rosie the Riveter Remembers." American Heritage. Feb-March 1984, p. 103.

Hart, James D. The Popular Book: A History of America's Literary Taste. Berkeley: Univ. of California Press, 1963.

Harvard Educational Review. The Rights of Children. Reprint Series No. 9. Cambridge, Mass.: Harvard Educational Review, 1974.

Haskell, Molly. From Reverence to Rape: The Treatment of Women in the Movies. New York: Holt, Rinehart and Winston, 1974.

_____. "Jodie Foster and Tatum O'Neal." In The National Society of Film Critics on the Movie Star. Ed. Elisabeth Weis. New York: Viking, 1981, pp. 227-231.

Heung, Marina. "Why E.T. Must Go Home: The New Family in American Cinema." Journal of Popular Film and Television, 111, No. 2 (1983), pp. 79-85.

"A Hidden Epidemic." Newsweek, 14 May 1984, pp. 30-36.

Higham, Charles, and Joel Greenberg. Hollywood in the Forties. New York: A. S. Barnes, 1968.

Holt, John. Escape From Childhood. New York: E. P. Dutton, 1974.

Jacobs, Lewis. The Rise of the American Film. New York:
    Teachers College Press, 1968.

Jones, Landon Y. Great Expectations: America and the
    Baby Boom Generation. New York: Ballantine Books,
    1980.

Jowett, Garth. "The First Motion Picture Audiences." In
    Movies as Artifacts. Ed. Michael T. Marsden, John G.
    Nachbar, and Sam L. Grogg. Chicago: Nelson-Hall,
    1982, pp. 14-25.

Kael, Pauline. I Lost It at the Movies. Boston: Little
    Brown, 1954.

Kane, Mark. "The Anatomy of a Blockbuster: Producer
    Kathy Kennedy on 'E.T.'" Film Journal, 85, No. 14
    (14 June 1982), p. 9.

Kaplan, Justin, ed. Walt Whitman: Complete Poetry and
    Selected Prose. New York: Library of America, 1982.

Kerr, Walter. The Silent Clowns. New York: Knopf, 1979.

Knight, Arthur. The Liveliest Art. New American Library,
    1979.

Koller, Marvin R., and Oscar W. Ritchie. The Sociology of
    Childhood. 2nd ed. Englewood Cliffs, N.J.: Prentice-
    Hall, 1978.

Kracauer, Siegfried. From Caligari to Hitler. Princeton:
    Princeton Univ. Press, 1947.

Kuhn, Reinhard. Corruption in Paradise: The Child in
    Western Literature. Hanover, N.H.: Univ. Press of
    New England, 1982.

Lee, Raymond. The Films of Mary Pickford. New York:
    A. S. Barnes, 1970.

Lewis, R. W. B. The American Adam: Innocence, Tragedy,
    and Tradition in the Nineteenth Century. Chicago: Univ.
    of Chicago Press, 1955.

Liebert, Robert M.; John M. Neale; and Emily S. Davidson. The Early Window: Effects of Television on Children and Youth. New York: Pergamon, 1978.

Lifton, Robert Jay, and Richard Falk. Indefensible Weapons: The Political and Psychological Case Against Nuclearism. New York: Basic Books, 1982.

Maltin, Leonard. The Disney Films. New York: Crown, 1973.

_____, and Richard W. Bann. Our Gang: The Life and Times of the Little Rascals. New York: Crown, 1977.

Marsden, Michael T.; John G. Nachbar; and Sam L. Grogg, eds. Movies as Artifacts. Chicago: Nelson-Hall, 1982.

Mead, Margaret. Coming of Age in Samoa: A Study of Adolescence and Sex in Primitive Societies. Melbourne: Penguin Books, 1943.

Meltzer, Milton. Brother Can You Spare a Dime? New York: New American Library, 1969.

Meyer, William R. The Making of the Great Westerns. New Rochelle, N.Y.: Arlington House, 1979.

Miller, Douglas T., and Marion Nowalk. The Fifties: The Way We Really Were. New York: Doubleday, 1977.

Mitchell, Alice Miller. Children and Movies. Chicago: Univ. of Chicago Press, 1929.

Mott, Frank Luther. Golden Multitudes: The Story of Best Sellers in the United States. New York: Macmillan, 1947.

Noble, David W. The Eternal Adam and the New World Garden. New York: George Braziller, 1968.

Nye, Russel. The Unembarrassed Muse: The Popular Arts in America. New York: Dial, 1970.

Osborne, Robert. Academy Awards 1974 Oscar Annual. Laltabra, Cal.: ESE California, 1974.

Peterson, Ruth C., and L. L. Thurstone. Motion Pictures and the Social Attitudes of Children. New York: Macmillan, 1933.

Place, J. A. The Non-Western Films of John Ford. Secaucus, N.J.: Citadel, 1979.

Platt, Anthony M. The Child Savers: The Invention of Delinquency. Chicago: Univ. of Chicago Press, 1969.

Plumb, J. H. "The Great Change in Children." Horizon, 13, No. 1 (Winter 1971), pp. 4-13.

Pollard, Arthur, gen. ed. Webster's New World Companion to English and American Literature. New York: Popular Library, 1976.

Postman, Neil. The Disappearance of Childhood. New York: Delacorte, 1982.

Rainer, Peter. Review of E.T. Mademoiselle, 88 (Sept. 1982), pp. 60-61.

Rice, Susan, comp. and ed. Films Kids Like. Chicago: ALA, 1963.

Richette, Lisa Aversa. The Throwaway Children. Philadelphia: J. B. Lippincott, 1969.

Rosow, Eugene. Born to Lose: The Gangster Film in America. New York: Oxford Univ. Press, 1978.

Russo, Vito. The Celluloid Closet: Homosexuality in the Movies. New York: Harper and Row, 1981.

Samuels, Stuart. "The Age of Conspiracy and Conformity: Invasion of the Body Snatchers." In American History/American Film: Interpreting the Hollywood Image. Ed. John E. O'Connor and Martin A. Jackson. New York: Ungar, 1979, pp. 203-217.

Sayers, Frances Clarke, and Charles M. Weisenberg. "Walt Disney Accused." Horn Book, 40 (Dec. 1965), pp. 602-611.

Schell, Jonathan. The Fate of the Earth. New York: Avon
    Books, 1982.

Sklar, Robert. Movie-Made America: A Cultural History of
    American Movies. New York: Vintage Books, 1975.

Slotkin, Richard. Regeneration Through Violence: The
    Mythology of the American Frontier, 1600-1860. Middle-
    town, Conn.: Wesleyan Univ. Press, 1973.

Smith, Henry Nash. Virgin Land: The American West as
    Symbol and Myth. New York: Vintage Books, 1957.

Sommerville, John. The Rise and Fall of Childhood. Sage
    Library of Social Research, vol. 140. Beverly Hills:
    Sage, 1982.

Spock, Benjamin. Baby and Child Care. New York: Pocket
    Books, 1946.

Steinberg, Cobbett. Reel Facts: The Movie Book of Records.
    Updated ed. New York: Vintage Books, 1982.

"Stolen Children." Newsweek, 19 March 1984, pp. 78-86.

Stone, Albert E. Jr. The Innocent Eye: Childhood in Mark
    Twain's Imagination. New Haven: Yale Univ. Press,
    1961.

Street, Douglas. Children's Novels and the Movies. New
    York: Ungar, 1983.

Tanner, Tony. The Reign of Wonder: Naivety and Reality
    in American Literature. Cambridge: At the University
    Press, 1965.

"Temple, Shirley." Current Biography. 1945 ed.

Turner, Frederick Jackson. "The Significance of the Fron-
    tier in American History." Rpt. The Frontier in Ameri-
    can History. New York: Holt, Rinehart, and Winston,
    1962.

U.S. Department of Health, Education, and Welfare, Office
    of Child Development. Infant Care. Washington, D.C.:
    U.S. Gvt. Printing Office, 1962.

Wagenknecht, Edward. The Movies in the Age of Innocence. New York: Ballantine Books, 1962.

Wertham, Frederic. Seduction of the Innocent. New York: Holt, Rinehart, and Winston, 1954.

Windeler, Robert. The Films of Shirley Temple. Secaucus, N.J.: Citadel, 1978.

Wolfe, Tom. "The Me Decade and the Third Great Awakening." In Mauve Gloves and Madmen, Clutter and Vine, and Other Stories, Sketches, and Essays. New York: Farrar, Straus, and Giroux, 1976.

Wolfenstein, Martha. "The Image of the Child in Contemporary Film." In Childhood in Contemporary Cultures. Ed. Margaret Mead and Martha Wolfenstein. Chicago: Univ. of Chicago Press, 1955, pp. 277-293.

Wood, Robin. "Images of Childhood." In Personal Views: Explorations in Film. London: Gordon Fraser, 1976.

Zierold, Norman. The Child Stars. New York: Coward-McCann, 1965.

FILMOGRAPHY

Watering the Gardener (1895)
    Directed by Louis and Auguste Lumiere

Feeding the Baby (1898)
    Directed by Louis and Auguste Lumiere

Life of an American Fireman, The (1902)
    Directed by Edwin S. Porter

Great Train Robbery, The (Edison, 1903)
    Directed by Edwin S. Porter

Adventures of Dolly, The (Biograph, 1908)
    Directed by D. W. Griffith

Lonely Villa, The (Biograph, 1909)
    Directed by D. W. Griffith

Battle at Elderbush Gulch, The (Biograph, 1913)
    Directed by D. W. Griffith

Cinderella (Famous Players, 1914)
    Directed by James Kirkwood; with Mary Pickford

Prince and the Pauper, The (Famous Players, 1915)
    Directed by Edwin S. Porter and Hugh Ford; with
    Marguerite Clark

Rags (Famous Players, 1915)
    Directed by James Kirkwood; with Mary Pickford

War Brides (Selznick-World, 1916)
    Directed by Herbert Brenon

Little Princess, The (Famous Players, 1917)
    Directed by Marshall Neilan; with Mary Pickford

Poor Little Rich Girl, The (Famous Players, 1917)
    Directed by Maurice Tourneur; with Mary Pickford

Rebecca of Sunnybrook Farm (Famous Players, 1917)
    Directed by Marshall Neilan; with Mary Pickford

Seven Swans, The (Famous Players, 1917)
    Directed by J. Searle Dawley; with Marguerite Clark

Stella Maris (Famous Players, 1917)
    Directed by Marshall Neilan; with Mary Pickford

Uncle Tom's Cabin (Famous Players-Laskey, 1918)
    Directed by J. Searle Dawley; with Marguerite Clark

Broken Blossoms (United Artists, 1919)
    Directed by D. W. Griffith; with Lillian Gish

Daddy Long Legs (First National, 1919)
    Directed by Marshall Neilan; with Mary Pickford

Pollyanna (United Artists, 1920)
    Directed by Paul Powell; with Mary Pickford

Little Lord Fauntleroy (United Artists, 1921)
    Directed by Alfred E. Green and Jack Pickford; with
    Mary Pickford

Kid, The (First National, 1921)
    Directed by Charlie Chaplin; with Jackie Coogan

My Boy (First National, 1921)
    Directed by Victor Heerman; with Jackie Coogan

Peck's Bad Boy (First National, 1921)
    Directed by Sam Wood; with Jackie Coogan

Through the Back Door (United Artists, 1921)
    Directed by Alfred E. Green and Jack Pickford; with
    Mary Pickford

Tol'able David (First National, 1921)
    Directed by Henry King; with Richard Barthelmess

Oliver Twist (First National, 1922)
    Directed by Frank Lloyd; with Jackie Coogan

Trouble (First National, 1922)
    Directed by Albert Austin; with Jackie Coogan

Circus Days (First National, 1923)
    Directed by Edward F. Cline; with Jackie Coogan

Daddy (First National, 1923)
    Directed by E. Mason Hopper; with Jackie Coogan

Little Annie Rooney (United Artists, 1925)
    Directed by William Beaudine; with Mary Pickford

Sparrows (United Artists, 1926)
    Directed by William Beaudine; with Mary Pickford

Champ, The (MGM, 1931)
    Directed by King Vidor; with Jackie Cooper

Alice in Wonderland (Paramount, 1933)
    Directed by Norman McLeod

Baby, Take a Bow (Fox, 1934)
    Directed by James Lachman; with Shirley Temple

Bright Eyes (Fox, 1934)
    Directed by David Butler; with Shirley Temple, Jane
    Withers

Little Miss Marker (Paramount, 1934)
    Directed by Alexander Hall; with Shirley Temple

Now and Forever (Paramount, 1934)
    Directed by Henry Hathaway; with Shirley Temple

Stand Up and Cheer (Fox, 1934)
    Directed by Hamilton McFadden; with Shirley Temple

Treasure Island (MGM, 1934)
    Directed by Victor Fleming; with Jackie Cooper

Anna Karenina (MGM, 1935)
    Directed by Clarence Brown; with Freddie Bartholomew

Curly Top (Fox, 1935)
    Directed by Irving Cummings; with Shirley Temple

David Copperfield (MGM, 1935)
    Directed by George Cukor; with Freddie Bartholomew

Dinky (WB, 1935)
    Directed by D. Ross Lederman and Howard Bretherton;
    with Jackie Cooper

Littlest Rebel, The (20th Century-Fox, 1935)
    Directed by David Butler; with Shirley Temple

Little Lord Fauntleroy (United Artists, 1936)
    Directed by John Cromwell; with Freddie Bartholomew,
    Mickey Rooney

Paddy O'Day (20th Century-Fox, 1936)
    Directed by Lewis Seiler; with Jane Withers

Pepper (20th Century-Fox, 1936)
    Directed by James Tinling; with Jane Withers

Poor Little Rich Girl (20th Century-Fox, 1936)
    Directed by Irving Cummings; with Shirley Temple

Stowaway (20th Century-Fox, 1936)
    Directed by William A. Seiter; with Shirley Temple

Captains Courageous (MGM, 1937)
    Directed by Victor Fleming; with Freddie Bartholomew,
    Mickey Rooney

45 Fathers (20th Century-Fox, 1937)
    Directed by James Tinling; with Jane Withers

Heidi (20th Century-Fox, 1937)
    Directed by Allan Dwan; with Shirley Temple

Wee Willie Winkie (20th Century-Fox, 1937)
    Directed by John Ford; with Shirley Temple

Always in Trouble (20th Century-Fox, 1938)
    Directed by Joseph Santley; with Jane Withers

Kidnapped (20th Century-Fox, 1938)
    Directed by Alfred M. Werker; with Freddie Bartholomew

Rebecca of Sunnybrook Farm (20th Century-Fox, 1938)
    Directed by Allan Dwan; with Shirley Temple

Susannah of the Mounties (20th Century-Fox, 1939)
    Directed by William A. Seiter; with Shirley Temple

Wizard of Oz, The (MGM, 1939)
    Directed by Victor Fleming; with Judy Garland

Blue Bird, The (20th Century-Fox, 1940)
    Directed by Walter Lang; with Shirley Temple

Citizen Kane (RKO, 1941)
    Directed by Orson Welles; with Buddy Swain

How Green Was My Valley (20th Century-Fox, 1941)
    Directed by John Ford; with Roddy McDowall

Journey for Margaret (MGM, 1942)
    Directed by Major W. S. Van Dyke; with Margaret O'Brien,
    Billy Severn

Jungle Book, The (United Artists, 1942)
    Directed by Zoltan Korda; with Sabu

Hitler's Children (RKO, 1943)
    Directed by Edward Dymtryk; with Bonita Granville

Meet Me in St. Louis (MGM, 1944)
    Directed by Vincente Minnelli; with Judy Garland, Mar-
    garet O'Brien, Joan Carroll

National Velvet (MGM, 1944)
    Directed by Clarence Brown; with Elizabeth Taylor, Mickey
    Rooney

Bells of St. Mary's, The (RKO, 1945)
    Directed by Leo McCarey; with Joan Carroll

Our Vines Have Tender Grapes (MGM, 1945)
    Directed by Roy Rowland; with Margaret O'Brien

Three Caballeros, The (Disney, 1945)
    Directed by Norman Ferguson

Tree Grows in Brooklyn, A (20th Century-Fox, 1945)
    Directed by Elia Kazan; with Peggy Ann Garner, Ted
    Donaldson

Bad Bascomb (MGM, 1946)
    Directed by S. Sylvan Simon; with Margaret O'Brien

Black Beauty (20th Century-Fox, 1946)
    Directed by Max Nosseck; with Mona Freeman

Song of the South (Disney, 1946)
    Directed by Wilfred Jackson and Harve Foster; with Glen
    Leedy, Bobby Driscoll, Luana Patten

Three Wise Fools (MGM, 1946)
    Directed by Edward Buzzell; with Margaret O'Brien

Yearling, The (MGM, 1946)
    Directed by Clarence Brown; with Claude Jarman, Jr.

Fun and Fancy Free (Disney, 1947)
    Directed by William Morgan; with Luana Patten

Miracle on 34th Street (20th Century-Fox, 1947)
    Directed by George Seaton; with Natalie Wood

Little Women (MGM, 1949)
    Directed by Mervyn LeRoy; with Margaret O'Brien,
    Elizabeth Taylor, Janet Leigh, June Allyson

Cheaper By the Dozen (20th Century-Fox, 1950)
    Directed by Walter Lang; with Jeanne Crain, Anthony
    Sydes, Roddy McCaskill, Norman Ollestad, Carole Nugent,
    Jimmy Hunt, Teddy Driver, Betty Barker

Kim (MGM, 1950)
    Directed by Victor Saville; with Dean Stockwell

Treasure Island (Disney 1950)
    Directed by Byron Haskin; with Bobby Driscoll

Member of the Wedding, The (Columbia, 1952)
    Directed by Frank Zinnemann; with Julie Harris, Brandon
    De Wilde

Story of Robin Hood, The (Disney, 1952)
    Directed by Ken Annakin

Shane (Paramount, 1953)
    Directed by George Stevens; with Brandon De Wilde

Sword and the Stone, The (Disney, 1953)
    Directed by Ken Annakin

Rob Roy, the Highland Rogue (Disney, 1954)
    Directed by Harold French

Bad Seed, The (WB, 1956)
    Directed by Mervyn LeRoy; with Patty McCormack

Invasion of the Body Snatchers, The (Allied Artists, 1956)
    Directed by Don Siegel

Houseboat (Paramount, 1957)
    Directed by Melville Shavelson; with Charles Herbert,
    Mimi Gibson, Paul Peterson

Old Yeller (Disney, 1957)
    Directed by Robert Stevenson; with Tommy Kirk, Kevin
    Corcoran

Shaggy Dog, The (Disney, 1959)
    Directed by Charles Barton; with Tommy Kirk, Kevin
    Corcoran

Pollyanna (Disney, 1960)
    Directed by David Swift; with Hayley Mills, Kevin
    Corcoran

Swiss Family Robinson, The (Disney, 1960)
    Directed by Bill Anderson; with Kevin Corcoran, Tommy
    Kirk

Toby Tyler (Disney, 1960)
    Directed by Charles Barton; with Kevin Corcoran,
    Barbara Beaird, Dennis Joel

Village of the Damned (MGM, 1960)
    Directed by Wolf Rilla; with Martin Stephens

Absent-Minded Professor, The (Disney, 1961)
    Directed by Robert Stevenson

Babes in Toyland (Disney, 1961)
    Directed by Jack Donohue; with Kevin and Brian Corcoran,
    Annette Funicello, Tommy Sands

Innocents, The (20th Century-Fox, 1961)
    Directed by Jack Clayton; with Martin Stephens, Pamela
    Franklin

Parent Trap, The (Disney, 1961)
    Directed by David Swift; with Hayley Mills

Children's Hour, The (United Artists, 1962)
    Directed by William Wyler; with Karen Balkin

Lolita (MGM, 1962)
    Directed by Stanley Kubrick; with Sue Lyon

Miracle Worker, The (United Artists, 1962)
    Directed by Arthur Penn; with Patty Duke

To Kill a Mockingbird (Universal, 1962)
    Directed by Robert Mulligan; with Mary Badham, Phillip
    Alford, John Megna

Father Goose (Universal, 1964)
    Directed by Ralph Nelson; with Sharyl Locke, Pip Sparke,
    Verina Grenlaw, Stephanie Berrington, Jennifer Berring-
    ton, Laurelle Felsette, Nicole Felsette

Mary Poppins (Disney, 1964)
    Directed by Robert Stevenson; with Karen Dotrice, Matthew
    Garber

Three Lives of Thomasina, The (Disney, 1964)
    Directed by Don Chaffey; with Karen Dotrice

That Darn Cat (Disney, 1965)
    Directed by Robert Stevenson; with Hayley Mills

Sound of Music, The (20th Century-Fox, 1965)
    Directed by Robert Wise; with Charmian Carr, Heather

Menzies, Nicholas Hammod, Duane Chase, Angela Cart-
wright, Debbie Turner, Kym Karath

Happiest Millionaire, The (Disney, 1967)
    Directed by Norman Tokar; with Ann Warren

Oliver! (Columbia, 1968)
    Directed by Carol Reed; with Mark Lester, Jack Wild

Rosemary's Baby (Paramount, 1968)
    Directed by Roman Polanski

Love Bug, The (Disney, 1969)
    Directed by Robert Stevenson

True Grit (Paramount, 1969)
    Directed by Henry Hathaway; with Kim Darby

Willy Wonka and the Chocolate Factory (Paramount, 1971)
    Directed by Mel Stuart; with Peter Ostrum

Cowboys, The (WB, 1972)
    Directed by Mark Rydell; with Alfred Barker, Jr., Nicolas
    Beauvy, Steve Benedict, Robert Carradine, Norman Howell,
    Jr., Stephen Hudis, Sean Kelly, Clay O'Brien, Mike
    Pyeatt

Other, The (20th Century-Fox, 1972)
    Directed by Robert Mulligan; with Chris and Martin
    Udvarnoky

Exorcist, The (WB, 1973)
    Directed by William Friedkin; with Linda Blair

Paper Moon (Paramount, 1973)
    Directed by Peter Bogdanovich; with Tatum O'Neal

Benji (Mulberry Square, 1975)
    Directed by Joe Camp; with Cynthia Smith, Allen Fiuzat

Bad News Bears, The (Paramount, 1976)
    Directed by Michael Ritchie; with Tatum O'Neal, Jack
    Earle Haley, Alfred W. Lutter, Brandon Cruz, Chris
    Barnes, Gary Lee Cavagnaro, Jaime Escobedo, Scott
    Firestone, George Gonzales, Brett Marx, David Pollock,
    Quinn Smith, David Stambaugh

Bugsy Malone (Paramount, 1976)
    Directed by Alan Parker; with Jodie Foster, Scott Baio,
    Florrie Dugger, John Cassisi, Martin Lev, Paul Marshall,
    Sheridan Russell, Albin Jenkins, Dexter Fletcher

The Devil Within Her (American International, 1976)
    Directed by Peter Sasdy

Omen, The (20th Century-Fox, 1976)
    Directed by Richard Donner; with Harvey Stevens

Sailor Who Fell from Grace with the Sea, The (Augo Embassy,
    1976)
    Directed by Lewis John Carlino; with Jonathan Kahn, Earl
    Rhodes

Taxi Driver (Columbia, 1976)
    Directed by Martin Scorsese; with Jodie Foster

Audrey Rose (United Artists, 1977)
    Directed by Robert Wise; with Susan Swift

Close Encounters of the Third Kind (Columbia, 1977)
    Directed by Steven Spielberg; with Cary Guffey

Exorcist II: The Heretic (WB, 1977)
    Directed by John Boorman; with Linda Blair

For the Love of Benji (Mulberry Square, 1977)
    Directed by Joe Camp; with Cynthia Smith, Allen Fiuzat

It's Alive (WB, 1977)
    Directed by Larry Cohen; with Daniel Holzman

Halloween (Compass International, 1978)
    Directed by John Carpenter; with Will Sadin, Brian
    Andrews, Kyle Richards

International Velvet (MGM, 1978)
    Directed by Bryan Forbes; with Tatum O'Neal

It Lives Again (WB, 1978)
    Directed by Larry Cohen

Black Stallion, The (United Artists, 1979)
    Directed by Carroll Ballard; with Kelly Reno

The Champ (MGM, 1979)
    Directed by Franco Zeffirelli; with Ricky Schroder

Kramer vs. Kramer (Columbia, 1979)
    Directed by Robert Benton; with Justin Henry

Little Romance, A (Orion/WB, 1979)
    Directed by George Roy Hill; with Diane Lane, Thelonious
    Bernard

Children, The (World-Northal, 1980)
    Directed by Max Kalmanowicz

Gloria (Columbia, 1980)
    Directed by John Cassavetes; with Juan Adames

Shining, The (WB, 1980)
    Directed by Stanley Kubrick; with Danny Lloyd

Annie (Columbia, 1982)
    Directed by John Huston; with Aileen Quinn

Author! Author! (20th Century-Fox, 1982)
    Directed by Arthur Hiller; with Eric Gurry

E.T. The Extraterrestrial (Universal, 1982)
    Directed by Steven Spielberg; with Henry Thomas, Drew
    Barrymore, Robert MacNaughton

Poltergeist (MGM/UA, 1982)
    Directed by Tobe Hooper; with Heather O'Rourke, Oliver
    Robins, Dominique Dunne

Raggedy Man (Universal, 1982)
    Directed by Jack Fisk; with Henry Thomas, Carey Hollis,
    Jr.

Savannah Smiles (Embassy, 1982)
    Directed by Pierre DeMoro; with Bridgette Anderson

Shoot the Moon (MGM, 1982)
    Directed by Alan Parker; with Dana Hill, Viveka Davis,
    Tracey Gold, Tina Yothers

Six Weeks (Columbia, 1982)
    Directed by Tony Bill; with Katherine Healy

Cujo (WB, 1983)
   Directed by Lewis Teague; with Danny Pintauro

Something Wicked This Way Comes (Disney, 1983)
   Directed by Jack Clayton; with Vidal Peterson, Shawn
   Carson

Table for Five (WB, 1983)
   Directed by Robert Lieberman; with Robbie Kiger, Roxana
   Zal, Son Hoang Bui

Without a Trace (20th Century-Fox, 1983)
   Directed by Stanley Jaffe; with Daniel Brian Corkill

Children of the Corn (New World, 1984)
   Directed by Fritz Kiersch; with John Franklin, Robby
   Kiger, Marie McEvoy

Firestarter (Universal, 1984)
   Directed by Mark L. Lester; with Drew Barrymore

Gremlins (WB, 1984)
   Directed by Joe Dante; with Zach Galligan, Phoebe Cates

Indiana Jones and the Temple of Doom (Paramount, 1984)
   Directed by Steven Spielberg; with Ke Huy Quan

Irreconcilable Differences (WB, 1984)
   Directed by Charles Shyerl; with Drew Barrymore

The Neverending Story (WB, 1984)
   Directed by Wolfgang Petersen; with Barrett Oliver, Noah
   Hathaway, Tami Stronach

Goonies, The (Universal, 1985)
   Directed by Richard Donner; with Sean Astin, Josh Brolin,
   Jeff Cohen, Corey Feldman, Kerri Green, Martha Plimpton,
   Ke Huy Quan

INDEX

(Film titles are underlined; book titles are in capital letters.)

Abbott, Jacob 22
Absent-Minded Professor, The
  (1961) 118, 207
Academy Awards 95, 130, 135,
  154, 156, 162
Adam (prelapsarian) 17, 18, 20
adolescence 99
adultified child, concept of 158
Adventures of Dolly, The
  (1908) 1, 34, 35, 200
Age of Innocence 47
Age of Prosperity 37, 38
Aiken, George 25
Alcott, Louisa May 24
Alford, Phillip 127
Alger, Horatio 26, 44
ALICE IN WONDERLAND (1866)
  26
Alice in Wonderland (1933) 64,
  202
Allyson, June 94
Always in Trouble (1938) 66,
  203
American Romantics 16, 19,
  20, 21
American Telegraph and Tele-
  phone 38
American West 17
"America's Sweetheart" (Pick-
  ford) 42
Anderson, James 128
Andrews, Julie 2, 125, 126
Anna Karenina (1935) 69, 202
ANNE OF GREEN GABLES
  (1908) 25
Annie (1982) 170, 210
Arthur, Jean 106
Arthur, T.S. 25
Astin, Sean 172

Atchison 38
atomic age (America's entrance
  into) 86
atomic bomb 10, 86, 88, 188
Audrey Rose (1977) 146, 209
Author! Author! (1982) 2,
  159, 164, 210

Babes in Toyland (1961) 118,
  207
BABY AND CHILD CARE 91,
  113
baby boom 9, 90, 91, 95, 101,
  102, 119, 126, 127, 133, 187
baby boom generation 150
  see also baby boom
Baby, Take a Bow (1934) 62,
  202
BABY TRAP, THE (1971) 150
Bad Bascomb (1945) 94, 205
Bad News Bears, The (1976)
  157, 158, 208
Bad Seed, The (1956) 2, 111-
  114, 137, 140, 141, 142,
  145, 146, 147, 148, 206
Bagnold, Enid 78
Baker, Joyce M. 89
Balkin, Karen 137
Ballard, Carroll 161
Bancroft, Anne 135
Barrymore, Drew 153, 169
Barrymore, Lionel 62
Barthelmess, Richard 39, 40
Bartholomew, Freddie 1, 67,
  68, 69, 70, 173
Barton, Charles 122
Basinger, Jeanine 7
Battle at Elderbush Gulch, The

(1913) 1, 35, 200
Baum, Frank L. 26
Bedham, Mary 127
Beecher, Catherine 22
Beery, Wallace 94, 162
Belasco, David 41
Bells of St. Mary's, The
  (1945) 95, 96, 97, 204
Benji (1974) 161, 208
Bergman, Andrew 3, 4, 5
Bernard, Thelonious 158
Best, Marc 7
BEULAH (1859) 24
Bible 17, 156
Biograph 34, 41
Black Beauty (1946) 98, 104,
  205
Black Stallion, The (1979)
  161, 209
Blackmer, Sidney 149
Blair, Linda 142, 156
Blatty, William Peter 141
Blue Bird, The (1940) 124,
  204
Bogdanovich, Peter 156
Boone, Daniel 18
Bossard, James H.S. 77
Boy Scouts of America 62
Bradley, Omar 88
Brenon, Herbert 37, 200
Bright Eyes (1934) 59-61, 66,
  202
Broken Blossoms (1919) 39,
  40, 43, 201
Brolin, Josh 172
Brown, Clarence 96
Brown vs. the Board of Educa-
  tion 129
"Buck Rogers" (radio show)
  64
Bugsy Malone (1976) 158, 209
Burdick, Loraine 7
Burke, Thomas 39
Burnett, Frances Hodgson 24,
  67
Burstyn, Ellen 142
Bushnell, Horace 22
"Buster Brown" (1902) (comic
  strip) 27

Canby, Vincent 143
Caprice, Jean 41
Capshaw, Kate 171
CAPTAINS COURAGEOUS (1897)
  26
Captains Courageous (1936) 69,
  70, 203
Carlyle, Thomas 19
Carmen, Jewel 41
Caron, Leslie 132
Carroll, Joan 96
Carroll, Lewis 26
Carter, Jimmy 148
Cary, Diana Serra (formerly
  Baby Peggy) 7, 42
CASE AGAINST HAVING CHIL-
  DREN, THE (1971) 151
Cassavetes, John 140
CELLULOID CLOSET, THE
  (1981) 4
Chafe, William 89
Champ, The (1931) 70, 202
Champ, The (1979) 162, 210
Chaplin, Charlie 1, 43, 47-53,
  183
Cheaper by the Dozen (1950)
  100, 101, 102, 104, 126, 205
CHILD STARS, THE (1965) 7
The Children (1980) 153, 210
Children of the Corn (1984)
  153, 162, 211
Children's Bureau of the United
  States Government 37
Children's Charter 64
Children's Hour, The (1962)
  137, 138, 207
"Chink and the Child, The"
  (story) 39
Christie, Julie 146
CHRISTMAS CAROL, A (1844)
  23
Cinderella (1914) 42, 200
"Cinemoppet" 59
Circus Days (1923) 53, 202
Citizen Kane (1941) 73, 74,
  204
Civil War 185
Clark, Candy 156
Clark, Marguerite 41, 200,
  201
Clayton, Jack 132

Close Encounters of the Third
  Kind (1977) 1, 165, 166,
  167, 168, 209
Cobb, Irvin S. 67
Cobberly, Elwood Patterson 53
Cohen, Jeff 172
Cohen, Larry 147
Cold War 10, 88, 103, 148
Collins, Joan 146
Columbia 104
COMING OF AGE IN SAMOA,
  THE (1928) 76
COMMON SENSE BOOK OF BABY
  AND CHILD CARE, THE
  (1946) 91
Communism 131
Connelly, John J. 113
Connors, Chuck 120
Coogan, Jackie 1, 47, 48, 53,
  54, 55, 56, 94, 201
Coogan, Jackie, Sr. 53, 54
Cooper, Frankie 89
Cooper, Jackie 1, 70, 148,
  156, 162
Coppola, Francis Ford 161
Corcoran, Kevin 119, 120, 121,
  122, 157
CORRUPTION IN PARADISE:
  THE CHILD IN WESTERN
  LITERATURE (1982) 3
Council of State Governments
  113
Cowboys, The (1972) 134,
  208
Cripps, Thomas 4
Crosby, Bing 95
Crowther, Bosley 107, 112,
  115, 135
Cuban Missile Crisis 126, 148
Cujo (1982) 162, 211
Cummins, Maria Susanna 24
Curly Top (1935) 62, 202

Daddy (1923) 53, 202
DADDY LONG-LEGS (1912) 25
Daddy Long-Legs (1919) 47,
  201
Dante, Joe 173
Darby, Kim 133
David, Lester and Irene 7, 8

DAVID COPPERFIELD (1850)
  23
David Copperfield (1935) 69,
  203
Demon Seed, The (1977) 146
Depression 3, 5, 56, 57, 59,
  60, 62, 63, 64, 65, 66-69,
  71, 72, 73, 92, 94, 100,
  128, 129, 150, 154
Devil Within Her, The (1976)
  146, 209
De Wilde, Brandon 104, 106,
  107, 157
"Dick Tracy" (radio show) 64
Dickens, Charles 23, 130
Dillon, Melinda 165
Dinky (1935) 148, 203
Dirks, Rudolph 27
DISAPPEARANCE OF CHILD-
  HOOD, THE (1982) 160
Disney, Walt 127
Disney Studios 118, 119, 122,
  123, 124, 165
Donaldson, Ted ("Pudge") 74
Donner, Richard 171
Dowdy, Andrew 4
Dreyfuss, Richard 166
Duke, Patty 137, 157
Dunne, Dominique 167
Durwood, Thomas 165
Duvall, Robert 128
Dymtryck, Edward 77

E.T., The Extraterrestrial
  (1982) 1, 5, 167, 169, 183,
  187, 210
Edelson, Edward 2, 7
Educational Pictures 58
Ehrlich, Paul 127, 150
Eisinger, Charles E. 88
Emerson, Ralph Waldo 16, 18,
  19, 20, 21
ESCAPE FROM CHILDHOOD
  (1974) 152
Evans, Augusta Jane 24
exorcism (in film) 142
Exorcist, The (1973) 2, 141,
  142, 143, 144, 145, 146,
  147, 148, 152, 156, 208
Exorcist II: The Heretic (1977)
  146, 209

Fairbanks, Douglas 43, 47
FAITH GARTNEY'S GIRLHOOD
    (1863) 24
Falk, Richard 88
family horror film, the 138
Farrow, Mia 140
Father Goose (1964) 131, 132,
    207
"Father Knows Best" (television
    show) 151
Faubus, Orville 129
Featherstone, Joseph 3
Feeding the Baby (1898) 31,
    200
Feldman, Corey 172
Ferrell, Sharon 147
Field, Erastus 22
Film Daily Critics Award 93
FILMS KIDS LIKE (1963) 7
FILMS OF SHIRLEY TEMPLE,
    THE (1981) 8
FILMS OF THE FIFTIES: THE
    AMERICAN STATE OF MIND
    (1973) 4
Fine, Benjamin 112
Firestarter (1984) 153, 211
FIVE LITTLE PEPPERS AND HOW
    THEY GREW, THE (1880)
    24
Fix, Paul 111
fix-it child in film 33, 34, 43-
    46, 59-62, 133, 134, 154,
    156, 174, 184, 188
"Flash Gordon" (radio show)
    64
Flynn, Errol 102, 103
For the Love of Benji (1977)
    161, 209
Ford, Harrison 171
Ford, Henry 39
Ford, John 62, 75
Forman, Henry James 7
45 Fathers (1937) 67, 203
Foster, Jodie 2, 158
Fourteenth Amendment 129
Fox Studios 58
Franklin, Pamela 132
FRANKLIN EVANS 26
FRECKLES (1904) 25
Freud, Sigmund 22
Friedkin, William 141

FROM CALIGARI TO HITLER
    (1947) 3
FROM REVERENCE TO RAPE
    (1974) 4
Fun and Fancy Free (1947)
    118, 205

Gaffrey, Maureen 7
Galton, Francis 22
Garland, Judy 1, 2, 71, 79,
    80, 94
Garner, Peggy Ann 74
Garnett, Gail 153
Gary Cooper Award for Human
    Values 129
"Gentle Boy, The" (story) 21
Gibson, Mimi 114
Gibson, William 135
Gipson, Fred 119
Gish, Lillian 39, 201
Gloria (1980) 2, 159, 164, 210
Golden Anniversary White House
    Conference on Children and
    Youth 136
Goldstein, Ruth M. 6, 7
Goldwyn, Samuel 92
Goodrich, Samuel 22
Goonies, The (1985) 171, 211
Gordon, Ruth 140
Grant, Cary 114, 115, 132
GREAT KIDS OF THE MOVIES
    (1979) 7
Great Train Robbery, The
    (1903) 33, 43, 200
Green, Keri 172
Greenleaf, Barbara Kaye 15
Gremlins (1984) 173, 211
Griffith, D.W. 1, 34, 35, 36,
    37, 39, 41, 42, 43, 170,
    183, 200, 201
Grogg, Sam L., Jr. 4
Grylls, David 14
Guffey, Cary 165

Habberton, John 24
Hall, Mordaunt 59
Hall, Stanley G. 22, 99
Halloween (1978) 147, 209
Happiest Millionaire, The (1967)

118, 208
Harris, Julie 104
Haskell, Molly 4, 143
Hawthorne, Nathaniel 21
Hearst, William Randolph 27
Heflin, Van 106
HEIDI (1884) 24
Heidi (1937) 62, 203
HELEN'S BABIES (1876) 24
Hellman, Lillian 137
Henry, Justin 162
Hepburn, Audrey 137
Herald Tribune 67, 86
Herbert, Charles 114
Heston, Charlton 9
HIDDEN HAND, THE (1859) 24
Higgins (the dog) 161
High Plains Drifter (1973) 6
Hiroshima 86
Hitler, Adolf 77
Hitler's Children (1942) 76,
    77, 204
Hoffman, Dustin 162
HOLLYWOOD'S CHILDREN
    (1979) 7
Holt, John 151, 152
Holzman, Daniel 147
Hooper, Tobe 167
Hoover, J. Edgar 113
Hopper, Hedda 57
Houseboat (1958) 114-117, 206
Hovick, Baby June 56
How Green Was My Valley
    (1941) 75, 204
HUCKLEBERRY FINN (1885) 21,
    26
Hyer, Martha 114

"Image of the Child in Con-
    temporary Films, The" (1954)
    (essay) 5
"Images of Childhood" (1976)
    (essay) 6
Indiana Jones and the Temple
    of Doom (1984) 171, 172,
    211
Industrial Revolution 14
INFANT CARE (1962) 37
Innocents, The (1961) 132,
    133, 135, 207

International Velvet (1978)
    161, 209
Interstate Compact on Juveniles
    113
Invasion of the Body Snatchers
    (1956) 139, 140, 206
Iron Curtain 88
Irreconcilable Differences
    (1984) 159, 164
It's Alive (1977) 147, 148, 209

"Jack Armstrong" (radio show)
    64
Jacobs, Lewis 3, 32, 37, 38
James, Henry 21, 132, 133
James, William 113
Janeway, James 15
Jarman, Claude 96, 157
Jenkins, Jackie ("Butch") 93
Jessop, Clytie, 132
Jones, Henry 111
Jones, Landon Y. 89, 101,
    127, 131, 148, 151
Journal of Popular Film, The
    4
Journey for Margaret (1942)
    94, 204
Jungle Book, The (1942) 76,
    77, 204
JUNGLE BOOKS, THE (1894-
    1895) 26

Kael, Pauline 133
Kahn, Jonathan 158
Kahn, Madeline 156
Kaler, James Otis 122
"Katzenjammer Kids, The"
    (comic strip) 27
Keller, Helen 2, 135, 137
Kelly, Nancy 111
Kennedy, John F. 10
Kennedy, Kathleen 167
Kerr, Deborah 132
Kerr, Walter 49, 50
Kid, The (1921) 1, 47-53, 54,
    56, 183, 201
Kidnapped (1938) 69, 203
Kim (1950) 102-104, 205
King, Henry 40

King, Stephen 153, 162
Kipling, Rudyard 26, 76, 102
Kirk, Tommy 119, 121
Kirkwood, James 200
Knight, Arthur 91
Korda, Zoltan 76
Korean war 148
Kracauer, Siegfried 3, 4
Kramer vs. Kramer (1980)
  162-164, 210
Kristofferson, Kris 158
Kuhn, Reinhard 3

Ladd, Alan 106
Laemmle, Carl 42
LAMPLIGHTER, THE (1854)
  24
Lane, Diane 158
Lang, Walter 101
Lawford, Peter 94
"Leave It to Beaver" (television
  show) 151
LEAVES OF GRASS 20
Lee, Harper 127
Lee, Raymond 43
Leigh, Janet 94
LeRoy, Mervyn 94, 111
Lester, Gladys 41
Lester, Mark 130, 131
Levin, Ira 140
Lewis, R.W.B. 16, 17
Life of an American Fireman,
  The (1902) 32, 33, 34, 200
Lifton, Robert Jay 88
LIMEHOUSE NIGHTS 39
Lincoln, Abraham (as portrayed
  in film) 62
Little Annie Rooney (1925)
  43, 45, 46, 202
LITTLE LORD FAUNTLEROY
  (1886) 24
Little Lord Fauntleroy (1921)
  43, 201
Little Lord Fauntleroy (1936)
  64, 67-68, 69, 203
LITTLE MEN (1871) 24
Little Miss Marker (1934)
  58, 59, 202
Little Nell 23
"Little Nemo" (comic strip) 27

"Little Orphan Annie" (radio
  show) 64
Little Rock School Board 129
Little Romance, A (1979) 158,
  210
LITTLE WOMEN (1868) 24
Little Women (1933) 64
Little Women (1949) 94, 205
Littlest Rebel, The (1935) 62,
  203
Lolita (1962) 138, 207
Lonely Villa, The (1909) 1,
  35, 200
Loren, Sophia 114, 115
Love Bug, The (1969) 118,
  208
Loy, Myrna 101
Lumiere, Auguste and Louis
  31, 48, 200
Lyon, Sue 138

MGM Studios 71, 77, 94, 96,
  138
MacLaine, Shirley 137
MacMurray, Fred 121
MacNaughton, Robert 169
Maltin, Leonard 120
Mann, Horace 22
Marsden, Michael T. 4
Martin, Vivian 41
Mary Poppins (1965) 5, 118,
  125, 126, 207
Matthau, Walter 157
McCarey, Leo 95
McCormack, Patty 111
McCullers, Carson 104
McDowall, Roddy 75
McGuire, Dorothy 119
McKay, Windsor 27
"me generation" 150
Mead, Margaret 76
Meet Me in St. Louis (1944) 6,
  79, 80, 93, 94, 204
Meltzer, Milton 64
Member of the Wedding (1952)
  104, 105, 106, 110, 205
Menjou, Adolphe 58
Meyer, William R. 134
"Mickey Mouse Club Show"
  (television show) 120

Miles, Susan 158
Mill, John Stuart 19
Mills, Hayley 124, 157
Minnelli, Vincente 79
Minter, Mary Miles 41
Miracle on 34th Street (1947)
    99, 100, 205
Miracle Worker, The (1962) 2,
    135, 136, 137, 207
monster child in film 137, 140,
    147, 149, 151-154, 174, 184,
    187, 188
Montgomery, Baby Peggy 7, 56
Montgomery, Lucy M. 25
Moody, Ron 130
Moore, Owen 42
MORE FILMS KIDS LIKE (1977)
    7
MOTHER'S DAY IS OVER (1973)
    151
mother's pension laws 53
Motion Picture Magazine 41
Motion Picture Production Code
    112
Mott, Frank Luther 24
MOVIE-MADE AMERICA (1975)
    4
MOVIES AS ARTIFACTS: CUL-
    TURAL CRITICISM OF POPU-
    LAR FILM (1982) 4
MOVIES FOR KIDS (1973) 7
MRS. WIGGS OF THE CABBAGE
    PATCH (1901) 25
Mulligan, Robert 127
My Boy (1922) 53, 201
My Darling Clementine (1946)
    6

Nabokov, Vladimir 138
Nachbar, John G. 4
Nagasaki 86
National Association for Re-
    tarded Children 136
National Velvet (1944) 77, 78,
    79, 96, 98, 100, 161, 204
Nazi Party (in film) 77
Nazimova, Alla 37
Neilan, Marshall 201
Nelson, Craig T. 167
Neverending Story, The (1984)

    170, 211
New Deal 63, 64
New York Central 38
New York Journal 27
New York Times 59, 107, 112
New York World 26
Night of the Living Dead (1968)
    6
Nixon, Richard M. 146
Nosseck, Max 98
Now and Forever (1934) 58,
    62, 202
Nugent, Frank S. 62

O'Brien, Margaret 2, 79, 93,
    94, 95
O'Connor, Joseph 130
OLD CURIOSITY SHOP, THE
    (1841) 23
Old Yeller (1958) 1, 118-121,
    123, 206
Oliver! (1969) 1, 130, 131,
    208
OLIVER TWIST (1838) 23
Oliver Twist (1922) 53, 130,
    201
Olivier, Laurence 159
Omen, The (1976) 2, 141, 144,
    145, 146, 148, 152, 209
Omen II: Damien (1978) 146
Omen III: The Final Conflict
    (1981) 146
"On the Good Ship Lollipop"
    (song) 60
1,000,000 DELINQUENTS (1954)
    112
"One Take Temple" (nickname)
    62
O'Neal, Ryan 5, 154
O'Neal, Tatum 2, 94, 154, 156,
    157, 158, 161
O'Rourke, Heather 167
Orpheum Theatre 47
Other, The (1972) 146, 148,
    208
Our Gang 55, 56, 57, 66, 171
OUR MOVIE MADE CHILDREN
    (1933) 7
Our Vines Have Tender Grapes
    (1945) 93, 204

Outcault, Richard 26
"Ozzie and Harriet" (television
    show) 151

Paddy O'Day (1936) 66, 203
Paper Moon (1973) 2, 5, 154-
    157, 184, 208
Paramount Studios 58, 106,
    114
Parent Trap, The (1961) 118,
    207
Parker, Fess 119
Parrish Children 56
Payne Fund Studies 6, 7
Peabody, Elizabeth 22
Pearl Harbor 72
Peck, Ellen 150
Peck, Gregory 96, 127, 144
Peck's Bad Boy (1921) 53, 201
Penn, Arthur 135
Pepper (1936) 67, 203
Peters, Brock 128
Peterson, Paul 114
Piaget, Jean 55
Pickford, Mary 41-47, 57, 62,
    66, 102, 124, 184, 185, 200,
    201
Place, J.A. 75
Plimpton, Martha 172
Polanski, Roman 140
POLLYANNA (1913) 25
Pollyanna (1920) 43-45, 46,
    201
Pollyanna (1960) 118, 124, 206
Poltergeist (1982) 167, 168,
    169, 210
Poor Little Rich Girl (1917)
    201
Poor Little Rich Girl (1936)
    62, 203
POPULATION BOMB, THE 127
Porter, Edwin S. 32, 33, 34,
    35, 36, 183, 200
Porter, Eleanor H. 25
Porter, Gene Stratton 25
Postman, Neil 9, 22, 160
Powell, Paul 43
precocious imp (filmic image of)
    154, 158, 160, 184, 187, 188
Prince and the Pauper (1919)

41, 200
Procreation Ethic 101, 102,
    127
Progressivism 15, 36
Puritanism 14, 15, 16

Quan, Ke Huy 171, 172
QUEECHY (1852) 24

"R" rating 143, 145
RAGGED DICK (1867) 26
Raggedy Man, The (1982)
    170, 210
Rags (1915) 42, 200
Raiders of the Lost Ark (1981)
    171
REBECCA OF SUNNYBROOK
    FARM (1903) 25
Rebecca of Sunnybrook Farm
    (1917) 42, 201
Rebecca of Sunnybrook Farm
    (1938) 61-62, 204
Reed, Carol 130
Remick, Lee 144
Reno, Kelly 161
Rhodes, Earl 158
Rice, Alan Hegan 25
Rice, Susan 7
Rilla, Wolf 138
RISE OF THE AMERICAN FILM,
    THE (1939) 3
Roach, Hal 54, 55, 56
Rob Roy, the Highland Rogue
    (1954) 118, 206
Robins, Oliver 167
Rode, Shirley L. 151
Rogers, Gil 153
Rogers, Will 58
Romantics, American see
    American Romantics
Rooney, Mickey 2, 56, 57,
    78, 94, 96, 161
Roosevelt, Franklin Delano 59,
    63
Roosevelt, Theodore 37
Rosemary's Baby (1968) 2,
    140, 141, 146, 208
Russo, Vito 4
Ryan, John 147

Sailor Who Fell from Grace with
    the Sea, The (1976) 2, 158,
    209
ST. ELMO (1867) 24
Samuels, Stuart 139
Sanders, George 138
Satanic theme in film 145
Savannah Smiles (1983) 170,
    210
Saville, Victor 102
SCARLET LETTER, THE (1850)
    21
Schell, Jonathan 87
SCREEN IMAGE OF YOUTH:
    MOVIES ABOUT CHILDREN
    AND ADOLESCENTS, THE
    6
Seaton, George 99
Sedgwick, Ruth Woodbury 67
"Self-Reliance" (1841) (essay)
    18
Seven Swans, The (1917) 41,
    201
Shaggy Dog, The (1959) 118,
    121, 122, 206
Shaker, Martin 153
Shane (1953) 1, 5, 106-110,
    121, 128, 129, 206
Shelley, Barbara 138
Shields, Brooke 2
Shining, The (1980) 162, 210
SHIRLEY TEMPLE 7
SHIRLEY TEMPLE SCRAPBOOK,
    THE (1975) 7
SHIRLEY TEMPLE STORY, THE
    7
Shoot the Moon (1982) 2, 159,
    164, 210
Sidney, Margaret 24
Silverman, Arnold 151
Six Weeks (1982) 170, 210
Skinner, B.F. 113
Sklar, Robert 4
SLOW FADE TO BLACK 4
Smith, Betty 74
Snow White 41
Something Wicked This Way
    Comes (1983) 170, 211
Sommerville, John 27, 114,
    133, 149, 164
Song of the South (1946) 118,

    200
Sound of Music, The (1965)
    126, 207
Southworth, E.D.E.N. 24
Sparrows (1926) 47, 202
Spielberg, Steven 2, 6, 165,
    167, 169, 170, 171, 172,
    173, 183, 187
Spock, Dr. Benjamin 91, 98,
    113, 124, 130, 136
"Spock babies" 130
Spyri, Johanna 24
Stand Up and Cheer (1934)
    58, 202
Stella Maris (1917) 43, 201
Stephens, Martin 132, 139
Stevenson, Robert 119
Stevenson, Robert Louis 26,
    70
Stimson, Henry L. 86
Stockwell, Dean 102
Stone, Robert E. 16
STORY OF MY LIFE, THE
    (Helen Keller) 135
Story of Robin Hood, The
    (1952) 118, 206
Stowaway (1936) 62, 203
Stowe, Harriet Beecher 25
Streep, Meryl 162
"super baby" trend 160
"super children" 187
Susannah of the Mounties
    (1939) 62, 204
Swiss Family Robinson, The
    (1960) 118, 206
Sword and the Rose, The
    (1953) 118, 206
Sydney, Sylvia 156

Table for Five (1983) 170, 211
tabula rasa theory 76
Tanner, Tony 19
Taxi Driver (1976) 158, 209
Taylor, Elizabeth 78, 94, 96
Taylor, William Desmond 41
Temple, Gertrude 58
Temple, Shirley 1, 2, 7, 58-
    64, 65, 66, 67, 71, 94, 95,
    102, 114, 116, 134, 147,
    154, 156, 173, 184, 185

TEN NIGHTS IN A BAR-ROOM
    AND WHAT I SAW THERE
    (1854) 25
"Terry and the Pirates" (radio
    show) 64
Texas Chainsaw Massacre (1974)
    167
That Darn Cat (1965) 118, 207
THEIR HEARTS WERE YOUNG
    AND GAY (1975) 7
"There Was a Child Went Forth"
    (1855, 1871) (poem) 20
Thomas, Henry 169
Thoreau, Henry David 16, 19,
    20, 21
THOSE ENDEARING YOUNG
    CHARMS (1971) 7
Three Caballeros, The (1945)
    118, 204
Three Lives of Thomasina (1964)
    118, 207
Three Wise Fools (1946) 94,
    205
Times 59, 62
To Kill a Mockingbird (1963)
    1, 127-130, 207
Toby Tyler (1960) 1, 118,
    122-124, 206
Tol'able David (1921) 40, 201
TOM SAWYER (1876) 26
Tramp, the 48-53
TREASURE ISLAND (1884) 26
Treasure Island (1934) 70, 205
Treasure Island (1950) 118
Tree Grows in Brooklyn, A
    (1945) 74, 75, 205
Trouble (1922) 53, 202
True Grit (1969) 133, 134,
    208
Tunberg, William 119
TURN OF THE SCREW, THE
    (1898) 21, 132
Turner, Frederick Jackson 17
Twain, Mark 21, 26, 41
Twentieth Century-Fox Studios
    71, 98, 99, 126, 132, 144,
    147

UNCLE TOM'S CABIN (1852)
    25, 26, 44

Uncle Tom's Cabin (1918) 41,
    201
United Artists Studios 43, 67,
    76, 102, 135
United States Children's Bureau
    65
United States Steel 38
United States Supreme Court
    92, 129, 150
Universal Studios 127

V-J Day 90
Valentino, Rudolph 47
Van Dyke, Dick 125
Vietnam war 8, 10, 126, 148,
    153
Village of the Damned (1960)
    138, 139, 140, 141, 206

Wagenknecht, Edward 39, 46
WALDEN 20
"Walking" (poem) 19-20
Wallace, Dee 169
Walt Disney Studios 118, 119,
    122, 123, 124, 165
Walton, Henry 22
War Brides (1916) 37, 38, 200
War of 1812 16
Warner, Susan 24
Warner Brothers Studios 111,
    144, 147
Watergate 10, 146, 148, 153
Watering the Gardener (1895)
    31, 48, 200
Waters, Ethel 104
Watson, John B. 22, 55, 113
Wayne, John 133, 134
Webb, Clifton 101
Webster, Jean 25
Wee Willie Winkie (1937) 62,
    203
Weimar Germany 3
Welles, Orson 73, 74
Wellman, William 137
WE'RE IN THE MONEY (1971)
    3, 5
"Where Is Love?" (song) 131
White House Conferences for
    Children 36, 37

White House Conference on
  Child Health and Protection
  64
White House Conference on
  Children in a Democracy
  73
White House Conference on the
  Care of Dependent Children
  53
White House Mid Century Con-
  ference on Children and
  Youth 98
Whitman, Walt 17, 20, 26
Whitney, A.D.T. 24
WIDE, WIDE WORLD, THE
  (1850) 24
Wiggin, Kate Douglass 25
Wilcox, Collin 128
Wild, Jack 130
Williams, Jobeth 167
Willy Wonka and the Chocolate
  Factory (1972) 162, 208
Windeler, Robert 8
Withers, Jane 1, 2, 60, 66,
  67, 94
Without a Trace (1983) 170,
  211
Wizard of Oz, The (1939) 64,
  71, 72, 79, 80, 124, 170,
  204
Wolfenstein, Martha 5

Women's Movement 143
WONDERFUL WIZARD OF OZ,
  THE (1900) 26
Wood, Natalie 99
Wood, Robin 6, 79, 144, 147
Woolworth, F.W. 39
Wordsworth, William 19
working mothers 91
World War I 31, 37, 38, 39
World War II 1, 2, 8, 9, 31,
  72, 80, 86, 88, 89, 90, 93,
  94, 98, 99, 100, 127, 132,
  144, 148, 153, 154, 184
Wyman, Jane 96
Wyngarde, Peter 133

Yearling, The (1946) 1, 96-
  98, 100, 104, 110, 205
"Yellow Kid, The" (comic
  strip) 26, 27
YOUNG CHRISTIAN, THE (1832)
  22

Zero Population Growth 127
Zierold, Norman 1, 7, 62, 66
Zinneman, Fred 104
Zornow, Edith 6, 7
Zukor, Adolph 42